CW00750719

Practical Guide to Using SQL in Oracle®

Richard Walsh Earp
and
Sikha Saha Bagui

Wordware Publishing, Inc.

Library of Congress Cataloging-in-Publication Data

Earp, Richard Walsh, 1940-
Practical guide to using SQL in Oracle / by Richard Walsh Earp and Sikha Saha Bagui.
p. cm.
Includes index.
ISBN-13: 978-1-59822-063-6
ISBN-10: 1-59822-063-2 (pbk.)
1. SQL (Computer program language. 2. Oracle (Computer file)
3. Database management. I. Bagui, Sikha Saha, 1964-. II. Title.
QA76.73.S67B344 2008
005.75'65--dc22 2008034585
CIP

1100 Summit Avenue, Suite 102
Plano, Texas 75074

Printed in the United States of America

ISBN-13: 978-1-59822-063-6
ISBN-10: 1-59822-063-2
10 9 8 7 6 5 4 3 2 1
0809

All inquiries for volume purchases of this book should be addressed to Wordware Publishing, Inc., at the above address. Telephone inquiries may be made by calling:

(972) 423-0090

Dedicated to my wife, Brenda,
and
my children, Beryl, Rich, Gen and Mary Jo

R.W.E.

Dedicated to my father, Santosh Saha, and mother, Ranu Saha,
and
my husband, Subhash Bagui,
and
my sons, Sumon and Sudip,
and
my brother and his wife, Pradeep and Shyamasri, and nieces,
Priyashi and Piyali

S. S.B.

Contents

Preface

Why This Book?

In recent years we have seen a dramatic increase in the popularity of Oracle. Oracle is now the most widely used database on the market. Due to this dramatic increase in popularity, more and more schools and training organizations are using Oracle to teach database principles and concepts. And given the current technological climate, the computer industry needs application developers who can write Oracle SQL code efficiently.

This book employs a step-by-step systematic approach to learning Oracle SQL, database principles, and concepts. It starts by presenting simple Oracle SQL commands and functions, and slowly moves into more complex query development and PL/SQL; it also introduces SQL/XML. Each chapter includes numerous examples, and if readers wish they can run these examples themselves using Oracle. Each chapter ends with a series of exercises that reinforce and build on chapter material. In doing these exercises, it is our hope and expectation that readers will learn SQL and the underlying principles of relational databases. As such, we do not include the "answers" to the exercises.

Oracle and SQL

SQL is an abbreviation for SEQUEL (Structured English Query Language), and was originally an IBM product. Since the 1970s, when SEQUEL was introduced, it has become the *de facto* standard "language" for accessing relational databases. SQL is not really a language as much as it is a database query tool. In this book, we will concentrate on using the Oracle database engine to learn and use SQL.

SQL allows you to define relational databases and create tables; in this sense, SQL is a Data Definition Language (DDL). Oracle also provides a utility called SQL*Loader to load the created database with data. After the database is created and populated, SQL provides a way to modify the database definition by using DDL. It also allows you to query the relational database in a most flexible way as well as change the data (i.e., perform data manipulation). Therefore, SQL is a Data Manipulation Language (DML) as well as a DDL.

This book covers SQL as it is invoked via SQL*Plus, which is a command-line system to launch interactive commands. SQL*Plus is a powerful Oracle product that takes your instructions for Oracle, checks them for correctness, submits them to the Oracle database engine, and then modifies or reformats the response Oracle gives. In short, SQL*Plus makes interacting with Oracle smooth and easy.

Audience and Coverage

This book can be used in conjunction with standard database texts used in universities and colleges; it can also be used as a "stand-alone" text to learn SQL and Oracle. For this latter scenario, we included a Prologue chapter. The Prologue provides basic database background material needed to begin using SQL and relational databases.

This book can be divided into two parts. Chapters 1 through 10 cover topics meant for introductory-level database learning or a beginning SQL/Oracle class. Chapters 11 through 14 contain a *preview* of advanced topics that are usually covered in advanced database classes. These chapters assume that the reader has some programming background or experience.

The Prologue introduces some of the database terms that will be used throughout the book and shows how and why the relational database model fits into the database world of today. Chapter 1 begins in a step-by-step manner, beginning with "signing on." Then it covers basic Oracle/SQL topics such as `SELECT`, `INSERT`, and `DELETE` (DML commands). Simple editing concepts are also introduced in this chapter. Chapter 2 covers additional beginning SQL commands and builds on the material in Chapter 1. Chapter 3 introduces joins, which is a way to put relational tables together. Chapters 4 and 5 get into basic Oracle functions and query development as well as the use of views and other derived structures. Chapter 6 covers simple set operations; Chapters 7, 8, and 9 cover more advanced queries including using subqueries, aggregate functions, and correlated subqueries. Chapters 10 through 13 introduce still more advanced SQL concepts such as the load utility, start files, reports, some introductory PL/SQL, and triggers. Chapter 14 introduces SQL/XML. As we mentioned earlier, we have included exercises at the end of every chapter to bolster the material in the chapter and incorporate a review of the chapter's topics.

Appendix A presents some common UNIX commands. Appendix B covers data dictionary concepts. Appendix C illustrates the Student-Course tables and other tables that have been used throughout the book. In addition, we have provided a glossary of terms and a list of important commands and functions for your reference.

Overall, we feel that this book is ideal for a beginning Oracle user to get an overview of what SQL and Oracle entails. The book gives a very good "feel" for what Oracle is and the many ways Oracle can be used.

Supplements

The exercises at the end of each chapter are drawn from databases that we created and that can be downloaded from http://www.cs.uwf.edu/~sbagui/. The download instructions are also available at this web site. The files can also be downloaded from http://www.wordware.com/files/sql-oracle.

Acknowledgments

Our special thanks are due to our editors, Tim McEvoy, Martha McCuller, and Beth Kohler.

We would also like to thank Dean Jane Halonen, Interim President Judy Bense, and Interim Provost Chula King for their inspiration, encouragement, support, and true leadership. We would also like to express our gratitude to Dr. Richard Podemski on the same endeavor.

Our sincere thanks also go to Dr. Leo TerHaar, chair, Computer Science Department, for his advice, guidance, and support, and encouraging us to complete this book, and Dr. Norman Wilde and Dr. Ed Rodgers for their continuing support and encouragement throughout past years. And, last but not least, we would like to thank our fellow faculty members and Diana Walker for their continuous support.

— Richard Earp and Sikha Bagui

Prologue

The Software Engineering Process and Relational Databases

This chapter is provided for those readers who wish to study SQL and database topics but feel that they lack sufficient relational database background. It is not intended to replace a course about databases; a theoretical database course is often taught concurrently with a study of this material.

We begin with some preliminary definitions and a short history of databases; this material is followed by a description of how and why the relational database model fits into the database world of today. We then delve into a more detailed description of relational databases and normal forms. Finally, we provide a brief explanation of software engineering. Some knowledge of how software

(SQL "programs," if you will) might be developed is useful in understanding why we suggest using some of the formats and conventions in this book.

What Is a Database?

Data — facts about something — must be stored in some fashion in order for it to be useful (that is, in order for it to be found). A *database* is a collection of associated or related data. For example, the collection of all the information in a doctor's office could be referred to as a "medical office database"; all data in this database would refer to information that is pertinent to the operation of a medical office.

Before the age of computers, databases were kept on paper (medical databases were kept in doctor's offices, personnel databases were kept in employment offices, and so on). Over the years, databases have migrated from paper to electronic media.

Regardless of the format (paper or electronic), information stored in databases is organized into files. *Files* are collections of data about one subject. A medical office database might well have files other than patient data. One might imagine that in a doctor's office there would be a pharmaceutical file, employee files, and so on. Individual data is stored in *records* within files. For example, Mr. Smith's medical records would be located in his doctor's patient files. Individual items in Mr. Smith's records would include his name, his address, and so on. Information such as name and address is referred to as a *field* or *attribute*. Thus, databases contain files, files contain records, and records contain fields (attributes).

Database Models

A conceptual way of thinking about data in a database is called a *logical model.* With a logical model, we conceptualize how data might be organized. The way that data is actually laid out on the disk — that is, where each bit is located — is called a *physical model.*

Over the past 40 years or so, three basic camps of logical database models evolved:

- The hierarchical model
- The network model
- The relational model

All three of these models represent ways of logically perceiving the arrangement of data in databases. As you will see, the hierarchical and network models can infer some knowledge of how the physical model operates, whereas the relational model virtually ignores the physical model. We will now give a little insight into each of these three historically significant models to see how the relational model has evolved into the dominant logical model.

The Hierarchical Model

The idea in a *hierarchical model* is that all data is logically arranged in a hierarchical fashion (also known as a parent-child relationship). As an example, suppose that your company had an employee database. Further, suppose that this database contained files about employees and files about the dependents of employees. Some employees have dependents; some do not. For those employees with dependents, there must be a reference in an employee's record to the location of corresponding dependent records in the dependent file.

If an employee had dependents, you could think of that employee as being the "parent" of the dependent. Thus, every dependent would have one employee-parent and every employee could have one or more dependent-children. (Please note that the parent and child inference is not necessarily meant to be a personal relationship: child and parent are not meant to be taken literally.) The connection of the employee to a dependent and vice versa is called a *relationship*. Figure 1 illustrates the hierarchical model.

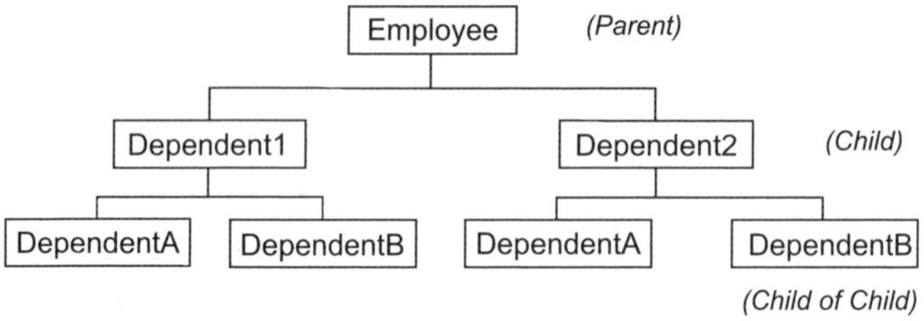

Figure 1: Hierarchical model

In logical models, all relationships between records have what are called structural constraints. *Structural constraints* indicate how many of one type of record is related to another (also called cardinality) and whether one type of record must have such a relationship (also called participation or optionality).

For example, suppose that an employee *may* have *one or more* dependents, and all dependents in a database *must* be related to *one and only one* employee. We would term the cardinality of this relationship of employee to dependent as *one to many*, or 1:M. Further, since we say that an employee may (or may not) have dependents, the participation constraint of the relationship from the employee side is *partial* or *optional*. Because a dependent must be associated with one employee, the participation from the dependent side is *full* or *mandatory*. Note that the words "one or more" and "one and only one" indicate cardinality. The words "may" and "must" indicate optionality or participation.

In a hierarchical model, there are either one-to-one (1:1) or one-to-many (1:M) relationships (as shown in Figures 2 and 3, respectively), but never many-to-one (M:1) relationships. The most common relationship in a hierarchical model is 1:M. In our example, a 1:M relationship means that one employee may have many dependents ("many" meaning one or more). Further, the 1:M employee-to-dependent relationship implies that each dependent has one and only one employee-parent.

Figure 2: One-to-one (1:1) relationship

Less common, but allowable in hierarchical models, is the 1:1 relationship shown in Figure 2. In our employee example, a 1:1 relationship would imply that one employee might have one designated dependent and a dependent would be related to only one employee. This relationship might infer a "next-of-kin" designation, for example.

Figure 3: One-to-many (1:M) relationship

Other Cardinalities

A many-to-one (M:1) relationship between employee and dependent would imply that a dependent might have multiple parents (multiple employees who "claimed" a particular dependent). But, because the relationship is M:1, it would infer that an employee could have at most one dependent. Again, the M:1 relationship is not allowed in hierarchical logical models.

The very common many-to-many (M:N) relationship, shown in Figure 4, is not allowed in hierarchical database models either. (Note that while M usually stands for many, M:N is used more often than M:M to stand for many-to-many because it's important not to infer that the values for M and N are equal; in fact, they usually are not.) We will discuss examples of these hierarchically unallowable relationships (M:1 and M:N) when we look at the network model.

Figure 4: Many-to-many (M:N) relationship

Before the advent of computers, hierarchical databases were implemented by choosing some way of physically connecting the parent and child records. Suppose that an employee, Mr. Smith, had three children: Sally, Ann, and Tom. If we think back to paper records, we might visualize that in the dependent file there could be a Sally Smith record, an Ann Smith record, and a Tom Smith record. Where would these independent records be in the dependent file? Suppose we put the dependent records in a filing cabinet and put the notation in Mr. Smith's record that his dependents were Sally (file drawer 1, record 2),

Ann (file drawer 3, record 12), and Tom (file drawer 2, record 13). Here, we are using a system to physically "point to" the dependent records from Mr. Smith's employee record. This scheme is called a *multiple-child pointer scheme*.

On a disk, just as with the paper model, one record "points to" physical locations for the dependent records. There are actually multiple ways to implement the hierarchical model. In addition to using a disk address instead of "file drawer x, record y," a different way to implement the employee-dependent relationship would be to have an employee record point to a disk location for the first dependent record. That dependent record would in turn point to the disk location of the next dependent, and so on. In this example, Mr. Smith would point to Sally, Sally would point to Ann, and Ann would point to Tom. This is called a *linked list of child-records* or, in older database books, a *chain* of records because they can be thought of as record-links that are chained together.

Regardless of how cleverly the physical record links are established, the hierarchical model has two major drawbacks:

- The choice of the way in which the files are physically linked impacts the way underlying database software is developed and hence impacts database performance both positively and negatively.
- Not all situations fall into parent-child (hierarchical) formats. What if one wanted to have a dependent (a child record) point to multiple employees (multiple parent records) and vice versa (that is, an M:N relationship)? This would not fit the hierarchical database model well.

To see a way around these drawbacks, let's take a look at the network model.

The Network Model

The *network model* handles the multiple parent concern of the hierarchical model. In the network model, you are not restricted to having one parent per child — a many-to-one (M:1) and a many-to-many (M:N) relationship is acceptable. As an example, if your network-modeled database consisted of your employee-dependent situation as in the hierarchical model, but it was necessary to allow multiple parents for each dependent person, then a dependent could have two or more "parents." Therefore, a dependent could relate to one or more employees. In this case, we would say that the relationship was many-to-many (M:N). An employee *may* have many dependents (zero or more) and a dependent *must* have a relationship to many (one or more) employees.

Implementing the employee-dependent M:N database in hierarchical databases involves creating redundant files. However, in network databases, you can simply have two or more connections or links from the dependent-child to however many parents there are. If you considered the multiple-child pointer scheme or the chaining system we described earlier in a network setting, you might imagine that the pointing schemes in networked databases are very complex. Indeed they are.

To illustrate the network model, suppose we consider a database of employees and projects to which they are assigned. Figure 5 is an example of a network model in which employees may be working on many projects, and the projects may have many employees working on them. This is a many-to-many (M:N) relationship between employee and project.

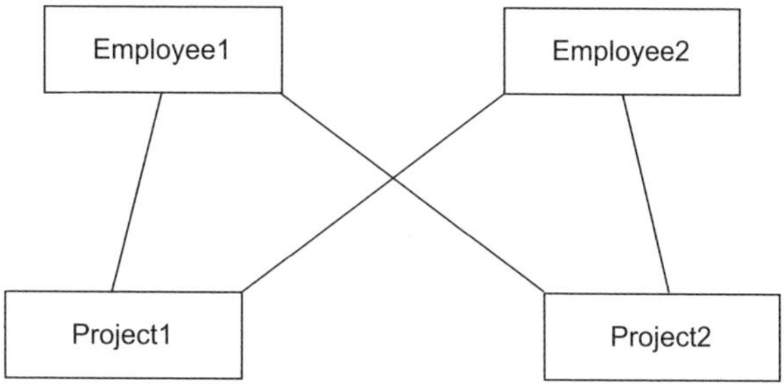

Figure 5: The network model

In both the hierarchical and network models, database software must be designed using some pointing scheme; we need some method of connecting or linking records. This choice of record connection then presents a hardware-implemented connection, which impacts performance both positively and negatively. Further, as the database becomes more complicated, the paths of connections and the maintenance problems with all the links become exponentially more difficult for the software to manage. As you can imagine, networked linking is more complicated than hierarchical linking. As records are updated, inserted, or deleted, all links must be maintained. The more complicated the system, the more danger there is for dead links (i.e., corrupted links or lost addresses).

Contemporary Databases: The Relational Model

Dr. Edgar F. Codd introduced the *relational model* around 1970 (Codd, 1970b). The relational model is based on the idea that if you ignore the way data files are connected and arrange your data into simple two-dimensional, unordered tables, then you can develop an algebra for queries and focus on the data as data, not as a physical realization of a logical model.

Before we delve into the details of the relational model, however, it is important that you understand some changes in terminology as databases evolved from file systems to relational databases. As you may know, current terminology refers to an *entity* as something we record information about. For example, we record information (data, facts) about employees; hence, an employee is an entity. Whereas we used to refer to the employee file, we now refer to the set of employee entities as an *employee entity set.* Likewise, employee records (now called *entities*) contain employee information fields (now called *attributes*) of the employee entity. The reason for using the terms entity set, entity, and attribute instead of file, record, and field, respectively, is to disconnect the idea of a physical file, record, and field from the logical notion of these things.

The relational model is truly logical in that one is no longer concerned with how data is physically stored. Rather, files (called *entity sets* in the relational model) are simply unordered, two-dimensional tables of simple data values (or sets of rows). Necessarily, there are rules that govern the way these tables "store" data. The first rule is that the data itself must be atomic — that is, not broken down into component parts. The tables of data are called *relations* and because the data is stored in tables, each table has columns (which represent the attributes) and rows (which represent the instances of each entity). A collection of tables is referred to as a *relational database.* Table 1 shows an example of an employee relation (a table with data in it).

Table 1: Example of an Employee relation (table)

Employee

name	address	project#
Smith	123 4th St.	101
Smith	123 4th St.	102
Jones	5 Oak Dr.	101

Employee is a table — a relation. The column names name, address, and project# are attributes. A row, such as

<Smith, 123 4th St, 102>

represents an employee entity occurrence (data about a person named Smith, Smith's address, and the project# that Smith is working on). In relational databases, the ordering of the rows in the table is not defined. The rows are considered a set of rows and sets do not have an order. Rows are either in the set or they or not, but where they are in the set is irrelevant. Thus, Table 2 is equivalent to Table 1.

Table 2: A reordered Employee table

Employee

name	address	project#
Smith	123 4th St.	102
Jones	5 Oak Dr.	101
Smith	123 4th St.	101

The First, Second, and Third Normal Forms

Obviously, databases contain more data than is illustrated in the Employee table shown above. To arrive at a workable way of deciding which pieces of data go into which tables and to arrange the tables so that Codd's relational algebra would work, Codd proposed something he referred to as *normal forms* (Codd, 1970a, Codd, 1970c, Codd, 1971). He originally defined three normal forms: the first, second, and third normal forms. We'll look at each of these next.

The First Normal Form

The *first normal form* (1NF) requires that data in tables be atomic and be arranged in a two-dimensional layout. Atomicity implies that there be no column that contains repeating groups. Repeating groups refers to columns that may contain multiple occurrences of data. A repeating group is an example of non-atomic data and violates the definition of a relational table. A problem with putting data in tables with repeating groups is that the table cannot be easily indexed or arranged in such a way that data in the repeating group can easily be found. Put another way, data in repeating groups cannot be found without searching each row individually.

An example of a table *not* in 1NF is where there is an employee entity with attributes (fields) name, address, and dependent name, as shown below:

```
Employee (name, address, {dependent name}),
```

where `{dependent name}` implies that the attribute is repeated, with rows containing data as illustrated below:

```
Smith, 123 4th St., {John, Mary, Paul, Sally}
Jones, 5 Oak Dr., {Mary, Frank, Bob}
Adams, 33 Dog Ave., {Alice, Alicia, Mary}
```

What do you do if you want to store data about employees and their dependents? Before tackling the problem of dealing with non-1NF data, it is helpful to understand the concept of a key. A *key* in a table is an attribute or group of attributes that identifies a row — a unique handle whereby one can find information in a table. In Table 2, the key could be the employee's last name. For example, if you wanted information about Jones, you would access Jones's row. Clearly, if there were two people named Jones, you would have to come up with a better key, such as adding a unique employee number to the table.

To resolve the non-1NF problem (and other NF problems that you will encounter), databases must be *normalized.* The normalization process involves splitting tables into two or more tables (also called *decomposition*). Data can be reunited from decomposed tables with a relational operation called a *join*. We will illustrate the normalization process by first solving the non-1NF problem. To eliminate the non-1NF problem, we do the following:

Non-1NF to First Normal Form (1NF)

The repeating group is moved to a new table with the key of the table from which it came.

For now, we will assume that the last name of the employee is the key in this version of Employee.

Non-1NF:

```
Smith, 123 4th St., {John, Mary, Paul, Sally}
Jones, 5 Oak Dr., {Mary, Frank, Bob}
Adams, 33 Dog Ave., {Alice, Alicia, Mary}
```

is decomposed into 1NF tables with no repeating groups, as shown in Tables 3a and 3b.

Table 3a: Employee table in 1NF

Employee1

name	address
Smith	123 4th St
Jones	5 Oak Dr
Adams	33 Dog Ave

Table 3b: Dependent table in 1NF

Dependent

dependentName	employeeName
John	Smith
Mary	Smith
Paul	Smith
Sally	Smith
Mary	Jones
Frank	Jones
Alice	Adams
Alicia	Adams
Mary	Adams

In Table 3a, name is the key of Employee1 — it uniquely identifies the rows. We would call name, as used here, a *primary key*. A primary key is the key that we choose to uniquely identify a row. In Table 3b, the primary key is a combination (concatenation) of dependentName and employeeName. Neither the dependentName nor the employeeName is unique in Table 3b, and hence both attributes are required to uniquely identify a row in the table. The employeeName in Table 3b is called a *foreign key* because it references a primary key: name in Table 3a. The original data could be reconstructed by combining all the rows in Table 3a with the corresponding rows in Table 3b where the employee names were equal. The combination of tables based on the equality of some attribute (column) is called an *equi-join* in a relational database.

The Second Normal Form

The *second normal form* (2NF) requires that data in tables depend on the whole key of the table. If a data item depends on only part of a compound key, it is said to be a *partial dependency*. Partial dependencies are not allowed in the second normal form. Consider for example a table called Employee2 with attributes name, job, salary, and address, as shown below:

```
Employee2(name, job, salary, address)
```

And suppose that it takes a combination of the name and job fields (which can also be shown as name + job) to identify a salary field, but the address field depends only on the name field. Name + job is a concatenated key and is the primary key of this table. *Dependence* here means identification. Since address depends on name, if you know the name, this will identify the person's address in this data. We would say that the dependence of address on name is a partial dependency because name is only part of the primary key of the table. Table 4 shows some sample data for the Employee2 table.

Table 4: A non-2NF table

Employee2

name	job	salary	address
Smith	Welder	14.75	123 4th St.
Smith	Programmer	24.50	123 4th St.
Smith	Waiter	7.50	123 4th St.
Jones	Programmer	26.50	5 Oak Dr.
Jones	Bricklayer	34.50	5 Oak Dr.
Adams	Analyst	28.50	33 Dog Ave.

Can you see the problem developing here? The address is repeated for each occurrence of a name. This repetition is called *redundancy* and leads to anomalies. An *anomaly* means that there is a restriction on doing something due to the arrangement of the data. There are insertion anomalies, deletion anomalies, and update anomalies. The key of this table is name + job. This is clear because neither attribute will, by itself, identify information in a particular row — it really takes both the name and job fields to identify a salary. (Try to answer the question "What is

Smith's salary?" without saying what the job is.) However, address depends only on the name, not the job. This is an example of a partial dependency. Address depends on only part of the key of this table.

A further rule of relational databases is that no part of a primary key of a relation may be null (have a undefined value); this is known as the *entity-integrity constraint*. What's wrong with null values in keys? If a null were allowed in a key, the key would have a non-unique value and hence not be a key at all.

An example of an insertion anomaly would be where one would want to insert a person into Table 4a, but the person to be inserted has not been assigned a job. This insertion cannot be done because a value would have to be known for the job attribute.

An example of an update anomaly would be where one of the employees changed his or her address. Suppose the person named Smith had a change of address. You would have to change three rows to accommodate this one address change.

An example of a delete anomaly would be where the person named Adams quits, so Adams' row is deleted. However, the information that the analyst pay is $28.50 is also lost. Therefore, a delete anomaly deletes more than is desired. How do we decompose a non-2NF table to fix these problems?

Non-2NF to 2NF

To make a non-2NF table a 2NF table, the partial dependency has to be removed to a new table. The attributes (columns or fields) that are fully dependent of the primary key (primary key here being name + job) are put together with the primary key (as shown in Table 5a). The salary is dependent on both parts of the primary key (name and job), so salary is placed with the name and job fields in Table 5a.

Table 5a: EmployeeSalary table

EmployeeSalary

name	job	salary
Smith	Welder	14.75
Smith	Programmer	24.50
Smith	Waiter	7.50
Jones	Programmer	26.50
Jones	Bricklayer	34.50
Adams	Analyst	28.50

Then, the fields that are not fully dependent on the primary key are placed with the part of the primary key that they are dependent on. In this case, the address field (which is only dependent on part of the primary key) is placed with name (the part of the primary key that address is dependent on). This is shown in Table 5b.

Table 5b: EmployeeInformation table

EmployeeInformation

name	address
Smith	123 4th St.
Jones	5 Oak Dr.
Adams	33 Dog Ave.

Hence the non-2NF table, Table 4, is decomposed to the 2NF tables as shown in Tables 5a and 5b.

The key of the EmployeeSalary table (Table 5a) is as before — the name and the job taken together. The key of the EmployeeInformation table (Table 5b) is just the name. Note that the "other" non-key attributes in both tables now depend on the key (and only on the key). Also, note the removal of redundancy and the elimination of possible anomalies. For practice, try adding, deleting, and updating rows and note that the anomalies are gone.

The Third Normal Form

The *third normal form* (3NF) requires that data in tables depend on the primary key of the table. 2NF problems only appear when there is a concatenated key to begin with; 3NF problems do not require a concatenated key. 3NF problems occur when some non-key data item is more properly identified by something other than the key of the table. A classic example of non-3NF relation could be shown by the Employee3 table below. Employee3 has the attributes name, address, project#, and project-location.

```
Employee3(name, address, project#, project-location)
```

In Employee3 we will assume that the name field is the primary key. Suppose that project-location in Employee3 means the location from which a project is controlled, and is defined by the project#. Some sample data will illustrate the problem, as shown in Table 6.

Table 6: A non-3NF table

Employee3

name	address	project#	project location
Smith	123 4th St.	101	Memphis
Smith	123 4th St.	102	Mobile
Jones	5 Oak Dr.	101	Memphis

Note the redundancy in Table 6. Project 101 is controlled in Memphis, but every time a person is recorded as working on project 101, the fact that they work on a project that is controlled in Memphis is recorded again. The same anomalies — insert, update, and delete — are also present in this table. You cannot add a project# or project location unless you have a name. (Remember that name cannot be null.) If you deleted Smith working on project 102 in Table 6, the "102, Mobile" information is also deleted. Suppose project 101's control location is moved to Tuscaloosa? How many changes would this require?

The name, project#, project-location situation is called a transitive dependency. This transitive dependency is resolved by decomposing into 3NF as follows.

Non-3NF to 3NF

To make a non-3NF table into a 3NF table, the transitive dependency has to be removed to a new table. Thus, Table 6 is decomposed into two tables: Tables 7a and 7b.

Table 7a: Employee table in 3NF

Employee3a

name	address	project#
Smith	123 4th St.	101
Smith	123 4th St.	102
Jones	5 Oak Dr.	101

Table 7b: Project table in 3NF

Project

project#	project location
101	Memphis
102	Mobile
101	Memphis

Again, observe the removal of the transitive dependency and the anomaly problem.

Before concluding our discussion of normal forms, note that there are other cases of non-normality that are beyond the scope of this brief overview. These other cases are not common, and a "good" relational database may be thought of as one that is in the 3NF.

In summary, there are rules that define a relational database. All data is laid out in two-dimensional tables. The tables have no sense of ordering of rows. In fact, the tables are often called "sets of rows." All data is atomic. A primary key is a chosen unique row-identifier; if one wants information from a row in a table, one gets it by the primary key value. The 3NF means that the data in a relation depends only on the primary key of the relation. Data in 3NF is assumed to be in the 1NF and 2NF. Data that is decomposed into the 3NF will avoid most redundancy and anomaly problems.

What Is the Software Engineering Process?

As a further bit of orientation to the material contained in this book, we wish to present some insight into the idea of how software is developed. The term "software engineering" refers to a process of specifying, designing, writing, delivering, maintaining, and finally retiring software. Many excellent references on the topic of software engineering (see Schach, 2005) are available to the interested reader.

A basic idea in software engineering is that to build software correctly, a series of standardized steps or phases are required. The steps ensure that a process of thinking precedes action. That is, thinking through "what is needed" precedes "what is written." One common version of presenting the thinking before acting scenario is referred to as a "waterfall model" as described in *Classical and Object-Oriented Software Engineering* (Schach, 2005). In the waterfall model the phases of software development are supposed to flow from one to another in a directional way without retracing.

Software production is like a life-cycle process — it is created, used, and eventually retired. The "players" in the software development life cycle may be placed into two camps, often referred to as the *user* and the *analyst*. Software is designed by the analyst for the user.

There is no general agreement among software engineers as to the exact number of phases in the waterfall-type software development model. For that matter, many software engineering practitioners do not support the waterfall model at all, and models vary greatly. A very brief description of a software development process goes like this:

Step 1 (or Phase 1). *Requirements*: find out what the user wants/needs.

Step 2. *Specification*: write out the user's wants/needs as precisely as possible.

Step 3. *Software is designed* to meet the specification from step 2.

Step 4. *Software is written (developed).*

Step 5. *Software is turned over to user (implementation).*

Step 6. *Maintenance* is performed on software until it is retired.

In most software engineering models, some feedback loops are allowed. For example, when completing step 2, it is possible to go back to step 1 if the analyst does not understand and communicate the user's requirements.

For SQL users, the software process involves retrieving data from a database. A database is a collection of facts stored on some electronic media. Often the question in SQL is "What does some user want to know?" This question is called a *query* because it is a question directed at the information contained in the database.

What does software engineering have to do with writing queries? We can draw a number of implications from the software engineering process. In the normal business world, the person who writes SQL queries is often not the person who wants to know something. Imagine a supervisor telling a SQL programmer to find the names of all the customers who spent over $1,000 this month. The SQL programmer has to design a query for this request. Does the SQL programmer understand the nature of the question? (requirements) Did the SQL programmer provide feedback to the supervisor and verify what he or she thinks the question is? (specification) What kind of query will the SQL programmer decide upon? (design) The query is written. Is it efficient? Does the query answer the original question? Is the execution of the query ready for turning over the result to the supervisor? (development/implementation) What if the question is changed and the supervisor now wants to change the amount in the query or the month or the format of the names? (maintenance)

If queries are written so that other people can immediately understand what the writer intended, then this is very good. Most of the money spent on software is on maintenance, which is a very time-consuming and expensive part of the software process — particularly if the software engineering process has not been done well. Maintenance involves correcting hidden software faults as well as enhancing the functionality of the software.

It is important to not only learn to write queries, but also to learn to write them so that other SQL programmers will know that you understood the requirements and so that your queries are open to maintenance. You must also learn ways to audit your query results. As with other programming, computers only do what you tell them to do. If you ask for garbage, you will get garbage. If your query is not correctly formed, SQL may give you an answer, but the answer may not be correct or make sense. You must ask yourself if the query really answers the question that was originally asked. Equally important is whether other SQL programmers will understand your query.

References

Codd, E.F., (1970a). "Notes on a Data Sublanguage," IBM internal memo (January 19, 1970).

Codd, E.F., (1970b). "A Relational Model of Data for Large Shared Data Banks," *CACM 13*, No. 6 (June, 1970).

Codd, E.F., (1970c). "The Second and Third Normal Forms for the Relational Model," IBM technical memo (October 6, 1970).

Codd, E.F. (1971). "A Database Sublanguage Founded on the Relational Calculus," IBM Research Report RJ893 (July 26, 1971).

Schach, S.R., (2005). *Classical and Object Oriented Software Engineering*, WCG McGraw-Hill, New York.

Chapter 1

Getting Started with Oracle

In this chapter, we will cover some elementary commands and statements that will allow us to use Structured Query Language (SQL). We will see generic operations that we can do with SQL and specific statements that pertain to the principal delivery system, Oracle. We will be concentrating on SQL*PLUS (often written as SQLPLUS and henceforth referred to as SQLPLUS), which is used to generate, store, and edit SQL queries and to control the database environment.

We start the chapter by showing you how to get started with Oracle in UNIX. Basic familiarity with the UNIX operating system is assumed. Then we present some basic system parameters, before introducing you to Oracle's commands — mainly the SELECT syntax. This leads to a discussion on basic editing. Next we show you how to access the tables in our Student-Course database. This is the database that is used throughout this book. The script to create this database is available at www.cs.uwf.edu/~sbagui or at the publisher's site at www.wordware.com/files/sql-oracle (download instructions are available at these web sites); the database structure is also presented in Appendix C of this book. We also discuss the creation and use of synonyms and introduce Oracle's data dictionary. Finally, toward the end of the chapter, we present a convention for writing SQL statements and show you how to save and print your work.

Getting Started with Oracle in UNIX

Before you can sign on to Oracle in UNIX, you need to first log on to the UNIX system. For logging on to UNIX, access the host UNIX machine and sign in to your UNIX account. Once you are at the UNIX prompt, you are now ready to sign on to Oracle.

Signing on to Oracle in UNIX

To sign on to Oracle and use SQL, type **sqlplus** from the UNIX prompt. The UNIX prompt is:

```
[whelk ~]$
```

as shown in Figure 1.1.

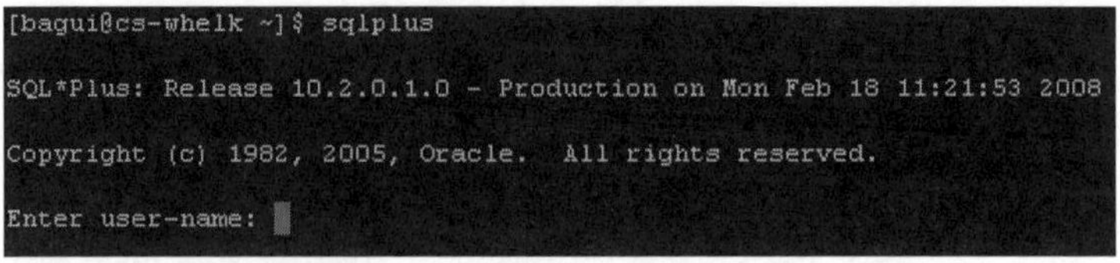
[baqui@cs-whelk ~]$ sqlplus
SQL*Plus: Release 10.2.0.1.0 - Production on Mon Feb 18 11:21:53 2008
Copyright (c) 1982, 2005, Oracle. All rights reserved.
Enter user-name:

Figure 1.1: The UNIX prompt

Note: sqlplus must be in lowercase letters because UNIX is case sensitive. While Oracle refers to SQL*Plus with mixed uppercase and lowercase letters and the asterisk (*), you do not type the invocation of the language with the * and the mixture of uppercase and lowercase letters; you just type sqlplus.

Once you type sqlplus at the UNIX prompt, as shown in Figure 1.1, the system will begin loading Oracle, and you will be asked to supply your SQL username and password. After you have typed in your SQL username and password, you will get the SQL prompt, as shown in Figure 1.2.

Connected to:
Oracle Database 10g Enterprise Edition Release 10.1.0.3.0 - 64bit Production
With the Partitioning, OLAP and Data Mining options
SQL>

Figure 1.2: The SQL prompt

You are now in SQLPLUS, and it awaits your instructions.

Setting Your System Parameters

Before you begin exploring SQL, you can set some parameters in SQLPLUS that will make your exploration easier. Setting these parameters is optional (you can use the defaults), but many programmers like to modify the environment in which they are working. Following are some examples of environmental control statements you can use should you choose to modify your environment.

The general form of the SET command for setting and unsetting environmental parameters is:

```
SET parameter [ON|OFF|value]
```

The notation [ON|OFF] means you are to choose either ON or OFF. Note that some commands require a value instead of ON/OFF.

Setting the PAUSE Parameter

The first useful parameter we will illustrate is PAUSE. When you execute a command that has a long output, the screen view of the result will scroll by very quickly. To keep your screen from scrolling, you can pause the screen and view results one screen at a time, then press the <Enter> key to move to the next screen. The command is:

```
SQL> SET PAUSE ON
```

Note: Oracle is case insensitive to commands, so "SET PAUSE ON" is the same as "Set pause on" or "set pause on." However, Oracle is case sensitive to data, as we will illustrate later. In this book, for consistency, we will use uppercase for all commands.

If you have a long result and you wish to terminate the command and you have pause on, you can use <Ctrl+C> and <Enter>. If you wish to reset SET PAUSE ON so the screen will keep scrolling (i.e., not pause) when you execute commands, type:

```
SQL> SET PAUSE OFF
```

Setting the Prompt Parameter

Another parameter that can be personalized is the prompt. The default for the prompt is:

```
SQL>
```

To change the default SQL prompt, you can type something like the following:

```
SQL> SET SQLPROMPT "Enter command->"
```

This `SET` command changes the prompt so that it looks like the one shown in Figure 1.3.

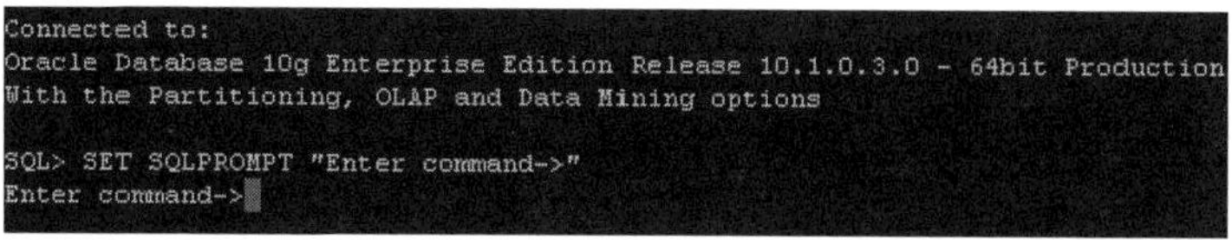
Connected to:
Oracle Database 10g Enterprise Edition Release 10.1.0.3.0 - 64bit Production
With the Partitioning, OLAP and Data Mining options
SQL> SET SQLPROMPT "Enter command->"
Enter command->

Figure 1.3: Setting the prompt parameter

To return to the default prompt, you can type:

```
SQL> SET SQLP SQL>
```

Note that `SET SQLPROMPT` may be abbreviated as `SET SQLP`.

Showing Timing Statistics

To show timing statistics for each SQL command that is executed, type:

```
SQL> SET TIMING ON
```

To reset the preceding, type:

```
SQL> SET TIMING OFF
```

Viewing a List of System Parameters

To view a list of all your system parameters, type:

```
SQL> SHOW ALL
```

Obviously, when you see this, you will note that there are plenty of other SET commands. We will look at additional commands later in the chapter.

Oracle's HELP Command in UNIX

If Oracle's HELP subsystem has been loaded into the UNIX system, you can type:

```
SQL> HELP
```

This will give you:

```
HELP
----
Accesses the SQL*Plus help system.  Enter HELP INDEX for a list of topics.
HELP [topic]
```

Then, to find the topics you can get help on, type:

```
SQL> HELP INDEX
```

This will give the list of available topics, as shown below:

```
@            COPY         PAUSE                    SHUTDOWN
@@           DEFINE       PRINT                    SPOOL
/            DEL          PROMPT                   SQLPLUS
ACCEPT       DESCRIBE     QUIT                     START
APPEND       DISCONNECT   RECOVER                  STARTUP
ARCHIVE LOG  EDIT         REMARK                   STORE
ATTRIBUTE    EXECUTE      REPFOOTER                TIMING
BREAK        EXIT         REPHEADER                TTITLE
BTITLE       GET          RESERVED WORDS (SQL)     UNDEFINE
CHANGE       HELP         RESERVED WORDS (PL/SQL)  VARIABLE
CLEAR        HOST         RUN                      WHENEVER OSERROR
COLUMN       INPUT        SAVE                     WHENEVER SQLERROR
COMPUTE      LIST         SET
CONNECT      PASSWORD     SHOW
```

We recommend that you explore a few of these topics. For example, to explore the help on the CLEAR command, you can type:

```
SQL> HELP CLEAR
```

This will give you:

```
CLEAR
-----
Resets or erases the current value or setting for the option,
CL[EAR] option ...
where option is one of the following clauses:
BRE[AKS]
BUFF[ER]
COL[UMNS]
COMP[UTES]
SCR[EEN]
SQL
TIMI[NG]
```

Using Oracle Commands

In this section we'll begin looking at the syntax and semantics of the SQL language.

Understanding SQL and Its Sublanguage

What we call "SQL" has several "sublanguages," and as you grow more familiar with SQL programming, you will want to distinguish between them:

- **SQLPLUS (SQL*PLUS)** (typified by SPOOL, HELP, LIST, HOST, SET, and so on) is an Oracle application language from which Oracle commands are launched.
- **PL/SQL** (as in BEGIN..END, EXIT, LOOP, IF, and so on) is a procedural language we will explore later in this text.

Note that SQL is a set language as opposed to a procedural language.

In addition, SQL itself is further subdivided into classes:

- **SQL — Data Definition Language (DDL)** (for example, `ALTER`, `CREATE`, `DROP`)
- **SQL — Data Manipulation Language (DML)** (for example, `SELECT`, `INSERT`)
- **SQL — transaction control** (for example, `COMMIT`, `ROLLBACK`)
- **SQL — session control** (for example, `ALTER SESSION`, `SET ROLE`)
- **SQL — system control** (for example, `ALTER SYSTEM`, `COMMENT`)
- **SQL — security control** (for example, `GRANT`, `REVOKE`)

SQL allows us to tell Oracle which pieces of information we want to:

- `SELECT` (retrieve data)
- `INSERT` (add data)
- `UPDATE` (modify data)
- `DELETE` (remove data)

from a database. In fact, these four verbs are the primary SQL commands that we will use to deliver Oracle instructions. `SELECT` is the main query verb.

Using SELECT Statement Syntax

The syntax of the most basic `SELECT` statement is:

```
SELECT result set FROM Table
```

The *result set* is what we want to see: a set of rows using columns that are available in a table. *Table* is the name of the table from which the data will be taken. The keywords SELECT and FROM are *always* present in a SELECT statement. Statements in Oracle are terminated by a semicolon, so to display a table called Student from our database you would enter:

```
SQL> SELECT * FROM rearp.Student;
```

Here, the asterisk (*) means "all columns" of the table Student.

Note: If your screen appears frozen, it may be because of the SET PAUSE ON command. To see the next screen of text or output, press the <Enter> key.

Say the Student table has a column called sname. If you wanted to see only the names of students, you would type:

```
SQL> SELECT sname FROM rearp.Student;
```

Note: As mentioned earlier, Oracle commands are not case sensitive, so SELECT Sname or SELECT SNAME will also work.

Re-executing a Command

You may need to re-execute a command. Each command you issue from the SQL prompt is stored in a buffer. To re-execute a command from the buffer (that is, without typing it back in), you can use a forward slash (/). At the SQL prompt, if you type the following:

```
SQL> /
```

you will re-execute the last command you ran.

Accessing Tables

Oracle allows you to set the access control of tables. For example, the table in the example mentioned above was created by Richard Earp, who is identified under Oracle as rearp. In this case, you have been given the privilege to view a table called Student, which was created by another user, rearp. To view the table, you need the name of the creator and the actual name of the table. You "qualify" the table name with the creator name, hence `rearp.Student` is used.

Suppose your name is S. Brown. If you had created a similar table under your own account, sbrown, and called it Student1, my statement (as executed from my account) would be `SELECT * FROM sbrown.Student1;` (assuming you gave me permission to view your table). You do not need to qualify your own tables; if you are sbrown and are logged in as sbrown, you would use `SELECT * FROM Student1;` from your own account to access your own table.

In Oracle, you can use as many lines as you wish to enter a statement. Oracle SQL acts like a "free-form" language. The system will not process a SQL statement until you enter a semicolon in a statement or a forward slash (/) on a line by itself in the first position. Actually, it is advantageous to enter statements on several lines in Oracle because it makes the statements easier to change and re-execute. So, you could enter the previous statement as:

```
SQL> SELECT *
  2  FROM rearp.Student;
```

This format, in which we capitalize keywords such as `SELECT` and `FROM` and use lowercase letters for user-supplied words, is preferred by many SQL programmers and is an excellent convention to follow.

Adding Comments to Statements

Software engineering suggests that we write statements in a standard and understandable way. To aid in statement elucidation, comments are often used in statements. Comments are ignored by SQLPLUS, but are very useful to programmers in determining what a statement does, when it was written, who wrote it, and so on. Comments can start with a double hyphen (--) and can be put into multi-line statements like this:

```
SQL> SELECT *              -- comment.. this statement will show only
  2  FROM rearp.Student   -- seniors and has an optional WHERE clause
  3  WHERE class = 4;
```

The WHERE clause in this example is a row filter. The result set in this query consists of rows in the table Student, with all columns, but only the rows WHERE the value of the class attribute is equal to 4 (that is, seniors) are selected for the result set.

Note: A comment cannot be on the same line with the semicolon.

You can also create a comment in SQL with a slash and asterisk (/* and */). Following is an example of a commented statement that uses the slash and asterisk format:

```
SQL> SELECT sname, class      /* get the sname and class */
FROM rearp.Student            /* from the Student table */
;
```

In some versions of Oracle you cannot start a command with a comment as your first word because you need a keyword such as SELECT for correct syntax.

A Few More Examples and Further Comments about Case

Although SQL is not case sensitive for commands, it is case sensitive for data. The following statements, which basically ask to show all student information about people whose name is "Smith," are equivalent as far as SQL is concerned:

```
SELECT * FROM rearp.Student WHERE sname = 'Smith';
Select * from rearp.Student where sname = 'Smith';
Select * FROM rearp.Student Where Sname = 'Smith';
```

However, the following examples would not retrieve any data:

```
SELECT * FROM rearp.Student WHERE sname = 'smith';
Select * from rearp.Student where sname = 'SMITH';
```

The reason for the non-return of data is that you need to match data in the database exactly. If the name in the sname column is stored as "Smith," then "SMITH" or "smith" won't match.

Editing SQL Statements

There are two ways to edit SQL statements. You can use an editor (the preferred method), or you can use SQLPLUS commands (such as `CHANGE`, `EDIT`, `APPEND`, `INPUT`, and `DELETE`). Use whichever method is the most comfortable for you when you need to change a command, but you should be familiar with both basic methods. We will illustrate how to use each of these methods next.

Option 1: Editing SQL Statements Using an Editor

If a command is entered at the SQL prompt and a change is desired, most programmers prefer to use an editor. An editor allows you to save your query as you are developing it.

Defining an Editor

UNIX has several editors, such as vi, joe, emacs, and others. The vi editor is one of the most popular UNIX editors, so in this book we will illustrate its use.

The first thing that must be done is to define the editor at the SQL prompt, as shown below:

```
SQL> define_editor=vi
```

Since the editor must be defined every time you log in to SQL, it is good practice to define the editor as soon as you log in; this way you are free to use the editor as and when you please.

Editing the Buffer

Let's say that after defining the editor you want to use (vi in this case), you type the following query at the SQL prompt:

```
SQL> SELECT cou
FROM rearp.Prereq;
```

This query returns an error message because cou is not a valid attribute name in the Prereq table. To correct this query (while it is in the buffer) using the vi editor, you can type:

```
SQL> EDIT
```

The vi editor screen will come up, as shown in Figure 1.4. You can now edit your query using normal vi commands. So, move your cursor to the end of the first line and press <**Esc**> and then type **i** to switch to Insert mode. Now you can insert whatever you want. For example, type **rse** at the end of "cou". Your query should now read:

```
SELECT course
FROM rearp.Prereq
```

Once you have finished editing your query, press <**Esc**> and type **:wq** to save it and quit vi. Note that every time you want to change modes in vi, you have to press the <**Esc**> key first. The buffer will be saved in a file named afiedt.buf (the default buffer name) and you will be returned to the SQL> prompt.

Figure 1.4: The vi editor screen

You can now execute the buffer by typing a forward slash (/), as shown below:

```
SQL> /
```

Note: Some useful vi commands are presented at the end of Appendix A of this book, in the section labeled "Using vi as Your Editor." If you need further help on the vi editor, you can use the "man vi" command in UNIX.

If you invoke EDIT again, you will be overwriting your default buffer, afiedt.buf. However, if you just want to fix a command and go on to a different command, you may not need to save the contents of afiedt.buf.

Note: You can use the HELP EDIT command to display a help screen that discusses editing options that may be useful.

If you define another UNIX editor or exit SQL, you will automatically exit vi.

Saving the Buffer

If you wish to save the contents of the default buffer (afiedt.buf) into a file you can later use, invoke the SAVE command as follows:

```
SQL> SAVE query1
```

You will get:

```
Created file query1
```

You have now saved the contents of your buffer into a file called query1.

To overwrite and replace the previous version of query1 you would type:

```
SQL> SAVE query1 REPLACE
```

The REPLACE command overwrites the previously saved version of query1.

Using GET

You can also retrieve an existing query, such as query1, at a later time and re-run it. To retrieve query1, use the GET command as shown below:

```
SQL> GET query1
```

This will give:

```
1* SELECT course_number FROM rearp.Prereq
```

Thus bringing query1 back into the buffer. You can now edit query1 by typing:

```
SQL> EDIT query1
```

The vi editor screen (see Figure 1.4) will come up again and you can edit the query as needed.

Using a Script File to Save Your Query

When you are writing longer queries, instead of using the default buffer, you will want to write and save your query in a script file using the editor. To create a script file using the editor, type:

```
SQL> EDIT filename
```

This will open up a blank vi editor screen (similar to Figure 1.4) where you can use vi commands and type your query. When you save the query, it will now be saved in a script file called *filename* instead of the default buffer, afiedt.buf.

To run this script file you would type:

```
SQL> @filename
```

Option 2: Editing SQL Statements or Queries Using SQLPLUS

SQLPLUS supplies several commands to make minor changes to statements or queries.

Using the CHANGE Command

If your change is simple (such as a misspelled word), you can use the CHANGE command. The format for the CHANGE command is:

```
CHANGE /old string/new string/
```

Note: The last forward slash (/) after *new string* is not required.

The CHANGE command works on one line at a time. For example, if you type:

```
SQL> SELECT * FROM rearp.Studens;
```

You get an error message because the word Student is misspelled as Studens. You can change the query by typing:

```
SQL> CHANGE /ens/ent/
```

or

```
SQL> c /ens/ent
```

By leaving off the ending forward slash you repair the current line of the command in the buffer. You then use the forward slash (/) to re-execute the line.

Note: The CHANGE command can be abbreviated to "c".

Using the LIST Command

If the query is a multi-line query, you should first use LIST to view the whole query. Then you can enter the line number that you want to change, CHANGE the line, type LIST again, and then re-execute the command with the forward slash. For example if you type:

```
SQL> SELECT cou
FROM rearp.Prereq;
```

you get an error on SELECT cou because cou is not a valid attribute name. To correct the error with the line editor, complete the following steps:

1. To see the whole buffer, type LIST:

   ```
   SQL> LIST
   ```

   This will give you:

   ```
   1  SELECT cou
   2* FROM rearp.Prereq
   ```

   Notice that the query is displayed with line numbers. The line with the asterisk (*) is the current line.

Note: The LIST command can be abbreviated to "l".

2. To make line 1 the current line of the buffer, type:

   ```
   SQL> 1
   ```

   and press <**Enter**>. This will give you:

   ```
   1  SELECT cou
   ```

   Line 1 is now your current line. Now you can use the CHANGE command on the current line.

3. To change cou to course_number, type:

```
SQL> CHANGE /cou/course_number/
```

This will give you:

```
    1* SELECT course_number
```

4. To see the whole buffer again, use LIST.

```
SQL> LIST
```

In this case, you will see lines 1 and 2:

```
1  SELECT course_number
2* FROM rearp.Prereq
```

5. Finally, to execute the corrected command, type:

```
SQL> /
```

This produces the following output:

```
COURSE_N
--------
ACCT3333
COSC3320
COSC3380
COSC3380
COSC5234
ENGL1011
ENGL3401
ENGL3520
MATH5501
POLY2103
POLY5501
CHEM3001

12 rows selected.
```

Using the APPEND Command

If you need to add something to the end of a line, you can use APPEND. For example, assuming that you followed the steps in the previous section, if you type LIST:

```
SQL> LIST
```

You will get:

```
1  SELECT course_number
2* FROM rearp.prereq
```

Now if you type **1** to make line 1 the current line, as shown below:

```
SQL> 1
```

You will get:

```
1* SELECT course_number
```

And line 1 is now the current line. So, now if you type `APPEND` and whatever you want to append, as shown below:

```
SQL> APPEND , prereq
```

Note: APPEND can be abbreviated to "a".

You will get:

```
1* SELECT course_number, prereq
```

Now if you type `LIST` again as follows:

```
SQL> LIST
```

You will get:

```
1  SELECT course_number, prereq
2* FROM rearp.prereq
```

Then, to run this query, type the forward slash at the SQL prompt as shown below:

```
SQL> /
```

To get the following output:

```
COURSE_N  PREREQ
--------  -------
ACCT3333  ACCT2220
CHEM3001  CHEM2001
COSC3320  COSC1310
COSC3380  COSC3320
COSC3380  MATH2410
COSC5234  COSC3320
ENGL1011  ENGL1010
ENGL3401  ENGL1011
ENGL3520  ENGL1011
MATH5501  MATH2333
POLY2103  POLY1201
POLY5501  POLY4103

12 rows selected.
```

Using the INPUT Command

INPUT allows you to add a line anywhere in your script. For example, if you type the following:

```
SQL> SELECT *
  2  FROM rearp.student
  3  /
```

You will get:

```
      STNO SNAME                MAJO      CLASS BDATE
---------- -------------------- ---- ---------- ---------
         2 Lineas               ENGL          1 15-APR-80
         3 Mary                 COSC          4 16-JUL-78
         8 Brenda               COSC          2 13-AUG-77
        10 Richard              ENGL          1 13-MAY-80
        13 Kelly                MATH          4 12-AUG-80
        14 Lujack               COSC          1 12-FEB-77
        15 Reva                 MATH          2 10-JUN-80
        17 Elainie              COSC          1 12-AUG-76
        19 Harley               POLY          2 16-APR-81
        20 Donald               ACCT          4 15-OCT-77
        24 Chris                ACCT          4 12-FEB-78
```

```
      .
      .
      .
      9 Romona               ENGL              15-APR-80
      6 Ken                  POLY              15-JUL-80
     88 Smith                                  15-OCT-79
    191 Jake                 MATH            2 10-JUN-80

48 rows selected.
```

Now, if you want to input a line at the end of your script, type **i** for the INPUT command, as shown:

```
SQL> i
```

You will get:

```
3
```

Note: INPUT can be abbreviated to "i".

Now type **WHERE class = 2;** as shown below:

```
3  WHERE class = 2;
```

Once you press <**Enter**>, you will get the following output:

```
      STNO SNAME                MAJO      CLASS BDATE
---------- -------------------- ---- ---------- ---------
         8 Brenda               COSC          2 13-AUG-77
        15 Reva                 MATH          2 10-JUN-80
        19 Harley               POLY          2 16-APR-81
       125 Sadie                MATH          2 12-AUG-80
       126 Jessica              POLY          2 16-JUL-81
       129 Cedric               ENGL          2 15-APR-80
       130 Alan                 COSC          2 16-JUL-77
       147 Smithly              ENGL          2 13-MAY-80
       148 Sebastian            ACCT          2 14-OCT-76
       191 Jake                 MATH          2 10-JUN-80
```

```
10 rows selected.
```

To view your complete script, type **LIST**:

```
SQL> LIST
```

You will get:

```
 1  SELECT *
 2  FROM rearp.student
 3* WHERE class = 2
```

Now, if you type /, as shown below:

```
SQL> /
```

You will get the same ten rows of output as shown above.

Using INPUT to Insert a Line

In the previous section, we showed you how you insert a line at the end of a script. But, what if you want to insert a line in the middle of a script? For example, if you type the following script at the SQL prompt:

```
SQL> SELECT sname
  2  WHERE class = 3;
```

You will get the following error message since you missed the FROM clause:

```
WHERE class = 3
*
ERROR at line 2:
ORA-00923: FROM keyword not found where expected
```

So you need to insert a line in the middle of the script. Let's start off by typing **LIST** to see our line numbers. (Although this may not appear to be useful in the short scripts that we are using for examples, you will need to do this as your scripts get longer to make it easier to track the line numbers.)

```
SQL> LIST
```

You will get:

```
1  SELECT sname
2* WHERE class = 3
```

Now type **1** to make line 1 your current line. (Note that INPUT will insert a line after the current line.)

```
SQL> 1
```

You will get:

```
1* SELECT sname
```

Now type **i** for INPUT, as shown below:

```
SQL> i
```

You will get:

```
2i
```

Type **FROM rearp.student**, as shown below:

```
2i FROM rearp.student
```

When you press <**Enter**> you will get:

```
3i
```

If you do not want to insert anything else, just press <**Enter**> to exit Input mode. To see your resulting script again, type **LIST**:

```
SQL> LIST
```

You will get:

```
1  SELECT sname
2  FROM rearp.student
3* WHERE class = 3
```

Using the DELETE Command

Next we will show you how to delete a line. So again, assuming that you have been following the previous steps, type **LIST** (it's always a good idea to first list out your script):

```
SQL> LIST
```

You will get:

```
1  SELECT *
2  FROM rearp.student
3* WHERE class = 3
```

If you want to delete line 3, you would type:

```
SQL> del 3
```

Now if you type **LIST**:

```
SQL> LIST
```

You will get:

```
1  SELECT *
2* FROM rearp.student
```

As you can see, line 3 has been deleted.

Displaying the Student-Course Database

It is now time to explore the actual database that you will be using for the exercises in this book. We will begin our exploration with simple queries. The exercises at the end of the chapter will ask you to modify these sample queries to produce other results.

Displaying the Course Table (the Course Relation)

The statement that displays the data in the Course table is:

```
SELECT *
FROM rearp.Course;
```

Note: From now on, we will usually display SQL queries or statements without the SQL> prompt.

This will give you all the rows and columns of the Course table as shown below:

COURSE_NAME	COURSE_N	CREDIT_HOURS	OFFE
ACCOUNTING I	ACCT2020	3	ACCT
ACCOUNTING II	ACCT2220	3	ACCT
MANAGERIAL FINANCE	ACCT3333	3	ACCT
ACCOUNTING INFO SYST	ACCT3464	3	ACCT
INTRO TO COMPUTER SC	COSC1310	4	COSC
TURBO PASCAL	COSC2025	3	COSC
ADVANCED COBOL	COSC2303	3	COSC
DATA STRUCTURES	COSC3320	4	COSC
DATABASE	COSC3380	3	COSC
OPERATIONS RESEARCH	COSC3701	3	COSC
ADVANCED ASSEMBLER	COSC4301	3	COSC

```
.
.
.
CALCULUS 3               MATH1503           3  MATH
Math Analysis            MATH5501           3  MATH

32 rows selected.
```

Note that:

- The word SELECT is necessary for all queries.
- The * means that all columns (attributes) will be in the result set.
- The word FROM is necessary for all SELECT commands as it defines the table from which you are selecting.
- Course is the name of the table you want to see. The "rearp." part of the table name is a necessary qualifier for our database.

Creating a Synonym for the Course Table

As mentioned earlier, because the tables you will use were created by someone other than yourself, you must qualify the table name by indicating the table creator (owner) (for example, rearp.Course). Here, "rearp" is the owner (the creator) of the table Course. Qualifying the name of the tables you use frequently becomes tiresome. Therefore, most programmers find it useful to create a synonym for qualified table names. The command for creating a synonym is:

```
CREATE SYNONYM x FOR y;
```

where *x* is the name you want to use, and *y* is the table you want to reference. For example, to create a synonym called "cou" for the Course table you would type:

```
CREATE SYNONYM cou FOR rearp.Course;
```

So, instead of typing:

```
SELECT *
FROM rearp.Course;
```

you can now type:

```
SELECT *
FROM cou;
```

It is a good idea to use meaningful synonym names, but simple names such as "test1" or even "x" are syntactically acceptable.

Deleting a Synonym

Once you have created a synonym, it exists until you delete it. To delete a synonym, type:

```
DROP SYNONYM synonym_name;
```

Introducing the Oracle Data Dictionary

The Oracle data dictionary is a set of tables that are used by the Oracle engine to keep track of the stored databases. The dictionary contains a vast set of tables and views that we will explore later in Appendix B. At this point we just want to introduce you to the dictionary. The dictionary holds descriptions of tables and objects that have been created by individual users, the system, and the database administrator (DBA). The tables in the dictionary are prefixed so that you can find:

- Objects that are created by you, which are prefixed by USER_ (e.g., USER_TABLES)

- Objects that are created by others, but where you have permission to query, which are prefixed by ALL_ (e.g., ALL_OBJECTS)
- Objects that are created by the system or the DBA, which are prefixed by DBA_
- Some dynamic tables, which have names like V$parameter (not prefixed)
- A few other tables such as ROLE_ROLE_PRIVS

To see the synonyms you have created, you can type:

```
SELECT *
FROM USER_SYNONYMS;
```

or

```
SELECT *
FROM ALL_SYNONYMS
WHERE table_owner = 'sql-id';
```

where 'sql-id' stands for your user ID.

Assuming that your user ID is SBROWN, you can type:

```
SELECT *
FROM ALL_SYNONYMS
WHERE table_owner = 'SBROWN';
```

Note: Since the 'sql-id' is case sensitive, you must exactly match the stored value. The stored value in the system (dictionary) tables is in all caps; for example, SBROWN if the table's owner is SBROWN.

Another command you will find useful is:

```
SELECT *
FROM USER_TAB_COLUMNS;
```

This will give you all the information about the columns you have created in tables. This is a very long list, so a much more useful command in Oracle is:

```
SELECT *
FROM TAB;
```

This gives you the tables and synonyms you have created. The keyword TAB is a public synonym for a view of the dictionary.

While TAB is still used, TABS (a synonym for a data dictionary table called USER_TABLES) and OBJ (a synonym for USER_OBJECTS) are more current versions. TABS contains a lot more information than TAB, which presents a display problem as it has 18 columns. For a simple version of "What tables do I have?" you can still use the SELECT * FROM TAB command.

If you wanted to use OBJ, you could type:

```
SELECT *
FROM OBJ;
```

However, as with TABS, you would be overwhelmed with information. To find out what OBJ stands for, look up OBJ in the dictionary table ALL_SYNONYMS.

For a display that looks like TAB, you could type:

```
SELECT SUBSTR(object_name,1,15) Name, object_type Type
FROM OBJ;
```

You could alternatively use SELECT * FROM TAB.

Using DESC

To see the attribute names in a table you use DESCRIBE *tablename*. DESC is a synonym for DESCRIBE. To use this very common command, type:

```
DESC Student
```

You will then see a screen like the one shown in Figure 1.5.

```
Name                                      Null?    Type
----------------------------------------- -------- ----------------
STNO                                      NOT NULL NUMBER(3)
SNAME                                              VARCHAR2(20)
MAJOR                                              CHAR(4)
CLASS                                              NUMBER(1)
BDATE                                              DATE
```

Figure 1.5: Description of a table

Note: The semicolon after the DESC Student command is not necessary, but it is allowed.

The `Dict` synonym is used for a table called Dictionary, which is owned by user SYS. To list all the tables you can "see," type:

```
SELECT *
FROM Dict;
```

Note: The result set is long and will scroll by quickly. You might consider setting "pause on" so you can see one screen at a time.

Using a Convention for Writing SQL Statements

Although there is no fixed rule for writing SQL statements, we suggest you follow a convention that will help you as your statements become more involved. The convention is this:

- Use uppercase for the keywords like `SELECT`, `FROM`, and `WHERE`. Use lowercase for user-supplied words.

- Align the keywords SELECT, FROM, and WHERE on separate lines like this:

```
SELECT *
FROM Student
WHERE class = 1;
```

  At the very least, start each command on a separate line (SELECT, WHERE, etc.).

Printing Query Results and Using Host

To print the result of a query or a command, you can use the SPOOL command to create a file of your output, and then print the spooled file.

The spooled file will be available through the operating system you are using. To activate SPOOL, type:

```
SQL> SPOOL ex1
```

and then type the following SQL statement:

```
SQL> SELECT * from rearp.Student;
```

The output will appear on the screen. ex1.lst will be the name of the file to which your output will be simultaneously redirected as it executes and displays on the screen. If you want, you can use some name other than ex1; however, Oracle will add the .lst extension to the filename if you do not add an extension yourself.

When you execute a series of commands, such as one or more SELECTs, you can examine the result from ex1.lst, as well as modify it or print it from the host operating system.

The command to turn off the spooler is:

```
SQL> SPOOL OFF
```

> **Note:** There is a SPOOL OUT command as well, which will automatically route the output of the spooler to a printer and turn off the spooling at the same time. However, *most* of the time it is easier to control the spooled output via SPOOL OFF rather than SPOOL OUT.

You can use HOST from SQLPLUS to temporarily exit to your host operating system and use the operating system commands to do whatever you need to do. Type EXIT from the host operating system prompt to return to SQLPLUS.

Following is a sequence of commands that shows how to go to the host, use it, and return to SQLPLUS.

At the SQL prompt, type:

```
SQL> host
```

Your screen will look similar to Figure 1.6:

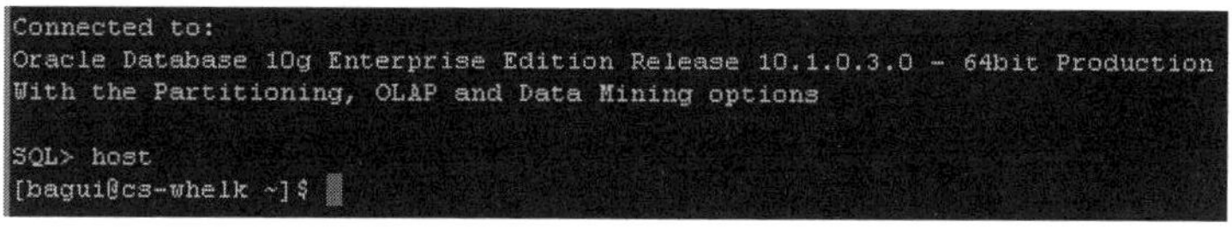
Connected to:
Oracle Database 10g Enterprise Edition Release 10.1.0.3.0 - 64bit Production
With the Partitioning, OLAP and Data Mining options
SQL> host
[bagui@cs-whelk ~]$

Figure 1.6: The host screen

To see a directory listing of the files that you had spooled from within SQLPLUS, type:

```
[bagui@cs-whelk ~]$ dir *.lst
```

as shown in Figure 1.7.

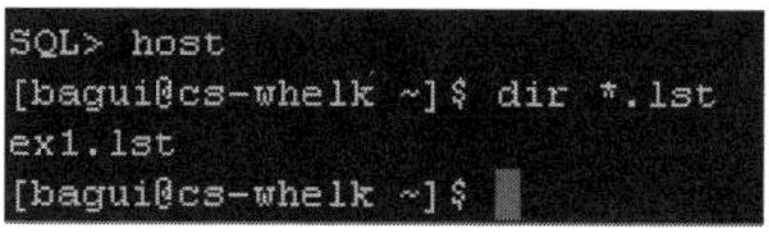
SQL> host
[bagui@cs-whelk ~]$ dir *.lst
ex1.lst
[bagui@cs-whelk ~]$

Figure 1.7: Viewing spooled files from host

To view the ex1.lst file that you had spooled from SQLPLUS, type:

```
[bagui@cs-whelk ~]$ type ex1.lst
```

To make a copy of your spooled file (for example, if you wanted to copy ex1.lst to a backup file called ex1.bak), type:

```
[bagui@cs-whelk ~]$ copy ex1.lst ex1.bak
```

To return to SQLPLUS from the host prompt, type:

```
[bagui@cs-whelk ~]$ exit
```

You must turn off the spooler before you can open the spooled file to read or copy it in the operating system.

Warning: If you turn off the spooler and then later turn it back on in the sequence SPOOL ex1, then SPOOL OFF, and then you type SPOOL ex1 again, you will write over the first version of ex1.lst with *no* warning, so be careful! Remember to use a new filename with the SPOOL command the next time you use it.

Signing Off from Oracle

To exit SQLPLUS, type:

```
SQL> EXIT
```

or

```
SQL> QUIT
```

Exercises for Chapter 1

Although we discussed spooling in this chapter, a shortcut to copy, save, and print your SQL output would be to copy and paste your output into a word processor file, and then save and print from there. We suggest you use the shortcut copy and paste method for these exercises. To keep a complete record of your work, it would be good idea to copy/paste your query as well as your query result.

1-1. Print a description of the Course table (use `DESC Course`). Use the `SELECT` statement to display the actual data. (Just a reminder — you will have to use "rearp." in front of all the table names since you are not the owner of these tables. So, you will have to type `rearp.Course` instead of just `Course` in your query.)

1-2. Create a synonym for the Student table. Display the table description using the synonym. Display all the data in the Student table using `SELECT`.

1-3. We have supplied a Student-Course database with the following tables (these tables are shown in Appendix C of this book):

Student
Course
Section
Prereq (for Prerequisite)
Grade_report
Department_to_major
Room

There are also other tables that will be used later in other exercises (such as Cap and Plants), but they are not tables connected with the Student-Course data. Create synonyms for the tables in the Student-Course database because you will use them extensively. You can shorten the name of the table in your synonym if you like, for example:

```
CREATE SYNONYM d2m FOR Department_to_major;
```

Using the synonyms and DESC, show the first few lines of all the tables in the Student-Course database. To display the column names and data types, use DESC. To display the first few lines of the table, use a WHERE on the table name like this:

```
SELECT *
FROM Student
WHERE rownum < 5;
```

Assume you created a synonym Stu for the Student table. The rownum is a *built-in* row counter (also called a *pseudo variable*). You can also use rownum in the result set of the query like this:

```
SELECT rownum, sname, major
FROM Stu
WHERE major = 'ACCT';
```

1-4. Using line editing:

a. Type and run the statement SELECT * FROM Prereq;

b. Use c (the CHANGE command) to edit the statement and display the Course table instead of the Prereq table.

c. Edit and then run the statement by appending a new line that says:

```
WHERE offering_dept = 'COSC'
```

So your query should now read:

```
SELECT *
FROM Course
WHERE offering_dept = 'COSC';
```

d. Edit the above query (use a line number and `c`) to select only course_name in the result set. (*Hint: Use course_name instead of* *.)

e. Delete the last line (`WHERE offering_dept = 'COSC'`) of your query and re-run it.

f. Add a line that says: `WHERE offering_dept = 'MATH'` to the query so it now reads:

```
SELECT *
FROM Course
WHERE offering_dept = 'MATH';
```

Re-run the query.

1-5. You can access system parameters using a dummy table called dual. Run the following statement:

```
SELECT sysdate, user FROM dual;
```

Oracle provides dual as a convenient table guaranteed to return at least one row and one column.

The system also keeps the time and you can show it like this:

```
SELECT TO_CHAR (sysdate,'dd-Mon-yyyy hh24:mm:ss') FROM dual
```

Other date formats are also available, and will be discussed later in this book.

Chapter 2

More "Beginning" SQL Commands

In this chapter, we start by expanding on the power of the SELECT command. Then we show you how to create tables, insert values into tables, change values in tables, and delete rows from tables. The next sections discuss the transaction processing commands ROLLBACK, COMMIT, and SAVEPOINT, which can be used in multi-user environments. Transaction processing commands can be used to undo changes in the database within a transaction. The chapter closes with a discussion of common data types available in Oracle, and includes an extended discussion of the DATE data type.

An Extended SELECT Statement

The SELECT is *usually* the first word in a SQL statement. The SELECT statement instructs the database engine to return information from the database as a set of records, a "result set." SELECT displays the result on the computer screen, but does not save the results.

The simplest form of the SELECT syntax is:

```
SELECT attributes
FROM Table;
```

A database consists of a collection of tables and each table consists of rows of data. The above statement returns a result set of zero or more rows drawn from specified columns (attributes) that are available in a table. In the above statement, *Table* is the name of the table in the database from which the data will be taken, and *attributes* are the selected columns (attributes) in the table. The keywords SELECT and FROM are always present in a SELECT statement.

For example,

```
SELECT name, address
FROM Old_Customer;
```

would select the attributes name and address from the table Old_Customer. The result set would consist of rows of names and addresses in no particular order.

An asterisk (*) in place of the attributes would mean "list all the attributes (or columns) of the table" (i.e., whole rows).

An example of using the asterisk would be:

```
SELECT *
FROM Student;
```

The asterisk (*) means return all columns from the table Student.

SELECTing Attributes (Columns)

All of the attributes (columns) and/or all of the rows do not have to be retrieved with a SELECT statement. What is shown is called the *result set*. Attribute names may be selected from a table, provided the exact name of the attribute is known. To find out the exact name of the attributes we can use DESC *tablename*. DESCRIBE was discussed in Chapter 1.

For example, in our Student-Course database we have a table called Student. Say we want to list all the student names from this Student table. First, we use DESC Student and find that the attribute name for student name is "sname":

```
SQL> DESC Student
```

Gives:

```
Name                              Null?    Type
--------------------------------- -------- --------------------
STNO                              NOT NULL NUMBER(3)
SNAME                                      VARCHAR2(20)
MAJOR                                      CHAR(4)
CLASS                                      NUMBER(1)
BDATE                                      DATE
```

So to show a listing of student names, we use the following query:

```
SELECT sname
FROM Student;
```

Note: All SQL statements require semicolons. SQLPLUS commands **do not** require semicolons or a terminating character, but if you use one, SQLPLUS is usually forgiving and will execute the command correctly anyway. In addition, DESC does not require a semicolon, while SELECT does.

This would give:

```
SNAME
--------------------
Lineas
Mary
Brenda
Richard
Kelly
Lujack
Reva
.
.
.

Smith
Jake

48 rows selected.
```

Note that the result set is unordered.

Using ORDER BY

The result set (output) of the query above contains all the sname values (student names) in the Student table. However, the sname rows in the result set are not ordered since a relational table does not keep its rows in any particular order. Rows in relational database tables are supposed to be mathematical sets (no particular ordering of rows and no duplicate rows); result sets are similar to mathematical sets in that no order is implied, but duplicates may occur. To show the contents of a table in a specific order, we can force the ordering of the result set using the `ORDER BY` clause in the `SELECT`.

For example, the following query will show the snames and majors of the Student table, ordered by sname. Here the output will be ordered in ascending order of sname because ascending order is the default of the ORDER BY clause.

```
SELECT sname, major
FROM Student
ORDER BY sname;
```

This will give:

```
SNAME                MAJO
-------------------- ----
Alan                 COSC
Benny                CHEM
Bill                 POLY
Brad                 COSC
Brenda               COSC
Cedric               ENGL
Chris                ACCT
Cramer               ENGL
Donald               ACCT
Elainie              COSC
Fraiser              POLY
.
.
.
Susan                ENGL
Thornton
Zelda                COSC

48 rows selected.
```

To order the output in descending order, add the DESC keyword to the appropriate attribute in the ORDER BY clause as follows:

```
SELECT sname, major
FROM Student
ORDER BY sname DESC;
```

This will give:

```
SNAME                MAJO
-------------------- ----
Zelda                COSC
Thornton
Susan                ENGL
Steve                ENGL
Stephanie            MATH
Smithly              ENGL
Smith
Sebastian            ACCT
Sadie                MATH
Romona               ENGL
Richard              ENGL
.
.
.
Bill                 POLY
Benny                CHEM
Alan                 COSC

48 rows selected.
```

The collection of names and majors are the same in both the previous result sets, but the names in the last result are in descending (reverse) order by sname.

We may also order within an order. For example, suppose we type:

```
SELECT sname, major
FROM Student
ORDER BY major DESC, sname;
```

The result is:

```
SNAME               MAJO
------------------- ----
Lionel
Smith
Thornton
Genevieve           UNKN
Lindsay             UNKN
Bill                POLY
Fraiser             POLY
George              POLY
Harley              POLY
Holly               POLY
Jessica             POLY
Ken                 POLY
Lynette             POLY
Jake                MATH
Kelly               MATH
Mario               MATH
Monica              MATH
Reva                MATH
Sadie               MATH
Stephanie           MATH
Cedric              ENGL
Cramer              ENGL
.
.
.
Donald              ACCT
Francis             ACCT
Harrison            ACCT
Sebastian           ACCT

48 rows selected.
```

Here the output is principally ordered by major in descending order and then by sname within major with the names in ascending order.

Note: Ascending order is the default of the ORDER BY clause.

SELECTing Rows

The output of rows in the result set may be restricted by adding a WHERE clause to the SELECT. When the WHERE clause is used, the database engine selects the rows from the table that meet the conditions given in the WHERE clause. If no WHERE clause is used, the query will return all rows from the table. In other words, the WHERE clause acts as a row filter.

The simplest format of the SELECT with a WHERE clause would be:

```
SELECT attribute(s)
FROM Table
WHERE criteria;
```

For example, to list the snames of only those students who are seniors, we would type:

```
SELECT sname
FROM Student
WHERE class = 4;
```

This will give:

```
SNAME
--------------------
Mary
Kelly
Donald
Chris
Holly
Jerry
Harrison
Francis
Jake
```

```
Benny

10 rows selected.
```

The comparison operators:

>	(greater than)
≠	(not equal)
=	(equal)
>=	(greater than or equal to)

are available for WHERE conditions. Other common operators include IN, EXISTS, and BETWEEN (each of which will be discussed later in the text).

Multiple conditions can be included in a WHERE clause by using the logical operators AND and OR. In addition there is also a BETWEEN operator. The following sections discuss the use of the AND, OR, and BETWEEN operators in the WHERE clause.

Using AND

By using AND in the WHERE clause of a SELECT we may combine conditions. The result set with WHERE..AND.. can never contain more rows than the SELECT with either of the conditions by themselves.

For example, consider the following query:

```
SELECT sname, class, major
FROM Student
WHERE class = 4
AND major = 'MATH';
```

This gives us:

```
SNAME                    CLASS MAJO
-------------------- ---------- ----
Kelly                        4 MATH
```

```
1 rows selected.
```

The `AND` clause means that both the conditions, `WHERE class = 4` *and* `major = 'MATH'` have to be met for the row to be included in the result set.

Using OR

Another way to combine conditions in a `WHERE` clause is by using the `OR` operator. The `OR` operator can used when either of the conditions can be met for a row to be included in the result set. For example, consider the following query:

```
SELECT sname, class, major
FROM Student
WHERE class = 4
OR major = 'MATH';
```

This gives us:

```
SNAME                     CLASS  MAJO
-------------------- ----------  ----
Mary                          4  COSC
Kelly                         4  MATH
Reva                          2  MATH
.
.
.
Benny                         4  CHEM
Mario                            MATH
Jake                          2  MATH

16 rows selected.
```

This result set is a tabulation of all students who are "either math majors or seniors" (`class = 4`). The `OR` means that either of the criteria (`WHERE class = 4` *or* major = 'MATH') has to be met for the row to be included in the result set.

It is not necessary to include all of the attributes used in the WHERE clause in the result set. It is a good idea to include the attributes when checking a query, but the following query is also legal:

```
SELECT sname
FROM Student
WHERE class = 4
OR major = 'MATH';
```

Giving:

```
SNAME
--------------------
Mary
Kelly
Reva
Donald
.
.
.

16 rows selected.
```

Using BETWEEN

The BETWEEN operator returns rows when a value occurs within a given range of values. The general syntax of the BETWEEN operator is:

```
SELECT ...
FROM ...
WHERE attribute
BETWEEN value1 AND value2;
```

If we want to find all the student rows with class values between 1 and 3 (inclusive), we could type:

```
SELECT sname, class
FROM Student
WHERE class
BETWEEN 1 AND 3;
```

This would give us:

```
SNAME                     CLASS
-------------------- ----------
Lineas                        1
Brenda                        2
Richard                       1
Lujack                        1
Reva                          2
Elainie                       1
Harley                        2
.
.
.
Gus                           3
Jake                          2

28 rows selected.
```

In Oracle SQL, *value1* has to be less than *value2*. Also note that the end points are included in the result set (BETWEEN is inclusive). The same result could be obtained using the query:

```
SELECT sname, class
FROM Student
WHERE class >=1
AND class <=3;
```

A Simple CREATE TABLE Command

The CREATE TABLE command allows us to create a table in which we can store data. A minimal syntax for the command is as follows (we will expand this CREATE TABLE syntax with more options in a later chapter):

```
CREATE TABLE Tablename (attribute_name data_type, attribute_name
data_type, ...);
```

In Example 1 below, we are creating a table called Customer. Suppose the table has two attributes: "cno" and "balance." The cno attribute is a fixed-length character attribute with a length of 3 and will represent customer-number. The balance attribute is numeric with five digits and no decimals. The appended DEFAULT 0 means that if no value is specified for balance when rows are inserted into the table, balance will be equal to zero.

Example 1

```
CREATE TABLE Customer
(cno CHAR(3),
balance NUMBER(5) DEFAULT 0);
```

Note: In this example, if DEFAULT 0 were not used, balance would default to null if no value was supplied. Null means "empty" and is Oracle's way of signifying that no value is present.

We could have also used other data types for the attributes. For example, another common character data type is VARCHAR2(*n*), which is a variable-length character string of length n. (We discuss data types in depth later in the chapter.)

Example 2

Here we are creating a table of names:

```
CREATE TABLE Names
(name VARCHAR2(20));
```

This table, Names, has one attribute called name. The name attribute is of data type VARCHAR2 (which means variable-length character), and each name in the table can have a maximum size of 20 characters.

Note: Older versions of SQL used a type called VARCHAR, but Oracle now uses and recommends the use of VARCHAR2.

Inserting Values into an Existing Table

Values may be inserted into a table using several methods. We will illustrate three such methods:

- INSERT INTO..VALUES
- INSERT INTO..SELECT
- Using the SQLLOADER procedure

In this chapter we will look at INSERT INTO..VALUES and INSERT INTO..SELECT. We will discuss SQLLOADER later in the text (in Chapter 10) because SQLLOADER is not a command, but rather a special Oracle procedure for loading tables.

INSERT INTO..VALUES

The INSERT INTO command with the VALUES option creates **one** row in a table. The following example inserts one row into the Names table:

```
INSERT INTO Names
VALUES ('Joe Smith');
```

(Note that the semicolon is required.)

where

- INSERT is the name of the command.
- INTO is a necessary keyword.
- Names is the name of the existing table.
- VALUES is another necessary keyword.
- 'Joe Smith' is a string of letters in agreement with the data type.

Note that 'Joe Smith' is surrounded by single quotes. "Joe Smith" would be invalid.

If you created a table with n attributes, you usually would have n values in the INSERT INTO..VALUES part of the command. For example, if you have created a table called Employee, like this:

```
CREATE TABLE Employee (name            VARCHAR2(20),
                       address         VARCHAR2(20),
                       employee_number NUMBER(3),
                       salary          NUMBER(6,2));
```

then the INSERT INTO..VALUES to insert a row would match column for column and would look like this:

```
INSERT INTO Employee
VALUES ('Joe Smith', '123 4th St.', 101, 2500);
```

The values in the VALUES part of the command correspond to the attribute names by their ordering. Note that character types must be enclosed in single quotes and numeric types are not in quotes. For example, 'Joe Smith' corresponds to the attribute name, and 2500 corresponds to the attribute salary. An INSERT that looks like the following is incorrect because it does not include all four attributes of the Employee table:

```
INSERT INTO Employee
VALUES ('Joe Smith', '123 4th St.');
```

However, if you do not have data values for all four attributes of the Employee table, and you wish to insert values into only two of the four attributes, you can name the attributes you want to insert and provide values for only those attributes you name. For example, you can use an INSERT like this:

```
INSERT INTO Employee (name, address)
VALUES ('Joe Smith', '123 4th St.');
```

In this case, the inserted row will contain nulls or default values for the attributes you did not use.

An INSERT that looks like the following is incorrect because it does not have the values in the same order as the definition of the table:

```
INSERT INTO Employee
VALUES (2500, 'Joe Smith', 101, '123 4th St.');
```

If the data had to be specified in this order, the statement could be corrected by specifying the column names like this:

```
INSERT INTO Employee (salary, name, employee_number, address)
VALUES (2500, 'Joe Smith', 101, '123 4th St.');
```

The following INSERT would also be legal if the address and the salary were unknown when the row was created, provided that the address and salary attributes allowed nulls:

```
INSERT INTO Employee
VALUES ('Joe Smith', null, 101, null);
```

Note: If you use non-numeric types like CHAR (fixed character size) or VARCHAR2 (variable character size), you must use single quotes in the INSERT command. If you use numeric types, you should not use quotes. Oracle will convert character strings to numbers, but it is never good to let a system do something that you should do yourself.

INSERT INTO..SELECT

With the `INSERT INTO..VALUES` option, you insert only one row at a time into a table. With the `INSERT INTO..SELECT` option, you may (and usually do) insert many rows into a table at one time. The syntax of the `INSERT INTO..SELECT` is:

```
INSERT INTO Table-name
"SELECT clause"
```

For example, the following statement will insert all the values from the table Customer into another table called Newcustomer:

```
INSERT INTO Newcustomer
SELECT *
FROM Customer;
```

Before using this above `INSERT INTO..SELECT` statement, you would have had to first create the Newcustomer table, and, although the attributes of Newcustomer do not have to be named exactly what they are named in Customer, the data types and sizes have to match. The size of the attributes that you are inserting into, that is, the size of the attributes of Newcustomer, have to be at *least* as large as the size of the attributes of Customer.

You can also use the `SELECT` to load less than the whole table (fewer rows or columns) as necessary. Some examples of restricted `SELECT`s for the `INSERT` command follow.

Suppose you have a table with only one attribute, which was created as follows:

```
CREATE TABLE Namelist
(customer_name VARCHAR2(20));
```

And assume that a second table exists that has the following structure:

```
Customer (cname, cnumber, amount)
```

where cname is `VARCHAR2(20)`. You can populate the Namelist table with the cname column from the Customer table as follows:

```
INSERT INTO Namelist
SELECT cname
FROM Customer;
```

This would copy all the names from Customer to Namelist.

Alternately, you can copy only certain names from Customer by restricting the `SELECT` as illustrated in the following example:

```
INSERT INTO Namelist
SELECT cname
FROM Customer
WHERE amount > 100
```

As with the `INSERT INTO..VALUES`, if you create a table with n attributes, you usually would have n values in the `INSERT INTO..SELECT` in the order of definition. Suppose that you had a table like the following:

```
Employee (name, address, emp_num, salary)
```

Further suppose that you wanted to load a table named Emp1 from Employee with the following attributes (address, salary, and employee number):

```
Emp1 (addr, sal, empno)
```

As with `INSERT INTO..VALUES`, the `INSERT INTO..SELECT` must match column for column and would look like the following:

```
INSERT INTO Emp1
SELECT address, salary, emp_num
FROM Employee;
```

The following `INSERT` would fail because the Employee table has four attributes, while the Emp1 table has only three:

```
INSERT INTO Emp1
SELECT * FROM Employee;
```

The following `INSERT` would also fail because the attribute order of the `SELECT` must match the order of definition of attributes in the Emp1 table:

```
INSERT INTO Emp1
SELECT address, emp_num, salary
FROM Employee;
```

As you might guess from the last `INSERT INTO..SELECT` example, you can load fewer attributes than the whole row of the Emp1 table with a statement like:

```
INSERT INTO Emp1 (address, salary)
SELECT address, salary
FROM Employee;
```

However, this would leave the other attribute, emp_num, with a value of null or with a default value. Therefore, although loading less than a full row is syntactically correct, you must be aware of the result.

One final caution: `INSERT INTO..SELECT` could succeed if the data types of the `SELECT` matched the data types of the attributes in the table to which you are inserting. For example, if you had another table called Emp2 with name, address as attributes (both defined as `VARCHAR2`), and if you executed the following, the command *could* succeed, but you would have an address in a name attribute and vice versa:

```
INSERT INTO Emp2
SELECT address, name
FROM Employee;
```

Note: We say "could" here because there are ways to prevent integrity violations of this type, but we have not introduced them yet.

Be careful with this INSERT INTO..SELECT command. Unlike INSERT INTO..VALUES, which inserts one row at a time, you almost always insert multiple rows with INSERT INTO.. SELECT. If types match, the insert will take place regardless of whether it makes sense or not.

The CREATE TABLE and INSERT INTO commands may be combined for creating backup copies of tables like this:

```
CREATE TABLE Course_copy AS
SELECT * FROM Course
```

The backup copy will be created and you will see the following confirmation message:

```
Table created.
```

The UPDATE Command

Another common command used for setting/changing data values in tables is the UPDATE command. As with the INSERT INTO..SELECT command, you often update more than one row at a time with the UPDATE command. To illustrate the UPDATE command, let's create a table called Customer1, like this:

```
CREATE TABLE Customer1
(cno CHAR(3), balance NUMBER(5), date_opened DATE);
```

Now suppose some values are inserted into the table using one of the above techniques. And then suppose that you would like to set *all* balances in the new table to zero. You can do this with an UPDATE command, as follows:

```
UPDATE Customer1
SET balance = 0;
```

This command sets all balances in all rows of the table to zero, regardless of their previous value.

Warning: UPDATE can be a dangerous command! Later in the chapter we will discuss a method in which to safeguard against accidental misuse by using the ROLLBACK command.

It is often useful and appropriate to include a WHERE clause on the UPDATE command so that values are set selectively. For example, the updating of a particular customer in our new table, Customer1, might be done with the following statement:

```
UPDATE Customer1
SET balance = 0
WHERE cno = 101;
```

This would update only the row(s) for customer 101. You could also set specific balances to zero with a statement like the following:

```
UPDATE Customer1
SET balance = 0
WHERE date > '01-JAN-09';
```

However, in this last example, multiple rows might be updated.

The DELETE Command

The `DELETE` command is used to delete rows from tables. A sample syntax for the `DELETE` command is:

```
DELETE FROM Table
WHERE (condition)
```

The (*condition*) determines which rows to delete.

Warning: With UPDATE and DELETE, multiple rows can be affected and hence these can be dangerous commands. Be careful when using them and learn to use ROLLBACK (discussed in a following section) before applying the commands.

An example of a multi-row delete from our sample Customer1 table might be:

```
DELETE FROM Customer1
WHERE balance < 10;
```

or

```
DELETE FROM Customer1
WHERE date_opened < '01-JAN-07';
```

Deleting a Table

To remove a table from the database, you would use the `DROP TABLE` command as follows:

```
DROP TABLE Table_name;
```

Once you drop a table, you cannot bring the table or its data back. Dropping tables cannot be undone.

ROLLBACK, COMMIT, and SAVEPOINT

When we make modifications to our database — using one or more INSERT, SELECT, DELETE, or UPDATE commands — we perform a transaction. A *transaction* is defined as "a logical unit of work." A transaction ends with a COMMIT command (either implied or explicit). Some commands contain implied COMMITs, which means if you execute one of these commands, it comes with a COMMIT. There is also an explicit COMMIT command.

If you make a mistake in a transaction, you can undo whatever modification you have done to your database with a ROLLBACK command. Also, COMMIT and ROLLBACK affect tables in a multi-user environment. In this section we will discuss how and when to perform a COMMIT and a ROLLBACK, as well as discuss the conditions for undoing a transaction.

All transactions have a beginning and an end. A common begin point for a transaction is when you log on to the database. Provided you have not issued an implied COMMIT, the end point of the transaction is when you sign off. You may also end a transaction by:

- Logging off your database session (an implied COMMIT)
- Issuing a command that contains an implied COMMIT (like the DROP TABLE command discussed in the previous section)
- Issuing an explicit COMMIT command
- Executing a ROLLBACK command

If you issue a COMMIT during a session, your transaction ends at that point and a new one begins. Data definition commands contain implicit COMMITs — they end the current transaction and start a new one. Data definition commands we have seen are: CREATE TABLE and DROP TABLE. If either of these two commands are issued, an implied COMMIT ensues and the current transaction ends and a new transaction begins. Several transactions may take place within a single session.

Sometimes you may need to divide your work into separate transactions. COMMIT and ROLLBACK are explicit transaction-handling commands. Suppose you had a table of values and you deleted some of the rows. You can undo the delete action by issuing a ROLLBACK command. For example, suppose while updating the Customer table you issued the following DELETE command:

```
DELETE FROM Customer
WHERE balance < 500;
```

This deletes all rows in the Customer table where balances are less than 500. Then you note that your boss actually asked you to delete customers where the balance was less than 50, not 500. You can rollback (undo) the previous command with:

```
ROLLBACK;
```

The ROLLBACK command resets the Customer table to whatever the values were at the beginning of the transaction. If you are sure that you have successfully executed the correct command, you may execute it and end the transaction with:

```
COMMIT;
```

At this point the modifications to the table will not be undoable. After the COMMIT, the transaction is history. We mentioned that ROLLBACK would work under certain conditions because some commands contain implied COMMITs. Implied COMMITs are:

- When you use Data Definition Language (DDL) commands. (DDL commands define or delete database objects. Examples of such commands include CREATE VIEW, CREATE TABLE, CREATE INDEX, DROP TABLE, RENAME TABLE, ALTER TABLE.)

- When you log off of SQL, implicitly COMMITting your work.

For valuable tables, an explicit backup (or two) should be made and permissions for updates and deletes should be judiciously managed by the table owner.

As an intermediate COMMIT/ROLLBACK action, you can also name a transaction milestone called a SAVEPOINT. For example, you can use the following command to mark a point in a transaction with the name point1:

```
SAVEPOINT point1
```

You can then rollback to point1 with the following command:

```
ROLLBACK TO SAVEPOINT point1
```

The naming of savepoints allows you to have several rollback places in a transaction — "milestones" if you will. These milestones allow partial rollbacks. COMMIT is much stronger than a SAVEPOINT because it commits all actions and wipes out the savepoints if there are any.

Following is an example of a transaction that includes a SAVEPOINT, ROLLBACK, and COMMIT.

Suppose we had a table, CustA, populated with attributes name and balance, defined as VARCHAR2(20) and NUMBER(5,2), respectively. Further suppose that we type:

```
SELECT *
FROM CustA;
```

And we get:

```
NAME          BALANCE
----------    -------
Mary Jo       25.53
Sikha         44.44
Richard       33.33
```

If we insert another row into CustA, as follows:

```
INSERT INTO CustA
VALUES ('Brenda',40.02);
```

We will get the following message:

```
1 row created.
```

We can now use this as a milestone, creating a savepoint by typing:

```
SAVEPOINT pointA;
```

We will then get the following message:

```
Savepoint created.
```

Now if we type:

```
SELECT *
FROM CustA;
```

We will get:

```
NAME         BALANCE
----------   -------
Mary Jo        25.53
Sikha          44.44
Richard        33.33
Brenda         40.02
```

If we type:

```
DELETE FROM CustA
WHERE balance < 35;
```

We will get the following:

```
2 rows deleted.
```

If we type:

```
SELECT *
FROM CustA;
```

We will get:

```
NAME        BALANCE
---------   -------
Sikha         44.44
Brenda        40.02
```

We could make this our next milestone, calling it pointB, by typing:

```
SAVEPOINT pointB;
```

Again, we will get the following message:

```
Savepoint created.
```

Now if we type:

```
DELETE FROM CustA;
```

We will get this message:

```
2 rows deleted.
```

If we now type:

```
SELECT *
FROM CustA;
```

We will get this:

```
no rows selected
```

If we feel that we have made a mistake, we can, at this point, rollback the transaction as follows:

```
ROLLBACK TO SAVEPOINT pointB;
```

We will get the following message:

```
Rollback complete.
```

If we now type:

```
SELECT *
FROM CustA;
```

We will get:

```
NAME          BALANCE
----------    -------
Sikha           44.44
Brenda          40.02
```

We can update CustA by typing:

```
UPDATE CustA
SET BALANCE = 55.55
WHERE name LIKE 'Si%';
```

This will give us the following message:

```
1 row updated.
```

If we now type:

```
SELECT *
FROM CustA;
```

We will get:

```
NAME          BALANCE
----------    -------
Sikha           55.55
Brenda          40.02
```

If we want to now rollback to pointA, we type:

```
ROLLBACK TO pointA;
```

We will get the following message:

```
Rollback complete.
```

If we now type:

```
SELECT *
FROM CustA;
```

We will get:

```
NAME         BALANCE
----------   -------
Mary Jo        25.52
Sikha          44.44
Richard        33.33
Brenda         40.02
```

At this point, if we COMMIT, we will basically wipe out the savepoints and we won't be able to rollback again. Suppose we issue a COMMIT:

```
COMMIT;
```

We get the following message:

```
Commit complete.
```

This completes the transaction in terms of making it impossible to rollback because the transaction is ended.

Most database situations occur in a multi-user environment. For example, suppose a CustomerN table exists with the following attributes:

```
CustomerN (name, address, credit_limit, balance)
```

Now suppose that two departments use the CustomerN table: the credit department and the billing department. In a database, data is shared. Now suppose that we have two users: Richard and Sikha. Richard works for the credit department and Sikha works for billing. At the same time Richard is updating the CustomerN table with new credit limits for some customers, Sikha is checking balances and credit limits.

The point is, although both are using the same table, as Richard updates CustomerN rows, Sikha will not see Richard's changes until Richard COMMITs the changes (ends his transaction). The judicious use of COMMIT is an underlying principle of shared databases and tables.

The ALTER TABLE Command

The ALTER TABLE command is used to alter the structure of a table. With the ALTER TABLE command you can add/delete columns from tables and/or alter the size or data types of columns.

The simplified syntax to add a column would be:

```
ALTER TABLE Tablename
ADD column-name data_type
```

For example, the following will add the address attribute (of data type VARCHAR2) to the Customer table created earlier in this chapter:

```
ALTER TABLE Customer
ADD address VARCHAR2(20);
```

To change a column's type, the simplified syntax would be:

```
ALTER TABLE Tablename
MODIFY column-name new_data_type
```

For example, the following will modify the balance attribute of the Customer table, making it a size of eight numbers with two decimal places:

```
ALTER TABLE Customer
MODIFY balance NUMBER(8,2);
```

We can only make attributes larger, not smaller, and we cannot violate any existing data with this command.

Using the ALTER TABLE command, we can define or change a default column value, enable or disable integrity constraints, manage internal space, and so on.

Note: If you modify a column, you can only make it bigger, not smaller, unless there is no data. Also, all the data in the database must conform to your modified type.

If you add a column, it will contain null values until you put data into it with an UPDATE or INSERT command to change the values in the new column.

Following is an example of using the ALTER TABLE command.

First, we use the DESC command to show all the attributes of the table Course_copy:

```
SQL> DESC Course_copy
```

Will give:

```
Name                                Null?     Type
----------------------------------- --------- -------------------
COURSE_NAME                                   CHAR(20)
COURSE_NUMBER                       NOT NULL  CHAR(8)
CREDIT_HOURS                                  NUMBER(2)
OFFERING_DEPT                                 CHAR(4)
```

Now, to alter the table, type:

```
SQL> ALTER TABLE Course_copy
     MODIFY offering_dept VARCHAR2(6);
```

This will give:

```
Table altered.
```

Now,

```
SQL> DESC Course_copy
```

Will give:

```
Name                              Null?    Type
--------------------------------- -------- -------------------
COURSE_NAME                                CHAR(20)
COURSE_NUMBER                     NOT NULL CHAR(8)
CREDIT_HOURS                               NUMBER(2)
OFFERING_DEPT                              VARCHAR2(6)
```

Now, an attempt to decrease the column:

```
SQL> ALTER TABLE Course_copy
     MODIFY offering_dept CHAR(2)

SQL> /
```

Will give:

```
modify offering_dept char(2)
       *
ERROR at line 2:
ORA-01441: cannot decrease column length because some value is too
 big
```

Data Types

A data type of an attribute defines the allowable values as well as the operations we can perform on the attribute. We commonly use the NUMBER data type for numbers and the CHAR and VARCHAR2 data types for character strings. In this section, we will explore these and other commonly used data types.

Common Number Data Types

The most commonly used numeric data types in Oracle are NUMBER and INTEGER. The NUMBER data type, with no parentheses, defaults to a number that is up to 38 digits long with eight decimal places. NUMBER may also be defined as having some maximum number of digits, such as NUMBER(5). Here, the (5) is referred to as the "precision" of the data type and may be from 1 to 38. If a second number is included in the definition, as shown in NUMBER(12,2), the second number is called the "scale." The scale defines how many digits will appear after the decimal point. Here, with NUMBER(12,2) we may have up to ten digits before the decimal point and two after.

A very common data type used in programming languages is type INTEGER. INTEGER holds whole numbers and is equivalent to NUMBER(38).

Usually, you enter a precision and/or a scale for your numbers with entries such as NUMBER(3) or NUMBER(6,2). NUMBER(3) implies you will have three digits and no decimal places. NUMBER(6,2) means that the numbers you store will be similar to 1234.56 or 12.34, with a decimal before the last two digits in a field that has a maximum of six numbers overall.

Here is an example to illustrate precision and scale with a numeric attribute. Type the following:

```
CREATE TABLE Testnum (x NUMBER(5,2));

INSERT INTO Testnum VALUES (20);
INSERT INTO Testnum VALUES (200);
INSERT INTO Testnum VALUES (2000);
```

The last INSERT gives an error:

```
INSERT INTO Testnum VALUES (2000);
*
ERROR at line 1:
```

```
ORA-01438: value larger than specified precision allows for this
 column
```

Then type:

```
INSERT INTO Testnum VALUES (200.12);
INSERT INTO Testnum VALUES (200.123);
```

Now,

```
SELECT *
FROM Testnum;
```

Will give:

```
         X
----------
        20
       200
    200.12
    200.12
```

If a number is inserted that is too large for the precision, an error results. If a number with too many decimal places is added, the decimal values beyond the scale are rounded up automatically, as shown by the following inserts:

```
INSERT INTO Testnum VALUES (123.99778);
INSERT INTO Testnum VALUES (333.333);
INSERT INTO Testnum VALUES (555.499999);
INSERT INTO Testnum VALUES (666.500004);
```

Now,

```
SELECT *
FROM Testnum;
```

Gives:

```
         X
----------
```

```
     20
    200
 200.12
 200.12
    124
 333.33
  555.5
  666.5
```

In addition to the above numeric data types, there are other specialty numeric types, including SMALLINT, BINARY DOUBLE, and others. There are also the FLOAT data types, which allow large exponential numbers to be stored, but they are rarely used. Float data types include FLOAT, REAL, and DOUBLE PRECISION.

CHAR Data Type

CHAR (pronounced "care") is a fixed-length character data type. This data type is normally used when the data will always contain a fixed number of characters. For example, if your field category codes are always exactly four characters long, they should be encoded as CHAR(4). Social Security numbers are also good candidates for this data type because they always contain nine digits, so CHAR(9) can be used. (Although Social Security numbers are digits, they are not used for calculation; hence, they may be stored as characters.) In a field defined as CHAR, if the requisite number of characters is not inserted, the attribute will be padded on the right with blanks. For example, if we defined the Social Security number as CHAR(10) instead of CHAR(9), there would be one blank space on the right of every nine-digit Social Security string. The default (or minimum size) for CHAR is one byte, and its maximum size is 2,000 bytes.

VARCHAR2 Data Type

As we mentioned earlier in the chapter, VARCHAR2 (pronounced "var-care") is Oracle's variable-length character data type. For this data type, maximum lengths should be specified, as in VARCHAR2(20), for a string of zero to 20 characters. When varying sizes of data are stored in an Oracle VARCHAR2, only the necessary amount of storage is allocated. This practice makes the internal storage of Oracle data more efficient. In fact, some Oracle practitioners suggest using only VARCHAR2(*n*) instead of CHAR(*n*). The minimum size for VARCHAR2 is one byte; the maximum size is 4,000 bytes. Since there is no default size for VARCHAR2, you must specify a size.

Note: Older versions of Oracle and other SQLs used VARCHAR instead of VARCHAR2. VARCHAR may not be supported in future versions, so we advise you to use VARCHAR2 instead.

NCHAR and NVARCHAR2 Data Types

NCHAR stores fixed-length character strings, and NVARCHAR2 stores variable-length character strings, both of which are Unicode data types that correspond to the national character set. The character set of NCHAR and NVARCHAR2 data types are specified at database creation time. The maximum size of an NCHAR data type is 2,000 bytes, and the maximum size of a NVARCHAR2 data type is 4,000 bytes.

Unicode is an encoding system that stores a unique number for every character in every known language. Thus, a database column that stores Unicode can store text written in any language. Oracle database users with global applications may need to use Unicode data for non-English characters.

LONG, RAW, LONG RAW, and BOOLEAN Data Types

The LONG data type is similar to VARCHAR2 and has a variable length of up to 2 GB. However, there are some restrictions in the access and handling of LONG data types:

- Only one LONG column can be defined per table.
- LONG columns may not be used in subqueries, functions, expressions, WHERE clauses, or indexes.

A RAW or LONG RAW data type is used to store binary data such as graphics characters or digitized pictures. The maximum size for RAW is 2,000 bytes while the maximum size for LONG RAW is 2 gigabytes. Thus, LONG RAW allows for larger sets of binary data.

In Oracle, there is also a BOOLEAN data type with values TRUE, FALSE, and NULL, but it is not often used.

Note: The BOOLEAN data type is only available when running the procedural language (PL/SQL). We will discuss PL/SQL in Chapters 11 and 12.

Large Object (LOB) Data Types

As of Oracle 8, four new large object (LOB) data types are supported: BFILE, BLOB, CLOB, and NCLOB. BFILE is an external LOB data type that only stores a locator value that points to the external binary file. BLOB is used for binary large objects, CLOB is used for large character objects, and NCLOB is a CLOB data type for multi-byte character sets.

Data in the BLOB, CLOB, and NCLOB data types is stored in the database, although LOB data does not have to be stored with the rest of the table. Single LOB columns can hold up to 4 GB and multiple LOB columns are allowed per table. In addition, Oracle allows you to specify a separate storage area for LOB data, greatly simplifying table sizing and data administration activities for tables that contain LOB data. Note that LOB data types consume large quantities of space.

Abstract Data Types

In Oracle, you can also define and use abstract data types. Where a data type defines a range of values and operations that can be performed on data declared to be of that type, an *abstract data type* (ADT) defines the operations explicitly (in methods or procedures) and should allow you to only access data of that type via the defined method. ADTs are created with the CREATE TYPE statement.

In addition to ADTs, CREATE TYPE allows you to create more complicated data types. For example, Oracle's *collection types* allow you to put a table within a table or allow a varying array in a table. Both of these concepts are non-third normal form (non-3NF) constructions and should be used only with a strong need to violate the 3NF assumption for relational databases. These more exotic data types also may present performance problems for large databases.

Note: A complete treatment of CREATE TYPE and abstract data types is beyond the scope of this book. We mention CREATE TYPE here only to alert you of its existence.

The XML Data Type

A new SQL data type, XMLType, has been created by Oracle to handle XML data. XML is a standardized textual coding technique used to exchange data over the Internet. Oracle needs an XML data type to transform XML data to a common SQL data type and vice versa. As with other data types, XMLType can be used as a data type for a column of a table or view. The maximum size of an XMLType attribute is 4 gigabytes.

Using XML involves data definition documents, style sheets, and other ancillary tools. The conversion of data to and from XML involves using CLOB data types in SQL and SQL procedures specifically designed to handle this new and exciting data type. For more information about SQL and XML, see the Oracle XML Technology Center website and *Advanced Functions in Oracle 10g* (ISBN 1-59822-021-7).

The DATE Data Type and Type Conversion Functions

The DATE data type allows the storage and manipulation of dates and times. There are functions to add, find the differences between dates, convert to a four-digit year, and so on. DATE data types store the century, year, month, day, hour, minute, and second. Here is an example of a table containing a DATE data type:

```
CREATE TABLE date_example
                  (day_test  DATE,
                   amount    NUMBER(6,2),
                   name      VARCHAR2(20));
```

Data is entered into the day_test date attribute in the character format 'dd-Mon-yy', which automatically converts the character string to a date format.

Note: The format of the DATE data type can be changed by the DBA (database administrator), but dd-Mon-yy is common.

Some examples of inserts for the date_example table would be:

```
INSERT INTO date_example (day_test)
VALUES ('10-oct-09')  /* valid */
INSERT INTO date_example (day_test)
VALUES ('10-OCT-09')  /* valid (month not case sensitive) */
INSERT INTO date_example (day_test)
VALUES (10-oct-09)    /* invalid (needs quotes) */
INSERT INTO date_example (day_test)
VALUES (sysdate)      /* valid (system date) */
INSERT INTO date_example (day_test)
VALUES ('10-RWE-09')  /*  invalid (bad month) */
INSERT INTO date_example (day_test)
VALUES ('32-OCT-09')  /*  invalid (bad day) */
INSERT INTO date_example (day_test)
VALUES ('31-OCT-09')  /*  valid */
INSERT INTO date_example (day_test)
VALUES ('31-SEP-09')  /*  invalid (bad day - Oracle
                          recognizes correct days per month) */
```

For dates in a form other than dd-Mon-yy, the `TO_DATE` function can be used to insert values. The `TO_DATE` function has two arguments: `TO_DATE(`*a*`,`*b*`)`, where *a* is the string you are using to enter the date and *b* is a recognized Oracle character format.

For example, to insert the date 2-1-09 in the format mm-dd-yy you would type:

```
INSERT INTO date_example (day_test)
VALUES (TO_DATE ('2-1-09','mm-dd-yy'))
```

Likewise, to enter the date 2/1/2009 in the format mm/dd/yyyy, you would type:

```
INSERT INTO date_example (day_test)
VALUES (TO_DATE ('2/1/2009','mm/dd/yyyy'))
```

To convert a DATE data type to a character data type, the TO_CHAR function is used. TO_CHAR is useful for displaying dates in formats other than the standard one. For example, if you type:

```
INSERT INTO date_example VALUES ('21-OCT-40',NULL,NULL);
```

And then you type:

```
SELECT *
FROM date_example;
```

You will get:

```
DAY_TEST        AMOUNT  NAME
--------- ---------- --------------------
21-OCT-40
```

And if you type:

```
SELECT TO_CHAR(day_test,'mm/dd/yy')
FROM date_example;
```

This will give:

```
TO_CHAR(
--------
10/21/40
```

And if you type:

```
SELECT TO_CHAR(day_test,'Month dd,yyyy')
FROM date_example;
```

This will give:

```
TO_CHAR(DAY_TEST,'
-----------------
October   21, 2040
```

Since the DATE data type stores more information than just the month, day, and year, you can expand the input date to include the hour (using a 24-hour clock) and minute. Suppose we create a table like this:

```
CREATE TABLE date_test2 (dte DATE);
```

We then INSERT some data as follows:

```
INSERT INTO date_test2
VALUES (TO_DATE('2-11-2009 16:05','mm-dd-yyyy hh24:mi'))
```

A simple SELECT will show only the day, month, and year, as follows:

```
SELECT dte FROM date_test2;
```

We then get:

```
DTE
---------
11-FEB-09
```

However, the other information that was stored can be fully displayed using TO_CHAR:

```
SELECT (TO_CHAR(dte,'dd-Mon-yyyy hh:mi:ss'))
FROM date_test2;
```

Will give:

```
(TO_CHAR(D,'DD-MON-Y
--------------------
11-Feb-2009 04:05:00
```

We can specify other data like this:

```
SELECT (TO_CHAR(dte,'dd-Mon-yyyy hh:mi:ss j q w PM cc'))
FROM date_test2;
```

where

- The "j" is the Julian days since Dec. 31, 4713 BC (here, 2454874).
- The "q" is the quarter of the year (1st quarter).
- The "w" is the week of the month (2nd week of February).
- The "PM" signifies PM if PM and AM if AM.
- The "c" specifies the century (21st).

To get:

```
(TO_CHAR(D,'DD-MON-YYYYHH:MI:SSJQWPMCC
------------------------------------
11-feb-2009 04:05:00 2454874 1 2 PM 21
```

Entering Four-Digit Years

There will often be times when we would want to enter and display four-digit years. If there is the possibility of confusion when entering dates, then entering four-digit years is safe and proper. To enter years as four digits, we use TO_DATE and a format to match the year part. For example:

```
INSERT INTO date_example (day_test)
VALUES (TO_DATE ('03-21-2009','mm-dd-yyyy'));
```

Now,

```
SELECT *
FROM date_example
WHERE TO_CHAR(day_test,'yyyy') = '2009'
```

Will give:

```
DAY_TEST        AMOUNT  NAME
---------  ----------  --------------------
21-MAR-09
```

And the code:

```
SELECT TO_CHAR(day_test,'Month dd, yyyy')
FROM date_example
WHERE TO_CHAR(day_test,'yyyy') = 2009;
```

Will give:

```
TO_CHAR(DAY_TEST,'
------------------
March     21, 2009
```

There are also two handy functions that deal with dates: MONTHS_BETWEEN and ADD_MONTHS. Following are examples of these functions.

Today's date can be found with a statement like this:

```
SELECT SYSDATE
FROM dual;
```

Dual is a dummy table that always returns one row. The Dual table and a query like the above are used for testing functions such as SYSDATE and/or variations such as TO_CHAR(SYSDATE,'mm-Day-yyyy'), as in:

```
SELECT TO_CHAR(SYSDATE,'mm-Day-yyyy')
FROM  dual;
```

Now, to show how the MONTHS_BETWEEN function works, consider this example:

```
SQL> SELECT SYSDATE FROM dual;
```

This will give:

```
SYSDATE
---------
04-MAR-08
```

```
SELECT MONTHS_BETWEEN(SYSDATE,'02-feb-07')
FROM dual;
```

Will give:

```
MONTHS_BETWEEN(SYSDATE,'02-FEB-07')
-----------------------------------
                         13.0869392
```

And for ADD_MONTHS, consider this:

```
SELECT ADD_MONTHS(SYSDATE,4)
FROM dual;
```

This will give:

```
ADD_MONTH
---------
04-JUL-08
```

Finally, to change the default date format, the ALTER SESSION statement may be used:

```
ALTER SESSION SET nls_date_format = 'dd-mon-yyyy';
```

Exercises for Chapter 2

As you do the exercises, it is a good idea to copy/paste your query as well as your query result into a word processor file.

2-1. a. Create a table called Cust with a customer number field as a fixed-length three-character string, an address field with a variable character string of up to 20, and a numeric balance of five digits.

b. Insert values into the table with INSERT INTO..VALUES. Use the form of INSERT INTO..VALUES that requires you to have a value for each attribute; therefore, if you have a customer number,

number, address, and balance, you must insert three values with `INSERT INTO..VALUES`.

c. Create at least five rows in the table with customer numbers 101 through 105 and balances of 200 to 2000.

d. Display the table with a simple `SELECT`.

2-2. Show a listing of the customers from Exercise 2-1 in balance order (high to low) and use `ORDER BY` in your `SELECT`.

2-3. From the Student-Course database, use the Student table to display the student names, classes, and majors for freshmen or sophomores (`class <= 2`) in descending order of class. (*Note:* If you haven't created the synonyms of all the tables in the Student-Course database as per the exercises in Chapter 1, you will need to use `rearp.Student` instead of `Student` in the query.)

2-4. From your Cust table, show a listing of only the customer balances in ascending order where `balance > 400`. (You can choose some other constant if you want. For example, `balance <= 600`, and so on. The results will depend on your data.)

2-5. a. Create another table with the same types as Cust but without the customer address. Call this table Cust1. Use attribute names cnum for customer number and bal for balance. Load the table with the data you have in the Cust table with one less row. Use an `INSERT INTO..SELECT` with appropriate attributes and an appropriate `WHERE` clause.

b. Display the resulting table. If it appears okay, `COMMIT` your work.

c. Assuming that you have `COMMIT`ted in step b, delete about half of your rows from Cust1 (use

"DELETE FROM Cust1 WHERE bal < some value" [or bal > some value]).

d. Show the table after you have deleted the rows.

e. Undelete the rows with ROLLBACK.

f. Display the table with the reinstated rows.

g. Delete one row from the Cust1 table and SAVEPOINT point1. Display the table.

h. Delete another row from the table and SAVEPOINT point2. Display the table.

i. ROLLBACK to SAVEPOINT point1, display the table, and explain what is happening.

j. Try to ROLLBACK to SAVEPOINT point2 and see what happens, then explain it.

2-6. a. Using the Cust1 table from the Exercise 2-5, COMMIT the table as it exists.

b. Alter the table by adding a date_opened column of type DATE.

After each of the following, display the table.

c. Set the date_opened value in all rows to '01-JAN-09' and COMMIT.

d. Set all balances to zero, display the table, then ROLLBACK the action and display again.

e. Set the date_opened value of one of your rows to 21-OCT-10 and display.

f. Change the data type of the balance attribute in Cust1 to NUMBER(8,2). Display the table. Set the balance for one row to 888.88 and display the table again.

g. Try changing the data type of balance to NUMBER(3,2). What happens? Why does this happen?

h. Change the values of all dates in the table to the system date using SYSDATE.

i. When you have finished the exercises (but be sure you are finished), use `DROP TABLE Cust1` to delete the table. Use `SELECT * FROM TAB` to be sure that you dropped Cust1.

For the next three problems, use the Student table from our Student-Course database.

2-7. Using the Student table, list the sname, major, and class of all students who are art majors and juniors.

2-8. Using the Student table, list the sname, major, and class of all students who are art majors or juniors.

2-9. From the Student table, list the sname, major, and class of all sophomores, juniors, and seniors. Use the `BETWEEN` operator for this.

Chapter 3

Joins

A *join* is a database operation whereby two tables are combined in a considered way. In this chapter we will focus on join operations. In the last couple of chapters we showed you how to retrieve data from one table. In real-world databases data is usually spread over multiple tables, and so when it is necessary to retrieve data from more than one table, you use joins.

We start the chapter with a discussion of Cartesian products, a most basic way of retrieving data from two tables, and then we introduce joins. We also discuss aliases, `COUNT`, and `rownum`, since these concepts are often used in conjunction with multiple tables. Later in the chapter we take a more in-depth look at joins and we cover outer joins.

The Cartesian Product

The *Cartesian product* is mathematical binary operation in which two objects are combined in an "everything in combination with everything" fashion. The Cartesian product in SQL *per se* is usually not wanted. If it is requested by accident, results are generally faulty.

Suppose we created a table called Emps with an employee number and a job code as shown below.

Note: Note that these two tables, Emps and Jobs, have not been created for you in the database. You will have to create these tables in order to try out this section.

Emps

```
    EMPNO  JOBCODE
---------  -------
      101    cp
      102    ac
      103    de
      104    cp
      105    cp
```

Then, suppose we created a second table called Jobs, which contained a job code and a job title as follows:

Jobs

```
JOBC    JOBTITLE
----    --------------------
de      dentist
cp      computer programmer
ac      accountant
ph      physician
```

We can display the data in the tables with:

```
SELECT *
FROM Jobs;
```

or

```
SELECT *
FROM Emps;
```

With SQL, we can retrieve the combination of both tables; however, we must be careful how we do so. If we connect the tables like this:

```
SELECT *
FROM Emps, Jobs;
```

we will get the Cartesian product — basically, all rows in Emps in combination with all rows in Jobs. The result of the above query would be:

```
    EMPNO  JO  JO  JOBTITLE
---------  --  --  --------------------
      101  cp  de  dentist
      102  ac  de  dentist
      103  de  de  dentist
      104  cp  de  dentist
      105  cp  de  dentist
      101  cp  cp  computer programmer
      102  ac  cp  computer programmer
      103  de  cp  computer programmer
      104  cp  cp  computer programmer
      105  cp  cp  computer programmer
      101  cp  ac  accountant
      102  ac  ac  accountant
      103  de  ac  accountant
      104  cp  ac  accountant
      105  cp  ac  accountant
      101  cp  ph  physician
      102  ac  ph  physician
      103  de  ph  physician
```

```
      104  cp  ph  physician
      105  cp  ph  physician

20 rows selected.
```

There would be 20 rows (5 times 4) in the result set with all combinations from Emps and Jobs. Here the result is truly a combination of tables, but it makes no sense.

The Join

A join can also be a Cartesian product followed by a row-reducing condition (usually an equality). To join tables, we use a `SELECT` command that includes both tables in the `FROM` clause and put our row-reducing condition in a `WHERE` clause that ties the connecting fields in the two tables together. Such a command could look like this:

```
SELECT *
FROM Emps, Jobs
WHERE Emps.jobcode = Jobs.jobc;
```

This `SELECT` requests a result set that will contain only those resultant rows that have jobcode in Emps equal to jobc in Jobs. This is an "equi-join" operation because the `WHERE` clause asks for rows in the Cartesian product where the two common columns have equal values. The result set of this join query would be:

```
     EMPNO  JO  JO  JOBTITLE
----------  --  --  --------------------
       101  cp  cp  computer programmer
       102  ac  ac  accountant
       103  de  de  dentist
       104  cp  cp  computer programmer
       105  cp  cp  computer programmer
```

Compare this result to the Cartesian product above and you will observe that the tables have the same structure but the second one has been row filtered by the WHERE clause to include only those rows where there is equality between Emps.jobcode and Jobs.jobc. Put another way, this table makes sense because it only presents those rows that correspond to one another with no extra, meaningless rows.

Note: In relational algebra, a *join* is defined as a Cartesian product followed by a relational select. Technically, a *relational select* is not the same as a SQL SELECT (which is broader), and the behind-the-scenes workings of the SQL SELECT may or may not actually follow the "Cartesian product, followed by the relational select scenario" internally for performance reasons. The result of the SQL join in SQL SELECT statements (when done correctly) is the same as the sense of the relational join in relational algebra.

Join Using ANSI Join Syntax

Although the most traditional way of formulating a join is by using a WHERE clause as shown above, the ANSI SQL standard join, which is now available in Oracle, may also be used. Let's look at an example ANSI SQL standard join. The simple join in ANSI SQL is performed with the use of an INNER JOIN clause. The previous query using ANSI SQL syntax would be:

```
SELECT *
FROM Emps INNER JOIN Jobs
ON Emps.jobcode = Jobs.jobc;
```

This will give the same result as shown before:

```
     EMPNO JO JO JOBTITLE
---------- -- -- --------------------
       101 cp cp computer programmer
       102 ac ac accountant
       103 de de dentist
       104 cp cp computer programmer
       105 cp cp computer programmer
```

As with most programming concepts, there are pros and cons to both join types, so we suggest that you learn and use both forms of the join.

Theta Joins

Joins with a comparison operator in the `WHERE` clause other than an equal sign are called *theta joins*. Tables in theta joins are combined using relational operators such as >, >=, <, <=, and <>. Theta joins with operations other than equality are rare though, and equi-joins are almost always used.

Qualifiers

The phrase `Jobs.jobc` uses a qualifier of Jobs for jobc — it says take jobc from the Jobs table. In this case, the qualifiers are not needed because the column name, jobc, is unique to the Jobs table. The same is true for jobcode and Emps, so the command will work without the qualifier, as follows:

```
SELECT *
FROM Emps, Jobs
WHERE jobcode = jobc;
```

This gives the same result as in the preceding section:

```
     EMPNO JO JO JOBTITLE
---------- -- -- --------------------
       101 cp cp computer programmer
       102 ac ac accountant
       103 de de dentist
       104 cp cp computer programmer
       105 cp cp computer programmer
```

We strongly urge you to never write a multi-table SELECT without qualifiers. There are several reasons for this:

- If the names of the attributes were the same in the two tables, you would have to use the qualifier. You never know when a table might be modified in the future; for example, someone could add a jobc column to the Emps table.
- When someone else looks at your query, he or she should not have to figure out which attribute came from which table. Tables with correct qualifiers are easy to modify.
- Many times, queries are enhanced by the addition of other tables with more joins or other constructions. If a new table has the same attribute name (like jobc), then qualification would be forced on the person that enhanced the query. If the query were correctly written in the first place with qualifiers, then maintenance problems would be minimized.

Table Aliases and an Introduction to Multi-table Joins

A *table alias* is a temporary variable name for a table that allows us to use a shorthand notation as we qualify attributes. Here is an example of a one-letter table alias:

```
SELECT *
FROM Emps e, Jobs j
WHERE e.jobcode = j.jobc;
```

The table alias is defined by a letter *after* the table name, so the table alias for Jobs here is "j" and the table alias for Emps in this example is "e". Although some people prefer a short, meaningful word or expression rather than a one-letter table alias, the one-letter alias is very common among SQL users. In this book we will use many table aliases in future statements and in most multi-table joins and queries.

Here is the same join in ANSI form with aliases (and it produces the same result as above):

```
SELECT *
FROM Emps e INNER JOIN Jobs j
ON e.jobcode = j.jobc;
```

Following are examples showing statements with and without table aliases.

Without table aliases:

```
SELECT   Student.stno, Section.course_num, Grade_report.grade
FROM     Student, Grade_report, Section
WHERE    Student.stno = Grade_report.student_number
AND      Grade_report.section_id = Section.section_id;
```

With table aliases:

```
SELECT   stu.stno, sec.course_num, gr.grade
FROM     Student stu, Grade_report gr, Section sec
WHERE    stu.stno = gr.student_number
AND      gr.section_id = sec.section_id;
```

As with the one-letter examples, the table aliases stu, gr, and sec are declared just after the table name in the FROM part of the SELECT.

In multi-table queries, it is not advisable to leave off qualifiers for attributes even if the database is well known. Most commonly, qualifiers are handled with table aliases. One never knows when the database will be expanded or when a query must be analyzed by another person. Aliases are not persistent; they are only active for the current statement or query. That is, table aliases are not saved after the query is run.

More on Comments

As we mentioned in Chapter 1, comments are often added to SQL statements to enhance their readability. As in programming languages, comments are ignored by the SQL engine but are invaluable for understanding and debugging. There are two ways of adding comments to SQL statements.

With the first method, comments can be added in the C programming style with /* and */, where everything between the two markers is ignored by the SQL parser. The /* ... */ comment is valid anywhere in a SELECT statement. Comments may cover several lines of code and are ignored when the statement is parsed prior to execution. An example of a commented SQL statement would be:

```
SELECT *                    /* the result set contains all columns */
FROM Emps e, Jobs j         /* using the Emps and Jobs tables */
WHERE e.jobcode = j.Jobc    /* the join condition for an equi-join */
;
```

Note: It is not necessary to line up comments, but it helps with readability.

Another method of inserting comments is with a double hyphen (--). The -- may be included on any line, but it does not span multiple lines like the /* ... */. The same example from above with -- would look like this:

```
SELECT *                     -- the result set contains all columns
FROM Emps e, Jobs j          -- using the Emps and Jobs tables
WHERE e.jobcode = j.Jobc     -- the join condition for an equi join
;
```

Either of these commenting methods is good programming practice as long as they do not obscure the code. In our example, the first and second comments are really superfluous because they are obvious to any SQL user. Obvious comments are annoying, whereas the comment on the join condition could be quite helpful.

Note: Comments should not be used on the first statement before the SELECT, or after the semicolon in a query. This could produce an error on some systems.

More on Multiple Table Joins and Join Conditions

While Cartesian products are rarely appropriate, there are times when they may be used — in some table loads, for example. However, in creating joins, it is imperative to avoid the Cartesian product. There is no warning that you have joined incorrectly except that you get an incorrect answer. Multiple tables can be joined using pairwise join conditions. In creating a join, there will always be $(n\text{–}1)$ join conditions for joining n tables.

If we join the Student and Grade_report tables, there are two tables and one join condition:

```
SELECT *
FROM Student s, Grade_report g
WHERE s.stno = g.student_number      /* the join condition */
;
```

If we join the Student, Grade_report, and Section tables, there are three tables and two join conditions:

```
SELECT *
FROM    Student s, Grade_report g, Section t
WHERE   s.stno = g.student_number     /* the Student-Grade_report
                                         join condition */
AND     g.section_id = t.section_id   /* the Grade_report-Section
                                         join condition */
;
```

Of course, it is valid and usual to include other conditions in the WHERE clause as necessary, as shown in the following example:

```
SELECT   sname, grade, class
FROM     Student s, Grade_report g, Section t
WHERE    s.stno = g.student_number    -- the Student-Grade_report
                                      -- join condition
AND      g.section_id = t.section_id  -- the Grade_report-Section
```

```
                                        -- join condition
AND      g.grade = 'B'
AND      s.class < 3;
```

This would be a three-table join of the Student, Grade_report, and Section tables where the result would be students who have a B in the Grade_report table and who are sophomores or freshmen. The output of this is:

```
SNAME                G    CLASS
-------------------- --   -----
Lineas               B        1
Lineas               B        1
Lineas               B        1
Brenda               B        2
Brenda               B        2
Lujack               B        1
Lujack               B        1
Lujack               B        1
Reva                 B        2
Reva                 B        2
Reva                 B        2
.
.
.
Sebastian            B        2
Lindsay              B
26 rows selected.
```

Since joins are pairwise operations, this "triple join" is actually either (Student join Grade_report) join Section or Student join (Grade_report) join Section. The choice of how the join is executed is usually made by the database's optimizer, based on the join conditions, indexes on tables, and any available statistics for the tables.

When you perform joins, we highly recommended that you do both of the following:

- Include a comment for each join condition in multiple table joins.

- Put each join condition on a separate line.

Here is the ANSI version of the above join:

```
SELECT sname, grade, class
FROM (Student s INNER JOIN Grade_report g
ON s.stno = g.student_number)
INNER JOIN Section t
ON g.section_id = t.section_id
AND g.grade = 'B'
AND  s.class < 3
```

Note the pairwise joining in the ANSI version. We can force which join is performed first by using parentheses. Here we chose to join the Student and Grade_report tables first and then join the Section table to that result.

Column Aliases

When writing a query, it is often useful to enhance the output and readability of a query in two ways: (a) by using the table alias in the column designation and (b) by using a column alias. Using the table alias in the column designation is good practice because it is likely that in large databases two tables will contain the same column names. Furthermore, maintenance (e.g., enhancements, changes) is aided by writing the query clearly in the first place.

A column alias is declared following the column designation in the SELECT statement. First let's look at a query with table aliases in column designations, but without column aliases:

```
SELECT s.sname, g.grade
FROM   Student s, Grade_report g
WHERE  s.stno = g.student_number     -- join condition
;
```

This produces the following result set:

```
SNAME                   G
--------------------    --
BURNS                   D
BURNS                   F
BURNS                   C
BURNS                   C
...
```

In this example, it is clear to anyone who looks at this query which table sname and grade came from. Now adding the column aliases involves placing them just after the column name in the SELECT statement. A query with a simple column alias would be:

```
SELECT s.sname Name, g.grade Grade
FROM   Student s, Grade_report g
WHERE  s.stno = g.student_number     -- join condition
;
```

This produces the following result set (note the change in the first column heading):

```
NAME                    G
--------------------    --
BURNS                   D
BURNS                   F
BURNS                   C
BURNS                   C
```

You can also use more complex column aliases. For example, if there is an embedded blank, the column alias is put in double quotes as follows:

```
SELECT s.sname "Student Name", g.grade "Grade Assigned"
FROM   Student s, Grade_report g
WHERE  s.stno = g.student_number     -- join condition
;
```

This produces the following result set:

```
Student Name         G
-------------------- --
BURNS                D
BURNS                F
BURNS                C
BURNS                C
```

You have probably noticed a result set presentation problem. No matter what the column alias, if the length of the output field is smaller than the alias or the name of the field, the result set display only uses the field length. To make the output conform to the column alias you used, you need to execute a SQLPLUS command to format the column. The command looks like this:

```
COLUMN "Grade Assigned" FORMAT a15
```

This would set the size of the Grade Assigned field to 15 alphanumeric characters and make our result look like this:

```
Student Name         Grade Assigned
-------------------- ---------------
BURNS                D
BURNS                F
BURNS                C
BURNS                C
```

Note: The COLUMN command should be executed just before the SELECT.

Scripting

In using column aliases, we are beginning to see output enhancements that make result sets of queries easier to read and understand. Other formatting features can also enhance outputs (for example, in reports). The examples of the use of column formats and aliases suggest that there ought to be a way to put these two features together. The solution is to use a *script*, which is an executable set of multiple SQL and SQLPLUS commands.

To put together and run a script, follow these steps:

1. First, define your editor, as shown below:

   ```
   SQL> define_editor=vi
   ```

2. Then, to open the editor and create a new file called run1.sql, at the SQL prompt type:

   ```
   SQL> EDIT run1;
   ```

   Your screen will look like Figure 3.1:

Figure 3.1: The vi editor screen

3. Press <**Esc**> and type **i** to go to Insert mode in vi. You will know that you are in Insert mode when you see "--INSERT--" at the bottom of your screen, as shown in Figure 3.2. Now type the following statements in the editor:

```
COLUMN "Student Name" FORMAT a20
COLUMN "Your Grade" FORMAT a20
SELECT  s.sname "Student Name",
   g.grade "Your Grade"
FROM    Student s, Grade_report g
WHERE   s.stno = g.student_number     /* join condition */
;
CLEAR COLUMNS
```

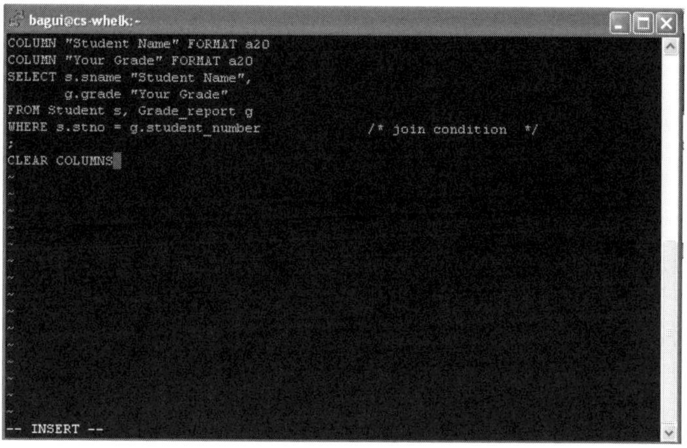

Figure 3.2: Typing a script file in an editor

Note: For information about other vi commands, please refer to the section "Using vi as Your Editor" at the end of Appendix A of this book.

4. To save the file press <**Esc**> and type **:wq** (colon, and w and q for write and quit).
5. To run the script you just created, type:

```
SQL> @run1
```

Note: A CLEAR COLUMNS command should be issued after formatting columns. The purpose of the CLEAR COLUMNS is to remove the formatting from the heading "Student Name." If the command is not issued, then any other time you use "Student Name" as a column alias, it would be formatted as a20. If that is what you want, then the CLEAR could be left off; however, it is good practice to leave the environment as you found it, so it is recommended that whatever you change, you return to its original condition at the end of the script.

COUNT and Rownum

When dealing with multiple tables, it is often desirable to explore the result set without actually displaying all of it. For example, we may want to know how many rows there are in a result set without actually seeing the result set itself. The "row-counter" in SQL is a function called COUNT. Although we will explore functions later in the text, COUNT is used so commonly that we want to introduce it to you here. For example, if you executed the statement:

```
SELECT *      -- all columns, all rows
FROM Student;
```

You would see all the rows of the Student table plus the values for all columns in those rows. If *all* you want to see is the number of rows in the result set, the statement would be:

```
SELECT COUNT(*) -- the count of the number of rows in the result set
FROM Student;
```

This would give you:

```
  COUNT(*)
----------
        48
```

Rownum is another handy Oracle command for exploring result sets. Rownum is called a pseudo-variable because it looks like a variable attribute. Rownum may also be referred to as a *pseudocolumn*. The following is an example of how rownum can be used. If you type:

```
SELECT rownum, sname
FROM   Student
WHERE  rownum < 5;
```

You will get:

```
    ROWNUM SNAME
---------- --------------------
         1 Lineas
         2 Mary
         3 Brenda
         4 Richard
```

Using COUNT

You can also count the occurrence of non-null attributes. For example, if you type:

```
SELECT COUNT(class)
FROM Student;
```

You will get:

```
COUNT(CLASS)
------------
38
```

COUNT(class) will count the rows where class is not null. Combining the two queries with COUNT(*) and COUNT(class) in them we can see that there are ten rows with null values for class. This suggests that judicious use of COUNT could allow us to audit the content of a database without actually looking at the data itself.

Using Rownum

There are two caveats to observe with using `rownum`. First, the `WHERE` clause must contain an inequality — an equality will not work. More specifically, if you use `rownum` in the `WHERE` clause, you must use either < or <=. It will not work with >, >=, =, or <>. `Rownum` appends a `COUNT` as the row is retrieved. In order for the pseudo-variable to work, it has to `COUNT` during retrieval, so a statement that includes `WHERE rownum = 5` will not work correctly.

Second, the following query is not allowed by SQL syntax:

```
SELECT rownum, *
```

If we wanted to see all columns plus a row number, we would have to use the `rownum` pseudo-variable and then list each of the columns.

Outer Joins

Thus far we have discussed equi-joins — the regular and usual inner joins. In this section we will discuss outer joins. Outer joins will include rows in the result set that are not found in inner joins.

In equi-joins, rows without matching row values are eliminated from the join result. For example, in the following join example we have lost the information on the physician from the Jobs table since no employee is a physician.

```
SELECT *
FROM Jobs j, Emps e
WHERE j.jobc = e.jobcode;
```

Will give you:

```
JO JOBTITLE                 EMPNO JO
-- -------------------- ---------- --
cp computer programmer        101 cp
ac accountant                 102 ac
de dentist                    103 de
cp computer programmer        104 cp
cp computer programmer        105 cp
```

At times it may be desirable to include not only rows that have matching values in another table, but also all the rows in one of the tables, matching or not. When you want all rows from one table regardless of whether they have matching values in the other table, the query is called an *outer join*. Although Oracle also uses the ANSI SQL standard of LEFT OUTER JOIN and RIGHT OUTER JOIN, Oracle typically uses the (+) to make a join an outer join. This is because Oracle uses the idea of a "driving table," which is the table that is accessed first. It "drives" the join and all of its rows will be included in the result set (whether or not they match with the other table). Syntactically, the driving table in Oracle is the one *without* the plus sign.

Next we will illustrate the left and right outer joins, first using the idea of the driving table of Oracle, and then using ANSI SQL standard syntax. Before proceeding with this material, we will add one more row to the Emps table:

```
INSERT INTO Emps VALUES (106,'ad');
```

We can assume that 'ad' stands for "administrator."

Left Outer Join

An outer join where we want to keep all the rows from the first mentioned table (or left relation) is called a *left outer join*. Following is an example of a left outer join:

```
SELECT *
FROM Emps e, Jobs j
WHERE e.JobCode = j.Jobc(+);
```

This will give:

```
    EMPNO JO JO JOBTITLE
--------- -- -- --------------------
      103 de de dentist
      105 cp cp computer programmer
      104 cp cp computer programmer
      101 cp cp computer programmer
      102 ac ac accountant
      106 ad

6 rows selected.
```

This left outer join result shows all rows of the Emps table, regardless of whether or not there is a match in Jobs. Here Emps is the "driving" table. Since we added another row to the Emps table with no matching row in the Jobs table, the added row <106,'ad'> is displayed with no matching "right side."

The ANSI SQL standard for a left outer join uses the phrase `LEFT OUTER JOIN` with an `ON` clause, so in ANSI SQL the left outer join would be written as:

```
SELECT *
FROM Emps e LEFT OUTER JOIN Jobs j
ON e.JobCode = j.Jobc;
```

This would give us the same output as shown above.

Right Outer Join

An outer join where we want to keep all the rows from the second table (or right table) is called the *right outer join.* Following is an example of a right outer join:

```
SELECT *
FROM Emps e, Jobs j
WHERE e.JobCode(+) = j.Jobc;
```

This will give:

```
     EMPNO JO JO JOBTITLE
---------- -- -- --------------------
       101 cp cp computer programmer
       102 ac ac accountant
       103 de de dentist
       104 cp cp computer programmer
       105 cp cp computer programmer
                ph physician

6 rows selected.
```

This lists all the job codes available in the table Jobs, even if there are no employees using those codes in Emps. Here Jobs is the driving table. Since no employee is a physician, that row contains nulls for e.empno and e.jobcode.

The ANSI SQL standard for a right outer join uses the phrase `RIGHT OUTER JOIN` with an `ON` clause, so in ANSI SQL the right outer join would be written as:

```
SELECT *
FROM Emps e RIGHT OUTER JOIN Jobs j
ON e.JobCode = j.Jobc;
```

Again, this would give use the same output as shown above.

Handling Full Outer Joins

In Oracle, an outer join cannot be symmetric. This means that two tables may not be outer joined to each other (the plus sign (+) cannot be on both sides of the condition at the same time) in Oracle. For example, the following symmetric outer join:

```
SELECT *
FROM  jobs j, emps e
WHERE j.jobc(+) = e.jobcode(+);
```

Gives us the following error:

```
where j.jobc(+) = e.jobcode(+)
                *
ERROR at line 3:
ORA-01468: a predicate may reference only one outer-joined table
```

In this example there is no driving table and hence Oracle disallows the full outer join (at least without a work-around). The ANSI SQL standard, however, has a full outer join. A *full outer join* is when you want to keep the unmatched rows from the first table (left) as well as the unmatched rows from the second table (right). The following example illustrates the use of the ANSI SQL standard `FULL OUTER JOIN` clause:

```
SELECT *
FROM Emps e FULL OUTER JOIN Jobs j
ON e.JobCode = j.Jobc;
```

This will give us:

```
     EMPNO JO JO JOBTITLE
---------- -- -- --------------------
       103 de de dentist
       105 cp cp computer programmer
       104 cp cp computer programmer
       101 cp cp computer programmer
       102 ac ac accountant
       106 ad
             ph physician

6 rows selected.
```

Here the two unmatched rows (unmatched in the equi-join) show up in the result set, <106,'ad'> on the left and <'ph','physician'> on the right.

Outer Join with an AND Condition

In this section we will see how an outer join behaves with the AND clause. If we want to join only where `Job.Job = 'cp'`, and we want all of the employees of the Emps table also, this would be a left outer join with an `AND` clause, as follows:

```
SELECT *
FROM Emps e, Jobs j
WHERE e.JobCode = j.Jobc(+)
AND j.Jobc = 'cp';
```

But this gives us:

```
     EMPNO JO JO JOBTITLE
---------- -- -- --------------------
       101 cp cp computer programmer
       104 cp cp computer programmer
       105 cp cp computer programmer
```

This give us all the employees where `j.jobc = 'cp'`, but it does not give the rest of the Empnos and JobCodes of the employees (from the Emps table). The effect of the left outer join in the `WHERE` clause is not apparent because no outer join has been included in the `AND` clause. To correct this, when using outer joins, the (+) must also be placed in the *other* conditions, as shown in the following query:

```
SELECT *
FROM Emps e, Jobs j
WHERE e.JobCode = j.Jobc(+)
AND j.Jobc(+) = 'cp';
```

This gives the result we want:

```
     EMPNO JO JO JOBTITLE
---------- -- -- --------------------
       105 cp cp computer programmer
       104 cp cp computer programmer
       101 cp cp computer programmer
       106 ad
       103 de
       102 ac
```

This table gives us the result of the join where `j.jobc = 'cp'` and also shows all the Empnos and Jobcodes of the employees (from the Emps table), even if there are no corresponding jobc equal to "cp" in the Jobs table. There are, of course, corresponding jobs for "de" and "ac", but they don't show up in the result set because of the `AND j.jobc(+) = 'cp'` restriction.

Chaining Outer Joins

As with ordinary joins, several levels of outer joins are possible. If a table A is outer joined to a table B, and then the outer join result is outer joined to a table C, this is known as *chaining* on the outer join.

Let us assume that we have another table, EmpN, as follows:

```
EMPNAME              EMPNO
--------------- ----------
Sam Miller             104
Susan Sommers          105
Kimmy Keebler          101
Patsy Cox              102
Mili Sinha             103
```

The example below shows an example of chaining of an outer join — the Jobs table is outer joined to the Emps table, which may then be thought of as being outer joined to the EmpN table:

```
SELECT *
FROM jobs j, emps e, empn n
WHERE j.jobc(+) = e.jobcode
AND e.empno(+) = n.empno;
```

This gives us:

```
JO JOBTITLE             EMPNO JO EMPNAME         EMPNO SUPEREMPNO
-- ------------------ ------- -- -------------- ------ ----------
de dentist                103 de Mili Sinha        103        102
cp computer programmer    105 cp Susan Sommers     105
cp computer programmer    104 cp Sam Miller        104        102
cp computer programmer    101 cp Kimmy Keebler     101        102
ac accountant             102 ac Patsy Cox         102        105
```

The important thing to note here is that the outer join has to be carried all the way through.

A table cannot be outer joined to more than one table at the same time, as in:

```
SELECT *
FROM jobs j, emps e, empn n
WHERE j.jobc = e.jobcode(+)
AND e.empno(+) = n.empno;
```

This would give the following error message:

```
where j.jobc = e.jobcode(+)
             *
ERROR at line 3:
ORA-01417: a table may be outer joined to at most one other table
```

Self Joins

A *self join* is where a table is joined to itself. In a self join, by the use of table aliases, the query "sees" two identical copies of the same table. An example of a self join would be if we added an employee's supervisor (superEmpno) to our EmpN table. So, assume that the EmpN table now looks like this:

```
EMPNAME              EMPNO  SUPEREMPNO
--------------- ---------- ----------
Sam Miller             104        102
Susan Sommers          105
Kimmy Keebler          101        102
Patsy Cox              102        105
Mili Sinha             103        102
```

From this table we can see that Patsy Cox supervises Sam Miller, Kimmy Keebler, and Mili Sinhar. Susan Sommers is Patsy Cox's supervisor. A listing of employees and their supervisor names could be shown by using a self join of this table as follows:

```
SELECT e.empname employee_name, s.empname supervisor_name
FROM empn e, empn s
WHERE s.empno = e.superempno;
```

This give us:

```
EMPLOYEE_NAME   SUPERVISOR_NAME
--------------- ---------------
Patsy Cox       Susan Sommers
Mili Sinha      Patsy Cox
Kimmy Keebler   Patsy Cox
Sam Miller      Patsy Cox
```

Self Join and Outer Join

A self join can also have an outer join. For example, if we want all the employee names, even if they do not have supervisors, we have to do an outer join of the self join. The following outer join will show all the employees and their supervisors, as well as the rest of the employees, whether they have a supervisor or not:

```
SELECT e.empname employee_name, s.empname supervisor_name
FROM empn e, empn s
WHERE s.empno(+) = e.superempno;
```

This gives us:

```
EMPLOYEE_NAME    SUPERVISOR_NAME
---------------  ---------------
Patsy Cox        Susan Sommers
Mili Sinha       Patsy Cox
Kimmy Keebler    Patsy Cox
Sam Miller       Patsy Cox
Susan Sommers
```

Exercises for Chapter 3

As you do the exercises, it is a good idea to copy/paste your query as well as your query result into a word processor file.

3-1. Create two tables, Stu(sname, majorCode) and Major(majorCode, majorDesc) with the data shown. Use `VARCHAR2(2)` for the codes and appropriate data types for the other attributes.

Stu

sname	majorCode
Jones	CS
Smith	AC
Evans	MA
Adams	CS

Major

majorCode	majorDesc
AC	Accounting
CS	Computer Science
MA	Math

a. Display the Cartesian product (no `WHERE` clause). Use `SELECT *`.... How many rows did you get? How many rows will you always get when combining two tables with n and m rows in them (Cartesian product)?

b. Display an equi-join of Stu and Major on majorCode. (Show this both ways: First using an appropriate `WHERE` clause, then using ANSI SQL standard syntax.) Use table aliases. How many rows did you get?

c. Leave off the column qualifiers (the aliases) on the equi-join in step b. What do you get? This will give an error because of ambiguous column names.

d. Use the `COUNT(*)` function instead of `SELECT *` in the query. Use `COUNT` to show the number of rows in the result set of the equi-join and the Cartesian product. Do the equi-join first with `COUNT`, then comment out the `WHERE` clause for the second answer (put a double hyphen (--) in front of the word `WHERE`).

e. Add two more major codes to the Major table as follows:

```
IT    Information Technology
ST    Statistics
```

Display all the student names (sname) and major descriptions (majorDesc), but also show all the majors, even if there are no students with that major. Display your query both ways: First using ANSI SQL standard syntax, and then using Oracle's driving table (+) concept.

f. Add two more students, Arpan and Ayona, to the Stu table with null values for majorCode. Display all the student names (sname) and major descriptions (majorDesc) whether or not the students have a major. Display your query both ways: First using ANSI SQL standard syntax, and then using Oracle's driving table (+) concept.

g. Display all the student names and major descriptions. Make sure all the students as well as all the majors are shown in the result set, whether or not the students have a major, and whether or not the major has students.

3-2. Create two tables: T1(ename, jobno) and T2(jobno, jobdesc). Let jobno be data type `NUMBER(3)`, and use appropriate data types for the other attributes. Put three rows in T1 and two rows in T2. Give T1.jobno values 100, 200, 300 for the three rows: <..., 100>,<..., 200,>,<..., 300>, where ... represents any value you choose. Give T2.jobno the values 100, 200: <100,...>,<200,...>.

a. How many rows are there in the equi-join (on jobno) of T1 and T2?

b. If the values of T2.jobno were <200,...>, <200,...> (with different jobdesc values), how many rows would you expect and why? Why would the rows have to have different descriptions?

c. If the values of T2.jobno were 400, 500 as in <400,...>,<500,...>, how many rows would you expect to get?

d. If the values of T1.jobno were <..., 100>, <..., 100>,<..., 100> (different names) and the values of T2.jobno were <100,...>, <100...> with different descriptions, how many rows would you expect to get?

e. If you have two tables, what is the number of rows you may expect from a equi-join operation (with what conditions)? A Cartesian product?

f. The number of rows in an equi-join of two tables, whose sizes are *m* and *n* rows, is from ____ to ____ depending on these conditions: ________________________________.

3-3. Use tables T1 and T2 in this exercise also. Create another table called T3(jobdesc, minpay). Let minpay be type `NUMBER(6,2)`. Populate the table with at least one occurrence of each jobdesc from table T2 plus one more jobdesc that is not in T2. Write and display the result of a triple equi-join of T1, T2, and T3. Use an appropriate comment on each of the lines of the `WHERE` clause where there are equi-join conditions. Note that you will need two equi-join conditions.

a. How many rows did you get in the equi-join?

b. Use the `COUNT(*)` function and display the number of rows (rows) in the equi-join.

c. How many rows would you get in this triple Cartesian product? (use `COUNT(*)`).

d. In an equi-join of *n* tables, you always have ________ equi-join conditions in the `WHERE` clause.

3-4. The data dictionary contains views of dictionary tables. Recall from previous exercises that you can display the dictionary and its entries just like any other query. To look at the dictionary itself, the command would be:

```
SELECT * FROM Dict;
```

a. Display the number of rows in the dictionary (just the number of rows, not the content of the rows).

b. Display data dictionary entries for the tables you have created. To look at a table in the dictionary, you use a statement like:

```
SELECT *      -- you could also choose specific columns
              -- rather than all of them
FROM X
WHERE Y
```

where *X* is the name of a dictionary table like USER_TABLES, ALL_SYNONYMS, and so on, and *Y* is whatever condition (row filter) you care to place on the query. Since USER_TABLES are *your* tables, you do not need a "*Y*-condition" on this query to answer this question.

c. Look at which views are available to you. Use SELECT * FROM ALL_SYNONYMS. You should also try SELECT * FROM *xxx*, where *xxx* is a synonym like TAB, TABS, or SYN. TAB, TABS, and SYN are public synonyms for dictionary tables (note that there are others).

d. Look at the description (DESC) for USER_TABLES, USER_OBJECTS, USER_VIEWS, and USER_SYNONYMS. Compare the DESC USER_TABLES to ALL_TABLES. What data is available in ALL_TABLES that is not in USER_TABLES? Are there any columns (attributes) that are in ALL_TABLES which are not in

USER_TABLES? What is the synonym for USER_TABLES?

e. Display the first five rows in the following tables: Dict, USER_TABLES, and ALL_SYNONYMS.

3-5. Using the tables in our Student-Course database, write a script to generate a result set that looks like the following:

```
Student Name            Grade Assigned
--------------------    --------------------
Lineas                    D
Lineas                    B
Lineas                    B
Lineas                    A
Etc.
```

You need show only the first 10 lines of the output. (Use WHERE..rownum < 11.. in the WHERE clause and do not put rownum in the result set, just after the SELECT.)

3-6. You created tables T1, T2, T3, Stu, and Major. These are tables you used for testing. When you have completed this exercise, delete these tables. Check the dictionary to ensure that you have deleted the tables.

3-7. Using the Student table from the Student-Course database, list all the student names (sname) of all the students who are more senior than the juniors (*Hint*: Use a self-join for this.)

Chapter 4

Functions

This chapter is designed to introduce more utilitarian features into the SELECT statement and to show the application of these enhancements. You can use some of the information introduced in this chapter for checking the feasibility of outputs. As we have seen, SQL does not prevent programmers from asking questions that have very long or even meaningless answers (see, for example, our discussion of Cartesian products in Chapter 3).

The main thrust of this chapter is to introduce functions and to demonstrate how to find information when a row contains strings. Functions come in two general varieties: aggregate functions (such as COUNT or SUM) and row functions (such as SQRT). We will place special emphasis on string functions (row functions). We will also demonstrate how functions and other constructions allow us to retrieve information (using LIKE and matching patterns).

The COUNT Function

As we have seen, COUNT is a function that generates a value of how many of something there are. A function that returns a result based on multiple rows is called an *aggregate* function or a group function. We prefer the term aggregate because it avoids confusion. Later we will study a GROUP BY option in the SELECT statement that uses aggregates, but aggregates can be used without using GROUP BY. The aggregate function combines or distills an answer into a smaller set. The COUNT with an asterisk as the argument returns a count of the number of rows in the result set. Following is the syntax for the COUNT function:

```
SELECT COUNT(*)
FROM table-name(s)      -- counts all rows in a table
```

Consider the following example:

```
SELECT COUNT(*)
FROM Grade_report;
```

This would give:

```
 COUNT(*)
----------
      209
```

There are 209 rows in the Grade_report table. The COUNT function can be quite useful because it can save you from unexpectedly long results. In addition, it is often used to answer "how many" queries without looking at the data itself. Recall that in Chapter 3 we generated a Cartesian product and a join. When dealing with larger tables, it is good to first ask the question, "How many rows can I expect in my answer?" This question may be vital if a printout is involved. For example, how many rows are in the Cartesian product of the Student, Section, and

Grade_report tables in our Student-Course database? This question can be answered by the following query:

```
SELECT COUNT(*)
FROM Student, Section, Grade_report;
```

The following output shows what the Cartesian product of this query would give:

```
  COUNT(*)
----------
   321024
```

The COUNT from the last statement equals the product of the table sizes of the three tables. Contrast the previous COUNT query and Cartesian product result to this query:

```
SELECT COUNT(*)
FROM  Student, Grade_report, Section
WHERE Student.stno = Grade_report.student_number
     -- join Student to Grade_report
AND   Grade_report.section_id = Section.section_id
     -- join Grade_report to Section
;
```

The result of this query is:

```
  COUNT(*)
----------
      209
```

What is requested here is a COUNT of a three-way equi-join rather than a three-way Cartesian product. Remember that we strongly advocate the idea of commenting the join conditions, hence the comment:

```
     -- join condition of ...
```

is appropriately appended to the join's WHERE conditions.

Using SELECT and COUNT with DISTINCT

To SELECT all grades from the Grade_report table, we use:

```
SELECT grade
FROM Grade_report;
```

This results in 209 rows of all the grades in the Grade_report table.

To SELECT all distinct grades, we use:

```
SELECT DISTINCT grade
FROM Grade_report;
```

This results in:

```
G
-
A
B
C
D
F

6 rows selected.
```

Observe that the syntax requires us to put the word DISTINCT before the string of attributes because DISTINCT implies distinct rows in the result set. The previous statement also produces a row for null grades (also regarded as a DISTINCT grade). To COUNT distinct grades, we could use:

```
SELECT COUNT(DISTINCT grade)
FROM Grade_report;
```

This results in:

```
COUNT(DISTINCTGRADE)
--------------------
                   5
```

This result does *not* count null values; hence, we have five distinct grades instead of six. So, the DISTINCT produces null values in the output, but the COUNT does not count the null values.

The syntax of SQL will not allow you to COUNT two columns with this query. Thus, the following query will not work:

```
SELECT COUNT (DISTINCT grade, section_id)
FROM Grade_report;
```

More Basic Functions

There are many more functions in SQL besides COUNT. For example, aggregate numeric functions, which work on sets of data, find table values such as sums (SUM), averages (AVG), minimums (MIN), and maximums (MAX). In addition, row-level string functions (such as LPAD, RPAD, LTRIM, RTRIM, SUBSTR, INSTR, and so on), work on values in one given row; they construct, break apart, and parse strings. Row-level date functions provide interesting ways to handle date values. There are also row-level conversion functions (such as TO_CHAR and TO_DATE) that convert dates, characters, strings, and numbers (covered in Chapter 2). In the following sections, we will explore several of the more common aggregate functions for numbers and strings. We will also illustrate special row-level functions that handle special situations that arise in SQL — notably the problem of null values.

Aggregate Functions

One of the more common things to ask of a database involves finding an aggregate function on a set of numeric values. We have seen the COUNT function already. The aggregate functions SUM, AVG, MIN, MAX, and others work in a similar way. For this example, suppose we have a table called Employee that looks like this:

```
name                wage        hours
------------------- ----------  ------------
Alice Adams         10          40
Barry Baker         15          30
Darrel Davis        18
Ed Evans                        10
Genny George        20          40
```

To find the sum of hours worked, we would use the SUM function as follows:

```
SELECT SUM(hours)
FROM Employee;
```

This produces the following output:

```
SUM(HOURS)
----------
       120
```

This SUM result is particularly interesting in that fields that contain null values are ignored by the SUM function (as they are by all aggregate numeric functions). The point about ignoring nulls can be illustrated by the following query, which also shows that several aggregate functions can be placed in the result set:

```
SELECT AVG(hours), MAX(wage), COUNT(hours)
FROM Employee;
```

This produces the following output:

```
AVG(HOURS)    MAX(WAGE)    COUNT(HOURS)
----------    ----------   ------------
        30            20              4
```

A most interesting result may be noted in the following example. If we type:

```
SELECT name, wage*hours
FROM Employee;
```

This produces the following output:

```
NAME              WAGE*HOURS
-------------     ----------
Alice Adams              400
Barry Baker              450
Darrel Davis
Ed Evans
Genny George             800
```

This example illustrates that if a null is contained in a calculation on a row, the result is always null!

Row-level Functions

Row-level functions work on one row at a time. In this section we will look at some row-level functions — the NVL function and several string functions.

The NVL Function

To handle the null problem, Oracle provides a row-level function that returns a value if a table value is null: NVL. The NVL function has the form:

```
NVL(column-value, value-returned)
```

NVL is not an aggregate function — it is a row/value function. It operates on values one at a time as opposed to an aggregate like SUM, which operates on multiple rows for a result.

NVL says if the *column-value* is NOT null, return the value, but if the value IS null, return *value-returned*. For example, if we wanted to multiply wage by hours and avoid the null problem as above, the NVL could be used as follows:

```
SELECT name, NVL(wage,0)*NVL(hours,0)
FROM Employee;
```

This produces the following output:

```
NAME            NVL(WAGE,0)*NVL(HOURS,0)
-------------   ------------------------
Alice Adams                          400
Barry Baker                          450
Darrel Davis                           0
Ed Evans                               0
Genny George                         800
```

NVL does not have to have a *value-returned* equal to zero. For example, if the number of hours was assumed to be 30 if the value were null, then the expression would be: ...NVL(Hours,30)....

Note: There is an Oracle function similar to NVL called NVL2. NVL2 takes three arguments and returns the second if the first is not null and the third if the first is null. NVL2 is not as well known or widely used as NVL.

String Functions

In this section we will discuss the string functions SUBSTR, INSTR, RPAD, LPAD, LTRIM, RTRIM, LENGTH, LIKE, UPPER, and LOWER.

String functions are also row-level functions. String functions operate on a value in a row as a row is retrieved. Let's begin by looking at an example of a string function. Using the previous Employee table, we can list the names of the employees with a statement like this:

```
SELECT name
FROM Employee;
```

This produces the following output:

```
NAME
------------
Alice Adams
Barry Baker
Darrel Davis
Ed Evans
Genny George
```

But suppose we would like to list the names like this:

```
Adams, A.
Baker, B.
Davis, D.
Evans, E.
George, G.
```

To do this, we need string functions to break name into parts and then reassemble those parts, hence the use of the two string functions SUBSTR and INSTR, as well as a concatenation operator.

The SUBSTR and INSTR Functions

SUBSTR (pronounced "substring") returns part of a string, while INSTR (pronounced "in-string") finds where a pattern is located in a string. SUBSTR might be called a "string extractor." To build a string, we use the concatenation operator (||). *Concatenation* means "to place together." We will start the string rearrangement process with INSTR to find the first space break in the name. Consider this example:

```
SELECT INSTR(name,' '),name
FROM Employee;
```

This produces the following output:

```
INSTR(NAME,'')      NAME
--------------      ---------------
             6      Alice Adams
             6      Barry Baker
             7      Darrel Davis
             3      Ed Evans
             6      Genny George
```

Again, note that `INSTR` (like all the string functions) is not an aggregate function. Like `NVL`, it is a row/value function that operates on one value, one row at a time. `INSTR` finds the occurrence of some search string pattern (second argument) in the string listed in the first argument. Here, the `INSTR` is looking for a blank space. The search string pattern does not have to be just one character long as it is in this case. If a blank space did not occur in the subject string name, the function would return a zero.

To illustrate concatenation, we will append something to each name. Consider the following example:

```
SELECT name||', Esq.'
FROM Employee;
```

This produces the following output:

```
NAME||',ESQ.'
---------------------
Alice Adams, Esq.
Barry Baker, Esq.
Darrel Davis, Esq.
Ed Evans, Esq.
Genny George, Esq.
```

As mentioned earlier, SUBSTR is a row-level, string extraction function. SUBSTR in Oracle is almost identical to the same function in many other programming languages. The form of the function is:

```
SUBSTR(subject-string, start, how-far)
```

The *start* attribute tells us where to start retrieving from *subject-string*, and *how-far* tells us how many characters to extract. If *how-far* is not supplied, the function returns the rest of the string from wherever you *start*. If *start* is negative, the function works from the right end of the string.

Consider the following example:

```
SELECT SUBSTR(name,2,4), SUBSTR(name,6), SUBSTR(name,-3)
FROM Employee;
```

This produces the following output:

```
SUBS    SUBSTR(NAM   SUB
----    -----------  ---
lice    Adams        ams
arry    Baker        ker
arre    l Davis      vis
d Ev    ans          ans
enny    George       rge
```

Strings in Oracle are indexed from 1 and not from 0 (zero). But, if we start at position 0, we get the same result as we would if we started at position 1, as shown here. If we type:

```
SELECT SUBSTR(name,0,2)
FROM Employee;
```

We get the following output:

```
SU
--
Al
```

```
Ba
Da
Ed
Ge
```

Likewise, if we type:

```
SELECT SUBSTR(name,1,2)
FROM Employee;
```

We get the following output:

```
SU
--
Al
Ba
Da
Ed
Ge
```

As you can see, both of these queries produce the same result.

Now we combine concatenation, SUBSTR, and INSTR to find the names in a "last name, initial" format. A query like the following is required:

```
SELECT SUBSTR(name, INSTR(name,' ')+1)||', '||SUBSTR(name,1,1)||'.'
FROM Employee;
```

This produces the following output:

```
SUBSTR(NAME,INSTR(N
-------------------
Adams, A.
Baker, B.
Davis, D.
Evans, E.
George, G.
```

The string SUBSTR(name, INSTR(name,' ')+1) extracts characters from name beginning in the position one past (+1) the blank space. Since there is no third argument, the function returns everything after the blank. If there were no blank space in the string, then the characters returned would be the entire string. Then, a comma and a space are appended to the last name with the concatenation operators (||', '||). Finally, the first initial is appended with a concatenated period: SUBSTR(name,1,1)||'.'.

In all of these examples, column aliases would "dress up" the output and provide a handle for ORDER BY and column formatting. Aliases are encouraged, so in the previous query, the first line could read:

```
SELECT SUBSTR
(name, INSTR(name,' ')+1)||', '||SUBSTR(name,1,1)||'.' Names
```

which would produce the following output:

```
Names
-------------------
Adams, A.
Baker, B.
Davis, D.
Evans, E.
George, G.
```

The RPAD and LPAD Functions

RPAD and LPAD could also be used to pad a string to some other string (or anything else). To add something to the right end of name, RPAD could be used as shown here:

```
SELECT RPAD (name,20,'.')
FROM Employee;
```

This would produce the following output:

```
RPAD(NAME,20,'.')
--------------------
Alice Adams.........
Barry Baker........
```

```
Darrel Davis........
Ed Evans............
Genny George........
```

This adds periods (.) after name until name has 20 characters.

To add something before name, LPAD could be used as shown here:

```
SELECT LPAD(name,20,'.')
FROM Employee;
```

This would produce the following output:

```
LPAD(NAME,20,'.')
--------------------
.........Alice Adams
.........Barry Baker
........Darrel Davis
............Ed Evans
........Genny George
```

This adds enough periods before name so that name is 20 characters.

The LTRIM and RTRIM Functions

LTRIM and RTRIM may be used to trim spaces from the left or the right end of a string. As we saw in the name rearrangement example, since we often break apart and reconstruct strings, these functions allow us to conveniently remove blanks if necessary.

There is also a function called TRIM that will edit strings even more flexibly from the left or right or both ends.

The LENGTH Function

To find the length of a desired string, LENGTH could be used as shown here:

```
SELECT LENGTH(name)
FROM employee;
```

This would produce the following output:

```
LENGTH(NAME)
------------
11
11
12
8
12
```

Matching Substrings Using LIKE

There are often times when we want to use part of an attribute as a condition in a query. For example, consider the Section table, which has the following structure:

```
section_id   course_num    sem      yr    inst
----------   -----------   -------  ----  --------------------
85           MATH2410      FALL     86    KING
86           MATH5501      FALL     86    EMERSON
.
.
.
```

We might want to know something about math courses (courses with the prefix MATH). We need to have a way to find a substring in an attribute. We could use SUBSTR, but there is another, more common way to handle this type of query — using the LIKE keyword. The LIKE keyword is used in two ways:

- As an existence match
- As a position match

LIKE as an Existence Match

Using LIKE as an existence match entails finding whether a character string exists in an attribute — if the string exists, the row is selected for inclusion in the result set. This existence type of LIKE query is useful when the position of the character string sought may be in various places in the substring. Oracle uses the wildcard character (%) at the beginning or end of a string when looking for the existence of substrings. For example, suppose we have a name attribute with a data type of VARCHAR(20). Suppose further that the names are in all caps. We want to find all students whose name is SMITH. Consider this example:

```
CREATE TABLE Tsmith (sname VARCHAR2(20));
INSERT INTO Tsmith VALUES ('JOE SMITH');

SELECT *
FROM Tsmith;
```

Which would give:

```
SNAME
--------------------
JOE SMITH
```

Now if we try:

```
SELECT *
FROM Student
WHERE sname = 'SMITH';
```

We get:

```
no rows selected
```

Why didn't we get any rows? Because when we write sname = 'SMITH', the entire name has to match the string "SMITH" (remember that data is case sensitive).

If we added another row to the Student table:

```
INSERT INTO Tsmith VALUES ('SMITH ');
```

We'd still get no match because our new SMITH row has an extra blank space after the last character.

To find "SMITH" we'd have to match all the blanks we put in the table, as follows:

```
SELECT *
FROM Student
WHERE sname = 'SMITH  '   --  a blank follows the H
;
```

Giving:

```
SNAME
--------------------
SMITH
```

To address all these issues, we use the wildcard character (%) and `LIKE` when trying to match or find data. Using a percent sign on both ends of the match string will find SMITH as well as people who have names with SMITH in them, such as SMITH, SMITHFIELD, SMITHSON, LOSMITH, and so on.

Now add some names to our test table, Tsmith, so it now looks like:

```
SNAME
--------------------
JOE SMITH
SMITH
AL LOSMITH
SUE SMITHLY
A. SMITHSON
```

Then using the query:

```
SELECT *
FROM Tsmith
WHERE sname LIKE '%SMITH%';
```

We get:

```
SNAME
--------------------
JOE SMITH
SMITH
AL LOSMITH
SUE SMITHLY
A. SMITHSON
```

Now consider the following examples:

```
SELECT * FROM Student
WHERE sname = 'SMITH'        -- matches only a five-character field
                             -- with SMITH in it
;

SELECT * FROM Student
WHERE sname LIKE '%SMITH%'   -- finds any SMITH pattern in sname
;

SELECT * FROM Student
WHERE sname LIKE 'SMITH%'    -- finds any pattern starting with
                             -- SMITH, ending with anything
;
```

To return to the original question of finding math courses in the Course table, we can use a wildcard match like this:

```
SELECT * FROM Section
WHERE course_num LIKE 'MATH%'   -- matches any course_num
                                -- starting with MATH
;
```

This would produce the following output:

```
SECTION_ID  COURSE_N  SEMEST  YE  INSTRUCTOR  BLDG     ROOM
----------  --------  ------  --  ----------  -------  -------
        85  MATH2410  FALL    98  KING        36       123
        86  MATH5501  FALL    98  EMERSON     36       123
       107  MATH2333  SPRING  00  CHANG       36       123
       109  MATH5501  FALL    99  CHANG       36       123
```

```
       112  MATH2410  FALL    99  CHANG        36       123
       158  MATH2410  SPRING  98               36       123

6 rows selected.
```

LIKE with a Positioned Match and a Wildcard

Another way to use the LIKE keyword is to find the occurrence of a given character sequence in a particular place in a string. For example, we might want to find courses that have a numeric identifier like 2*xxx* in the last four positions, where *xxx* is any letter (presumably a sophomore course). This LIKE form includes the use of the underscore character for the positions of the attribute where we don't care what the contents are. In this case, the SELECT would be:

```
SELECT *
FROM  Section
WHERE course_num LIKE '____2___';
```

This matches any character in the first four positions, then matches a 2, and then any character in the last three positions, as shown here:

```
SECTION_ID  COURSE_N  SEMEST  YE  INSTRUCTOR  BLDG     ROOM
----------  --------  ------  --  ----------  -------  -------
        85  MATH2410  FALL    98  KING        36       123
        95  ACCT2220  SPRING  99  RODRIGUEZ   74
        96  COSC2025  FALL    98  RAFAELT     79       179
       101  POLY2103  SPRING  00  SCHMIDT
       107  MATH2333  SPRING  00  CHANG       36       123
       112  MATH2410  FALL    99  CHANG       36       123
       158  MATH2410  SPRING  98              36       123
       201  CHEM2001  FALL    99              58       114

8 rows selected.
```

This technique is used primarily in fixed-length strings.

The UPPER and LOWER Functions

If the database data is in all caps, then the previous queries will behave as discussed. However, you can never count on what people will store in a database, and what you think might be SMITH could be Smith or SMith (with a leading blank), and so on. If the data in the database is in mixed case or all lowercase letters, then a query that includes the phrase `LIKE '%SMITH%'` will not match — the query will return "no rows." The way around this is to uppercase the comparison using the `UPPER` function. The `UPPER` function converts strings to all uppercase for display and testing (the actual data in the database is unaffected). If the data in the database is in mixed case or, more usually, if you do not know what the case is, you can add `UPPER` to a query like this:

```
SELECT *
FROM  Student
WHERE UPPER(sname) LIKE '%SMITH%';
```

Or, alternatively, you can add `LOWER` to a query like this:

```
SELECT *
FROM  Student
WHERE LOWER(sname) LIKE '%smith%';
```

Both of these queries will produce the same result, as follows:

```
STNO       SNAME                MAJO      CLASS BDATE
---------- -------------------- ---- ---------- ---------
147        Smithly              ENGL          2 13-MAY-80
151        Losmith              CHEM          3 15-JAN-81
88         Smith                                15-OCT-79
```

The Data Dictionary Revisited

In defining what a database is, we use the term *metadata* to define "data about data." Metadata is kept in a series of tables and views called the data dictionary. We have seen glimpses of the data dictionary earlier in this book, but we will use the material presented in this chapter to expand our exploration.

The data dictionary in Oracle is arranged into views so that users, developers, analysts, and DBAs can find out what objects exist, how big they are, when they were created, who they were created by, and so on.

Note: People often mix the terms "view" and "table" when talking about dictionary views. The correct term is "view"; however, "dictionary table" is so common that it is an accepted colloquialism.

The objects that are monitored by the dictionary include tables, tablespaces (subdivisions where tables are located), views, catalogs, synonyms, and other objects (including one category called "objects").

The dictionary has four levels of access defined in views: USER, ALL, DBA, and "other." The view names are a combination of the access/owner and the object. Some examples follow:

- USER_TABLES, which holds tables created by a user.
- ALL_VIEWS, which shows all views accessible to a user.
- DBA_CONSTRAINTS, which shows constraint definitions on all tables.

In multi-user environments, the subject of "grants" is vitally important. A *grant* is a permission conveyed to someone other than the object's owner. If you create something, you own it. If I create a table and I want you so see the contents, I grant you SELECT permission on my table.

"Other" views in the dictionary (not USER_TABLES, ALL_VIEWS, or DBA_CONSTRAINTS) contain more general information. For example, there is a view called COLUMN_PRIVILEGES that describes the grants on columns for which the user is the grantor, grantee, owner, or an enabled role or PUBLIC is the grantee. Spelling is critical when accessing these views because ALL_VIEW is not known, whereas ALL_VIEWS is. To avoid spelling and case problems for matching, you should always use LIKE and UPPER or LOWER appropriately.

There is a list of table synonyms in the dictionary. For example, CAT is a synonym for the view USER_CATALOG.

```
DESC USER_CATALOG
```

Gives:

```
Name                             Null?    Type
-------------------------------- -------- ---------------------
TABLE_NAME                       NOT NULL VARCHAR2(30)
TABLE_TYPE                                VARCHAR2(11)
```

```
DESC CAT
```

Gives:

```
Name                             Null?    Type
-------------------------------- -------- ---------------------
TABLE_NAME                       NOT NULL VARCHAR2(30)
TABLE_TYPE                                VARCHAR2(11)
```

```
SELECT *
FROM CAT
WHERE rownum < 3;
```

Will give:

```
TABLE_NAME                     TABLE_TYPE
------------------------------ -----------
BIN$SEXLA2YTI9DgRAgAIMRjOQ==$0 TABLE
TSMITH                         TABLE
```

There are also system tables that may be viewed. These tables/views have synonyms that begin with the prefix V$. You may or may not be able to display the table/view even though you may see it in the dictionary. One you can see and view is called `V$VERSION`, which tells you the version of Oracle you are using.

Finally, because the dictionary contains a lot of information, it is prudent to access the views therein cautiously. The suggested step-by-step approach outlined in the following exercises show you how to first describe and count before accessing these tables and views. Finally, note that the owner of dictionary tables and views is `SYS`. It is not appropriate to try to modify the dictionary directly.

Exercises for Chapter 4

As you do the exercises, unless it is stated otherwise, you will be using the tables from our standard Student-Course database. Also, as you do the exercises, it will be a good idea to copy/paste your query as well as your query result into a word processor file.

4-1. Display the `COUNT` of rows in each of the tables: Grade_report, Student, and Section. How many rows would you expect in the Cartesian product of all three tables? Display the `COUNT` (*not* the resulting rows) of the Cartesian product of all three and verify your result. Use `SELECT COUNT(*)...`.

4-2. Display the COUNT of section IDs from the Section table, and then the COUNT of DISTINCT section IDs from the Grade_report table. What does this information tell you? *Hint:* section_id is the primary key of the Section table.

4-3. Write, execute, and print a query to list student names and grades (just two attributes) using the table alias feature. Restrict the list to students that have either an A or B in courses with ACCT prefixes only.

Here's how to complete this problem:

a. Get the statement to work as a COUNT of a join of the three tables, Student, Grade_report, and Section. Use table aliases in the join condition (remember to use /* comments */). Note that a join of n tables requires (n–1) join conditions, so here you have to have two join conditions — one to join the Student and Grade_report tables, and one to join the Grade_report and Section tables. Note the number of rows that you get (expect no more rows than is in the Grade_report table). Why?

b. Modify the query and put the accounting (ACCT) condition in the WHERE clause. Note the number of rows in the result — it should be a good bit less than in (a).

c. Again, modify the query and add the grade constraints. The number of rows should decrease again. Note that if you have WHERE x AND y OR z, parentheses are optional, but the criteria will be interpreted according to precedence rules.

The reason that we want you to "start small" and add conditions is that it gives you a check on what you ought to get and it allows you to output less nonsense. Your minimal starting point should be a COUNT of the join with appropriate join conditions. If you are unsure of the join, use `rownum` and look at the first five or ten rows as you go along.

4-4. Do not assume any particular case (upper- or lowercase) for the data for this problem (or ever, for that matter!).

  a. How many students have names like SMITH or Smith?
  b. How many have names that contain the letter sequence SMITH?
  c. How many student names end in LD?
  d. Would `SELECT * FROM Student WHERE sname LIKE 'SMITH%'` find someone whose name was:
    (i) LA SMITH
    (ii) SMITH-JONES
    (iii) SMITH JR.
    (iv) SMITH, JR
  e. Would you call `UPPER` or `LOWER` aggregate functions? Why or why not?
  f. Pad all the student names in the Student table with periods (...) on the right.

4-5. List the junior level COSC courses (`LIKE COSC3`*xxx*) and the name of the course. Use the Course table.

4-6. Using the `COUNT` feature, determine whether there are duplicate names or student numbers in the Student table.

4-7. Assume that all math courses start with MATH. How many math courses are there in the Section table? From the `COUNT` of courses, does it appear that there are any math courses in the Section table that are not in the Course table? Again, using `COUNT`, are there any math courses in the Course table that are not in the Section table? Does it appear that there are any courses that are in the Grade_report,

Section, or Course tables that are not in the others? (We will study how to ask these questions in SQL in a later chapter.) Note that a query like the following would not work:

```
SELECT g.section_id
FROM Grade_report g, Section t
WHERE g.section_id <> t.section_id;
```

Explain why `WHERE..<>..` will not work to produce the desired output.

4-8. Display dictionary views for the tables we have in the Student-Course database (refer to Appendix C for all the table names). Use `ALL_TABLES` as the dictionary view. Do the query as follows:

   a. Describe the table with `DESC ALL_TABLES;`.

   b. Display the number of rows in `ALL_TABLES`. Use `SELECT COUNT(*) FROM ALL_TABLES;`.

Observe that when you are exploring the dictionary, it is *not* a good idea to simply `SELECT * FROM` *`whatever`*, where *whatever* is some dictionary view. Dictionary views are often long and wide — wide in that there are often many attributes and many of those attributes are not necessarily interesting.

   c. Display the owner and table_name from `ALL_TABLES` where `owner = 'your userid'`.

   d. Are the attributes different in `ALL_TABLES` and `USER_TABLES`? What is the difference in the two views?

   e. Display the first two rows (use `WHERE rownum < 3`) of the `ALL_TABLES` table.

f. Repeat this exercise (steps a, b, and c) for `ALL_CATALOG`, `ALL_OBJECTS`, `ALL_SYNONYMS`, and `ALL_TAB_COLUMNS` (synonym is `COLS`). The point of this exercise is twofold:

- To drive home the admonition to be very careful to look at what you will get before you actually ask for it (use `DESC` and `COUNT(*)` prudently), and
- To familiarize you with the dictionary contents.

g. How many objects are in the dictionary? Use `Dict` for the dictionary (Dict is the synonym for dictionary). How many `USER` tables are there? How many `ALL_` tables? How many `DBA_` type tables? How many other tables? *Hint:* `SELECT FROM Dict` and use `LIKE` appropriately for each query.

h. Using the table `ALL_USERS`, find out your user ID number and when your account was created.

i. Determine what session privileges you have available (`SESSION_PRIVS`).

j. Determine which version of Oracle we are using. Also determine which `V$` tables you can "see" in the dictionary and which you can and cannot actually view. *Hint:* Look at the `V$` tables in `Dict` and try to describe each one.

4-9. For all the tables in the Student-Course database — Student, Grade_report, Section, Room, Course, Prereq, and Department_to_major, list the attributes, number of rows, number of distinct rows, and number of rows without nulls. As you gather the information, put the information in a tabular format, as shown below. (*Note:* You may want to create this table in your word processor as you gather the information.)

Table	Attribute	Rows	Distinct Rows	Rows without Nulls
Student	stno	48	48	48
	sname		47	48
	major		8	45
	class		etc., etc.	
Section	section_id	etc.		

Also, note that there is probably no "one" query that will give you this information. You will have to find this information using separate queries, and then put the information together in a tabular format.

Hint: You can use:

```
SELECT COUNT (*)
FROM Student
WHERE sname IS NULL
```

4-10. a. Find the count, sum, average, minimum, and maximum capacity of rooms in the database. (*Hint:* Use the Room table for this question.)

b. Where there is a null value for the capacity, assume the capacity to be 40, and find the average room size again.

4-11. Using the Student table, display the first 10 rows (`WHERE rownum < 11`) with an appended initial. For the appended initial, choose the middle letter of the name, so that if a name is Evans, the initial is A (half of the length +1). If the name is Conway, the initial is W. You do not need to round up or down, just use `(LENGTH(Name)/2)+1` as the starting place in the `SUBSTR` function to create the initial. Use appropriate column aliases. Your result should look like this (actual names may vary depending on the current database):

```
PERSON#     NAMES
----------  ------------------------
         1  Lineas, E.
         2  Mary, R.
```

```
 3  Brenda, N.
 4  Richard, H.
 5  Kelly, L.
 6  Lujack, A.
 7  Reva, V.
 8  Elainie, I.
 9  Harley, L.
10  Donald, A.
```

4-12. In Chapter 2, we introduced some date functions, namely ADD_MONTHS and MONTHS_BETWEEN. Use the MONTHS_BETWEEN and other appropriate functions to write *one* query that returns the number of years between the oldest and youngest student in the Student table.

Chapter 5

Query Development, Privileges, and Derived Structures

In this chapter we show you how to approach and develop a query. One way to create long queries is to begin modestly, and to build up to the query of interest. In this process of "building up" the query, parentheses often need to be appropriately placed. We will illustrate this stepwise approach by developing a few queries in this chapter, and we will discuss how parentheses can aid in query development.

Another way to develop queries is to use derived structures. Derived structures include temporary tables, views (both real and inline views), and snapshots (also known as *materialized views*). Each of these derived structures allows us to easily manipulate partial displays of the database, which can then be connected to answer a complicated database query. This chapter also discusses the security measures (privileges) that can be enabled/disabled on derived structures as well as tables.

Whether we are deriving a long query or working to devise a derived structure, we will likely need to store and retrieve queries, so we will begin our discussion on query development with a brief review of how to use the SAVE and EDIT commands.

Query Development

Recall from Chapter 1 that you can handle editing in two ways: Using the statement buffer or working with a named file. You can name a query file with SAVE (as shown in step 1 of the following section) or you can name the file initially with EDIT (as shown in step 2 of the following section).

Using SAVE and EDIT

Queries are sometimes developed after some initial experimentation, while other times they are the result of modifying previously stored queries. In either case we use the SAVE and EDIT commands.

Let's look at how the query-building process works. Suppose we want to find the names of all students who major in computer science (COSC) and who have earned a grade of B in some course. To do so, we follow these steps:

1. From the SQL prompt, we begin by devising a query to find students who major in computer science (COSC):

```
SELECT *
FROM Student
WHERE major = 'COSC';
```

This gives us:

```
STNO     SNAME                MAJO  CLASS     BDATE
-------- -------------------- ----  --------- ---------
3        Mary                 COSC          4 16-JUL-78
8        Brenda               COSC          2 13-AUG-77
14       Lujack               COSC          1 12-FEB-77
17       Elainie              COSC          1 12-AUG-76
121      Hillary              COSC          1 16-JUL-77
128      Brad                 COSC          1 10-SEP-77
130      Alan                 COSC          2 16-JUL-77
142      Jerry                COSC          4 12-MAR-78
31       Jake                 COSC          4 12-FEB-78
5        Zelda                COSC            12-FEB-78

10 rows selected.
```

We save this query by typing:

```
SQL> SAVE q1
```

Note: When saving queries, CRE (meaning "create") is the default option. Use of CRE assumes q1 does not exist. In this example, SAVE q1 CRE would also work. The file q1.sql would be created in the directory of the host operating system. SAVE q1 REP (REP means "replace") would save a new version of q1 over the previously saved version of q1.

2. Whether we started with a query in the buffer (as in step 1) or we created a named query (with `EDIT q1`), we now need to modify the saved query, q1. At this point, in case you have not already done so, define your editor. For the vi editor we use:

```
SQL> define_editor=vi
```

Now suppose we wish to restrict the output of q1 to just names. We call up the file that was just created (q1) by typing:

```
SQL> EDIT q1
```

Warning: If we just say SQL> EDIT, the default editor will open up with the last command that was in the buffer, which is not what we want to do here. We want to edit the saved q1 query using an editor we choose.

Once in the vi editor, position your cursor on the * and press <**Esc**>, then type **i** (for Insert mode). Next, type **sname** and delete the *. So we edit the first line to:

```
SELECT sname
```

The query should now read:

```
SELECT sname
FROM Student
WHERE major = 'COSC';
```

We then save the file by pressing <**Esc**> and type **:wq** to close the editor.

Note: For information about other vi editor commands, refer to the section "Using vi as Your Editor" in Appendix A of this book.

3. To run (start) our saved query, we use the @ symbol. We start our query like this:

```
SQL> @q1
```

After pressing <**Enter**>, we will get the following output:

```
SNAME
--------------------
Mary
Brenda
Lujack
Elainie
Hillary
Brad
Alan
Jerry
Jake
Zelda

10 rows selected.
```

4. Because we want to see those students who major in computer science (COSC) *and* have earned a B in some course, we must edit the query again and as the next step add the Grade_report table by a join. The query now looks like this:

```
SELECT stu.sname
FROM   Student stu, Grade_report g
WHERE  stu.major = 'COSC'
AND    stu.stno = g.student_number      /* join condition
                                         Student-Grade_report */
;
```

5. Save q1 and restart query q1. This will give us the following output:

```
SNAME
--------
Mary
Mary
Mary
.
.
Elainie
Elainie
Brenda
```

```
Hillary
Brad
Alan
Jerry
Jake
Zelda
Zelda
Brenda
.
.
Jerry
Jerry

48 rows selected.
```

6. To add the condition for B's, we need to add another AND clause. Edit q1 again and add a fifth line so that we end up with the following query:

```
SELECT stu.sname
FROM  Student stu, Grade_report g
WHERE stu.major = 'COSC'
AND   stu.stno = g.student_number    /* join condition
                                      Student-Grade_report */
AND   g.grade = 'B';
```

7. Save and restart the query again. This will give us the following output:

```
SNAME
------------------
Mary
Mary
Mary
Mary
Mary
Brenda
Lujack
Lujack
Lujack
Hillary
```

```
Zelda
Brenda
Hillary
Hillary

14 rows selected.
```

This query successfully gives us all the students who are majoring in computer science (COSC) and who earned a grade of B in some class. The point of this process is that it allows us to test as we go, verify that the query works up to that point, and ensure that we have a reasonable result before we move on to the next enhancement.

Note: It is a good idea to adopt the convention of using query names like q1, q2, and so on or q51 (for exercise 5, query 1). It is also a good idea to keep old queries. You can always delete, replace, rename, copy, move, or add to them. As mentioned earlier, the queries will be stored in the host as q1.sql, q2.sql, and so on.

Deleting a Query

We can go to the host and delete a stored query. To go to the host, type:

```
SQL> HOST
```

This will take us to the host prompt:

```
[bagui@cs-whelk ~]$
```

To get a listing of all our queries (.sql files) in host, we type **dir *.sql**, as shown here:

```
[bagui@cs-whelk ~]$ dir *.sql
```

If we want to delete the query we just created, we type **rm** (short for remove) as shown below:

```
[bagui@cs-whelk ~]$ rm q1.sql
```

Note: Remember that UNIX is case sensitive, so the UNIX commands are in lowercase.

Parentheses in SQL Expressions

In programming languages like C, we can write a statement like this:

```
x = y + z * w
```

What is the result? It depends on precedence rules. Usually in programming languages (and in SQL), parentheses have the highest precedence. The authors of this book advocate fully parenthesized expressions for two reasons:

- It makes the expression easier to debug.
- It tells anyone else who looks at your expression that you knew what you wanted because you explicitly and unambiguously wrote the expression in a fully parenthesized way.

In SQL, the precedence problem occurs with AND and OR. For example, what does the following query request?

```
SELECT *
FROM  Student
WHERE class = 3 OR class = 4 AND stno < 100;
```

Does AND or OR have precedence, or is the rule "left to right"? The point is that we do not have to know the rule to write an unambiguous expression. If we use parentheses appropriately, we can make the expression clear and unambiguous. Ask yourself what these statements mean:

```
SELECT *
FROM  Student
WHERE class = 3 OR (class = 4 AND stno < 100);
```

This will result in the following output:

```
STNO       SNAME              MAJO  CLASS  BDATE
---------  -----------------  ----  -----  ---------
3          Mary               COSC  4      16-JUL-78
13         Kelly              MATH  4      12-AUG-80
20         Donald             ACCT  4      15-OCT-77
24         Chris              ACCT  4      12-FEB-78
49         Susan              ENGL  3      11-MAR-80
62         Monica             MATH  3      14-OCT-80
122        Phoebe             ENGL  3      15-APR-80
131        Rachel             ENGL  3      15-APR-80
143        Cramer             ENGL  3      15-APR-80
31         Jake               COSC  4      12-FEB-78
151        Losmith            CHEM  3      15-JAN-81
160        Gus                ART   3      15-OCT-78

12 rows selected.
```

If you type this:

```
SELECT *
FROM  Student
WHERE (class = 3 OR class = 4) AND stno < 100;
```

It will result in the following output:

```
STNO       SNAME              MAJO  CLASS  BDATE
---------  -----------------  ----  -----  ---------
3          Mary               COSC  4      16-JUL-78
13         Kelly              MATH  4      12-AUG-80
20         Donald             ACCT  4      15-OCT-77
24         Chris              ACCT  4      12-FEB-78
49         Susan              ENGL  3      11-MAR-80
62         Monica             MATH  3      14-OCT-80
31         Jake               COSC  4      12-FEB-78
```

```
7 rows selected.
```

In the preceding two statements, there is no ambiguity. In the first statement, the AND is performed first. In the second statement, the OR is performed first. Each is made clear by appropriate parentheses. In an unparenthesized set of conditions, OR is always evaluated first, then AND, and then NOT.

Derived Structures

Derived structures may become necessary as queries get larger. For larger queries, we may begin modestly and build the queries in a step-by-step approach (checking as we go). Here we will discuss the most commonly used derived structure, a view. The other derived structures, like temporary tables, inline views, and snapshots, will be discussed later in this chapter.

Views

The first and most common derived structure is a view. A view (also called a *virtual table*) is a mechanism that procures a restricted subset of data that is accessible in ways similar to ordinary tables. We use the word "similar" because some operations on views (such as some updates and deletes) may be restricted where they would not be if they were performed on the database itself.

A view serves several purposes: It is a convenient way to develop a query by isolating parts of it, and it is used to restrict a set of users from seeing part of the database, which increases security.

Using the CREATE OR REPLACE VIEW Statements

The simple version of the CREATE VIEW syntax is:

```
CREATE OR REPLACE VIEW view-name AS subquery
```

This syntax is used for views (and for other objects, as we will see later in the chapter). We could use the phrase CREATE VIEW (if a view did not exist) and we could DROP an existing view and recreate it with another CREATE VIEW (although we cannot say REPLACE VIEW by itself). However, the usual development scenario is to CREATE OR REPLACE VIEW when we write it or develop it. So, if we wanted to create a view of students called Namemaj, which was just names and majors, we could write:

```
CREATE OR REPLACE VIEW Namemaj AS
SELECT sname, major
FROM   Student;
```

We could then get our list of names and majors by using the view name in a query like this:

```
SELECT *
FROM   Namemaj;
```

This produces the following output:

```
SNAME                MAJO
-------------------- ----
Lineas               ENGL
Mary                 COSC
Brenda               COSC
Richard              ENGL
Kelly                MATH
Lujack               COSC
Reva                 MATH
Elainie              COSC
Harley               POLY
Donald               ACCT
Chris                ACCT
```

```
Lynette              POLY
Susan                ENGL
Monica               MATH
.
.
.

48 rows selected.
```

As with a table, the view can be filtered and used in a SELECT just like an ordinary table, as follows:

```
SELECT n.major Major, n.sname "Student Name"
FROM  Namemaj  n, Department_to_major  d
WHERE n.major = d.dcode
AND   UPPER(d.dname) LIKE 'COMP%';
```

This will produce the following output:

```
MAJO  Student Name
----  ------------
COSC  Mary
COSC  Brenda
COSC  Lujack
COSC  Elainie
COSC  Hillary
COSC  Brad
COSC  Alan
COSC  Jerry
COSC  Jake
COSC  Zelda

10 rows selected.
```

Adding ORDER BY to CREATE OR REPLACE VIEW Statements

If we want to order our output, we can add an ORDER BY to a CREATE OR REPLACE VIEW statement, as shown here:

```
CREATE OR REPLACE VIEW Namemaj AS
```

```
SELECT sname, major
FROM   Student
ORDER BY sname;
```

If we then type:

```
SELECT *
FROM Namemaj;
```

We will get the output ordered by name, as follows:

```
SNAME                MAJO
-------------------- ----
Alan                 COSC
Benny                CHEM
Bill                 POLY
Brad                 COSC
Brenda               COSC
Cedric               ENGL
Chris                ACCT
Cramer               ENGL
Donald               ACCT
Elainie              COSC
Fraiser              POLY
Francis              ACCT
Genevieve            UNKN
George               POLY
Gus                  ART
Harley               POLY
.
.
.
Susan                ENGL
Thornton
Zelda                COSC

48 rows selected.
```

Developing a Query Using Views

One way to develop a query using views is to get the query working in parts. For example, if we start by typing:

```
SELECT sname, major
FROM  Student;
```

We name this query q2. We can then create the view by inserting a line before the `SELECT` in q2, so that the query looks like this:

```
CREATE OR REPLACE VIEW Namemaj AS
SELECT sname, major
FROM   Student;
```

We would then use start q2 (`@q2`) to create the view.

Creating Special View Column Names

We can create special column names that are different from the names of the columns in the underlying table for use with the view. Column names can be placed just after the named view in the definition command as follows:

```
CREATE OR REPLACE VIEW Namemaj (name, maj) AS
SELECT sname, major
FROM   Student;
```

Now if we type:

```
SELECT *
FROM Namemaj;
```

We will get the following output:

```
NAME                 MAJ
-------------------- ----
Lineas               ENGL
Mary                 COSC
```

```
Brenda                COSC
Richard               ENGL
Kelly                 MATH
Lujack                COSC
Reva                  MATH
Elainie               COSC
Harley                POLY
Donald                ACCT
Chris                 ACCT
Lynette               POLY
Susan                 ENGL
Monica                MATH
.
.
.

48 rows selected.
```

When the view definition has column names, those names must be used to access the view. If we type the following:

```
SELECT maj, name
FROM  Namemaj
WHERE maj LIKE 'CO%';
```

We will get the following output:

```
MAJ   NAME
----  --------------------
COSC  Mary
COSC  Brenda
COSC  Lujack
COSC  Elainie
COSC  Hillary
COSC  Brad
COSC  Alan
COSC  Jerry
COSC  Jake
COSC  Zelda

10 rows selected.
```

Views can also be created using aliases instead of column names. We would have the same effect if the CREATE statement were:

```
CREATE OR REPLACE VIEW Namemaj AS
SELECT sname name, major maj
FROM   Student;
```

Note: Oracle has different forms for the CREATE VIEW command. The optional WITH CHECK OPTION (after the table name in the FROM clause) keeps you from creating a view that you could not use because of other security issues. The WITH CHECK OPTION guarantees that inserts and updates performed through the view will result in rows that the view subquery can select. The FORCE option allows you to create a view if the underlying tables do not exist or if you do not have privileges on the underlying table. Note that you should not need FORCE at this time.

Granting and Revoking Privileges on Tables and Views

Security is an extremely important issue when accessing of a table from a foreign account. The creator of the account has no restrictions on access and may or may not pass along manipulation privileges to others. The SQL statements controlling security are GRANT and REVOKE. The version of the GRANT command we will use looks like this:

```
GRANT {priv|ALL}
ON object-name
TO {specific user|PUBLIC}
```

The vertical bar (|) means "or" as in GRANT priv or GRANT ALL, and *priv* means some DML command like SELECT or INSERT. To allow another user to see the tables we created, for example, to allow any user to be able to SELECT data from our table named Student, we must run a command like the following for each table:

```
GRANT SELECT
ON Student
TO PUBLIC;
```

If we want to disallow previously granted access to a table such as Student, we could type:

```
REVOKE SELECT
ON Student
FROM PUBLIC;
```

Instead of PUBLIC, we can identify individuals in either case (GRANT or REVOKE) with statements like:

```
GRANT SELECT
ON Student
TO jsmith;
```

One of the great benefits of views involves security. A person can create a view, grant access to the view, and revoke access to the underlying table. For example, if the Student table contained some information that we did not want someone named Joe Smith to see, we could create a view of Student containing just the information that Joe was allowed to see. We could then grant Joe access to that view and then revoke all privileges on the underlying Student table from him.

Query Development and Derived Structures

In this section we will first look at query development and then we will show you how derived structures can be used in query development.

Our problem will be to list the names, student numbers, and department name of students who are freshman or sophomores and computer science majors, from our Student-Course database. In Step 1 we will develop a query, and in Step 2 we will show how to use this query with a derived structure. We will show several options with the derived structures. Option 1 shows how the query can be turned into a view. Option 2 shows how the query can be turned into a temporary table. In Option 3 we show how the query can be turned into an inline view, and in Option 4 we show how to create a snapshot.

Step 1: Developing a Query Step-by-Step

1. The first step in any query is to find out which attributes we need, and in which tables these attributes are found. For our example problem, we need student names (sname) and numbers (stno), which are found in the Student table. We also need Department names (dname), which are found in the Department_to_major table. In order to find the department names that correspond to the student majors, we have to join the Student and Department_to_major tables. To join these two tables, we link the major field from the Student table to the dcode field from the Department_to_major table as follows (since the statements will be eventually filtered by class, we will include class in the result set):

```
SELECT s.sname, s.stno, d.dname, s.class
FROM   Student s, Department_to_major d
WHERE  s.major = d.dcode;
```

Once we type the above query and run it, we will get:

```
SNAME                  STNO DNAME                   CLASS
------------------ -------- -------------------- ---------
Lineas                    2 English                     1
Mary                      3 Computer Science            4
Brenda                    8 Computer Science            2
```

```
Richard                 10 English              1
Kelly                   13 Mathematics          4
Lujack                  14 Computer Science     1
Reva                    15 Mathematics          2
Elainie                 17 Computer Science     1
.
.
.
Romona                   9 English
Ken                      6 Political Science
Jake                   191 Mathematics          2

45 rows selected.
```

2. Save this query as stucosc.
3. The next step in our query development scenario would be to edit stucosc to include only freshmen and sophomores (class 1 and 2) from the Student table. Therefore, we add `AND (s.class = 1 OR s.class = 2)` to stucosc, so it now reads:

```
SELECT s.sname, s.stno, d.dname, s.class
FROM   Student s, Department_to_major d
WHERE  s.major = d.dcode
AND (s.class = 1 OR s.class = 2);
```

This query will now give the following output:

```
SNAME                  STNO DNAME                    CLASS
------------------ -------- -------------------- ---------
Lineas                    2 English                      1
Brenda                    8 Computer Science             2
Richard                  10 English                      1
Lujack                   14 Computer Science             1
Reva                     15 Mathematics                  2
Elainie                  17 Computer Science             1
Harley                   19 Political Science            2
Lynette                  34 Political Science            1
Hillary                 121 Computer Science             1
Sadie                   125 Mathematics                  2
Jessica                 126 Political Science            2
```

```
Steve                127  English              1
Brad                 128  Computer Science     1
Cedric               129  English              2
Alan                 130  Computer Science     2
George               132  Political Science    1
Fraiser              144  Political Science    1
Smithly              147  English              2
Sebastian            148  Accounting           2
Lindsay              155                       1
Jake                 191  Mathematics          2

21 rows selected.
```

4. Resave this query by typing the following:

```
SAVE stucosc REP;
```

Now we have all the freshmen and sophomores along with their department names in our result set. To find the computer science majors from this group, edit stucosc again and add the line `AND s.major = 'COSC'` to the query so it now reads:

```
SELECT s.sname, s.stno, d.dname, s.class,
FROM   Student s, Department_to_major d
WHERE  s.major = d.dcode
AND   (s.class = 1 OR s.class = 2)
AND    s.major = 'COSC';
```

This finally give us the student names, student numbers, and department names of students who are freshman or sophomores and computer science majors, as shown below.

```
SNAME                   STNO  DNAME                  CLASS
------------------  ---------  -------------------  ---------
Brenda                     8  Computer Science           2
Lujack                    14  Computer Science           1
Elainie                   17  Computer Science           1
Hillary                  121  Computer Science           1
Brad                     128  Computer Science           1
```

```
Alan                      130  Computer Science            2

6 rows selected.
```

5. Resave this query as stucosc again:

```
SAVE stucosc REP;
```

Step 2: Using a Derived Structure

In this section we will see how to use the query that we developed above and turn it into queries that use derived structures — a view, temporary table, inline view, or snapshot. Each of these derived structures will produce the same end result, but each one has special uses.

Option 1: Make Your Query a View

Views are quite useful when we want to simplify frequently used queries or use certain security procedures. Views are also useful when we need to develop complex queries. In addition, views in Oracle occupy practically no disk space, making them even more desirable. When we use a view for queries, we use it just as we would the underlying tables. Although views depend on the underlying tables, the data in views is not stored as a separate table. Therefore, a view is like a mask over an underlying table.

To create a view from the query we just developed, stucosc, follow these steps:

1. Edit stucosc and insert a `CREATE VIEW` statement in the first line so that it reads:

```
CREATE OR REPLACE VIEW vustu AS
SELECT s.sname, s.stno, d.dname
FROM   Student s, Department_to_major d
WHERE  s.major = d.dcode      -- join condition
AND    (s.class = 1 OR s.class = 2)
```

```
AND    s.major = 'COSC';
```

This command, when run, will create a view called "vustu."

2. Save this query as Student_view.
3. Start Student_view by typing:

```
@Student_view
```

This will create the view.

4. We can then SELECT from the view:

```
SELECT *
FROM vustu
WHERE UPPER(sname) LIKE 'SMI%';
```

Option 2: Create a Temporary Table

If we were going to use the view of names, student numbers, and department names of freshmen and sophomore computer science majors often, and we did not need absolutely current information, we might want to create a temporary table rather than a view. A drawback of the temporary table is that if data in the original tables is changed, it will not get changed in the temporary table. In a view, whatever "happens" in the table "happens" in the view. On the plus side, a temporary table can be indexed, you can use a query to change the ORDER BY, and views of the temporary table can be made — sort of a hierarchy of views.

We can create a temporary table from the query developed in Step 1 by following these steps:

1. Edit stucosc so that it now reads:

```
CREATE TABLE Tempstu AS
SELECT s.sname, s.stno, d.dname
FROM   Student s, Department_to_major d
WHERE  s.major = d.dcode      /* join condition Student-D2m */
AND    (s.class = 1 OR s.class = 2)
```

```
AND    s.major = 'COSC';
```

2. Save this query as Temp_student.
3. Start Temp_student by typing:

```
@Temp_student
```

This creates the temporary table named Tempstu that has the attributes sname, stno, and dname.

4. We could query our temporary table like this:

```
SELECT *
FROM Tempstu;
```

This would give us the following output:

```
SNAME                  STNO  DNAME
-------------------- ------ --------------------
Brenda                    8  Computer Science
Lujack                   14  Computer Science
Elainie                  17  Computer Science
Hillary                 121  Computer Science
Brad                    128  Computer Science
Alan                    130  Computer Science

6 rows selected.
```

This is the same result that Option 1 would give us. However, remember that *data in a temporary table is only as current as the last time it was refreshed.* Maintenance of the temporary table falls to the creator, so the creator should arrange to refresh the table. When everyone is finished with the table, the creator should DROP it.

Option 3: Use an Inline View

We can put a query in the FROM clause of a SELECT statement and create what is called an *inline view*. An inline view exists only during the execution of a query. The main purpose of an inline view is to simplify the development of a query. For example, you could devise the inline view, inner select, test it, examine the result, and wrap it in parentheses, then continue with the overall query development.

Let's look at an example of an inline view in our sample problem. In this example, we write a query. Suppose we start with this:

```
SELECT s.sname  name, s.stno, d.dname
FROM  Student s, Department_to_major d
WHERE s.major = d.dcode       /* join condition Student-D2m */
AND  (s.class = 1 OR s.class = 2)
AND   s.major = 'COSC';
```

Notice that a column alias is used for the student name (name), whereas the other columns in the inline view result set are not aliased. Now to create the inline view, we wrap the query we just created in parentheses and use the result set from above like a table. We create an alias called "v" for our inline view/virtual table:

```
SELECT v.name, v.dname
FROM
(SELECT s.sname name, s.stno, d.dname
FROM  Student s, Department_to_major d
WHERE s.major = d.dcode         /* join condition Student-D2m */
AND  (s.class = 1 OR s.class = 2)
AND   s.major = 'COSC') v;
```

In the final result set of the outer query, the column names reference the names used or aliased in the inline view result set. Here v.name corresponds to the alias of s.sname, *name*, and v.dname corresponds to *d.dname*. It is usually better to use column aliases throughout the inline view to avoid confusion. Therefore, we may want to use something like the following:

```
SELECT v.iviewname, v.iviewdname
FROM
(SELECT s.sname iviewname, s.stno iviewstno, d.dname iviewdname
```

```
FROM  Student s, Department_to_major d
WHERE s.major = d.dcode            /* join condition Student-D2m */
AND  (s.class = 1 OR s.class = 2)
AND   s.major = 'COSC') v;
```

Option 4: Use a Snapshot

Snapshots (also known in Oracle as *materialized views*) are a sort of middle ground between temporary tables and views. Snapshots are usually used in distributed databases, where a table is kept at some remote location and where a current version of data is not needed right away. Snapshots can also be created locally and can serve as non-current views of data. In "snapshotting," the data can be automatically updated so that the entity acts like a view and like a temporary table at the same time. By using a snapshot, the user is seeing the table as it was (yesterday, an hour ago, last week, and so on), but the database does not have to refresh a view each time the snapshot is used. Likewise, the user does not have to see what is always an old "snapshot" as they would in a temporary table.

Note: To create a snapshot, the table must have a primary key defined.

To add a primary key to a table, we use the following syntax:

```
SQL> ALTER TABLE Tablename
ADD(constraint name_pk PRIMARY KEY (attribute_name));
```

Note: All the tables in our Student-Course database already have a primary key defined.

We can then type the statement for creating a snapshot as follows:

```
CREATE SNAPSHOT qsnap1
REFRESH COMPLETE NEXT SYSDATE + 7
AS
SELECT * FROM Student WHERE stno < 20;
```

Here, the snapshot "view" is `SELECT * FROM Student WHERE stno < 20`. The snapshot is named qsnap1. The difference between this view and other derived structures is the `REFRESH` clause, which refreshes the query every seven days (`SYSDATE + 7`) from the time the snapshot is first created. If we wanted a refresh every day, then the `NEXT` clause would read `...SYSDATE + 1`. If we wanted an hourly refresh, it would read `...SYSDATE + (1/24)`.

Snapshots are used just like views with statements like `SELECT * FROM qsnap1`. Unfortunately, `CREATE OR REPLACE` is not allowed, so to develop a snapshot we have to `DROP` the snapshot and recreate it. Snapshots are not widely used except in situations where a database is distributed. Creating snapshots requires privileges that may not be typically granted to users. Also, the DBA (database administrator) may have to execute special scripts to allow snapshots.

The details of when the snapshot was created and last updated, what the query is, and so on may be found in the dictionary view `USER_SNAPSHOTS` or `ALL_SNAPSHOTS`. In later versions of Oracle, the appropriate dictionary view is *x_mviews*, where *x* could be `USER`, `ALL`, or `DBA`. The `SELECT ANY TABLE` privilege is required for a user to see `ALL_SNAPSHOTS`.

Exercises for Chapter 5

As you do the exercises, unless it is stated otherwise, you will be using the tables from our standard Student-Course database. Also, as you do the exercises, it will be a good idea to copy/paste your query as well as your query result into a word processor file.

5-1. Develop and execute a query to find the names of students who had HERMANO as an instructor and earned a grade of B or better in the class. Develop the query by first finding sections where HERMANO was the instructor. Save this query. Then, recall (`EDIT`) it and modify the query to join the Section table with the Grade_report table. Then add the grade constraint. Save this query (with the `REPLACE` option). Then, recall it and go from there. Show all steps of your output.

5-2. Create a duplicate table (call it Stutab) in your account from the Student table that contains all tuples from the Student table. Hint: Use `DESC Student` to see the attributes of the Student table. Create the Stutab table with a `CREATE TABLE` command and use `INSERT INTO Stutab...SELECT` to populate it.

a. List student names and majors from the Stutab table for students who are juniors or seniors only.

b. List student names and computer science (COSC) majors from the Stutab table.

c. Create a view (call it vstu) that contains student names and majors, but only for COSC majors. (Use `CREATE OR REPLACE VIEW....`)

d. List the student names and majors from the vstu view in descending order by name.

e. Modify a tuple in your view of your table so that a student changes his or her major.

f. Re-execute the display of the view. Did modifying your vstu view also change the parent table, Stutab?

g. Try to modify the view again, but this time change the major to COMPSC — an obviously invalid field in the Stutab table because the attribute was defined as four characters. Can you do it? What happens?

5-3. a. Repeat the CREATE VIEW part of the exercise in 5-2c with a column name in the CREATE OR REPLACE VIEW statement like this:

```
CREATE OR REPLACE VIEW vx (Na, Ma) AS SELECT...
```

using the Stutab table you created in exercise 5-2. Display the view. What is the effect of the (Na, Ma)?

b. Repeat exercise 5-3a, but this time use column aliases in the view definition. Are there any differences noted between explicitly defining the view columns in the heading part of the statement versus using a column alias?

5-4. Perform an experiment to determine the precedence in a query with three conditions linked by AND and OR. Find out whether AND, OR, or left-to-right take precedence. Use statements like this (actual attribute names may be found using DESC Student):

```
SELECT *
FROM  Student
WHERE stno < 100 AND major = 'COSC' OR major = 'ACCT';
```

Then run the following two queries and answer whether the non-parenthesized statement gives you:

```
SELECT *
FROM Student
WHERE (stno < 100 AND major = 'COSC') OR major = 'ACCT';
```

or:

```
SELECT *
FROM  Student
WHERE stno < 100 AND (major = 'COSC' OR major = 'ACCT');
```

What happens if you put the OR first instead of the AND and run the query without parentheses?

5-5. Develop a query to find the instructor name and course name for computer science courses (use the Section table). Order the table by instructor name.

   a. Convert your query into a view.

   b. Remove the ORDER BY clause and convert the query into an inline view with column aliases and test it.

   c. Put the ORDER BY clause outside the inline view in the main query and run your query again.

5-6. Repeat the dictionary view (exercise 8) from Chapter 4 for USER_VIEWS and ALL_VIEWS. Be careful to DESCRIBE and COUNT(*) before (and if) you run the SELECT *... version. How many rows are in the USER_ version? How many rows are in the ALL_ version? Are the two views (ALL_ and USER_) the same? If not, what is different?

5-7. Type:

```
DESC ALL_SNAPSHOTS;
```

Use this information to answer the following questions:

   a. When was the snapshot qsnap1 last updated?

   b. What are the first five rows of a query of snapshot qsnap1?

   c. Who is the owner of qsnap1?

Chapter 6

Set Operations

Previous chapters looked at how data can be retrieved from multiple tables using joins. Data can also be retrieved from multiple tables using set operations. In this chapter we will look at the different set operations available in SQL.

A *set* is a collection of objects. In relational databases, a table is a set of rows. Elements in a set are not ordered. Whereas elements in mathematical sets do not have duplicate entries, duplicate rows may occur in relational tables unless they are explicitly disallowed.

Three set operations are used in SQL: UNION, INTERSECT, and MINUS (set difference). A *binary union* is a set operation on two sets where the result contains all the unique elements of both sets. A *binary intersection* generates unique values in common between two sets. Finally, a *binary set difference* gives us values in one set less those contained in another.

Like tables, result sets are sets of rows. Set statements allow us to combine two distinct sets of data (two tables or two result sets) provided we ensure union compatibility. *Union compatibility* is a commonly used SQL terminology for "set compatibility" and means that when using set operations, both sets must match in number of items and must have compatible data types. So what does "compatible data types" mean? It means all numeric columns are compatible with one another, all string columns are compatible with one another, and all date columns are compatible with one another.

As we will see, union compatibility can take place in several ways, such as:

- By unioning (or another appropriate set operation) two tables that have identical attributes (which implies same domains)
- By taking two subsets from a table and combining them
- By using views from two tables with the attributes chosen so that they are compatible

The general format of a set statement is:

```
set OPERATOR set
```

Here, *OPERATOR* can be a `UNION`, `MINUS`, or `INTERSECT`, and *set* is defined by a `SELECT`.

UNION Operations

Union operations take result sets from two or more queries and return all rows from the result sets as a single result set, removing duplicates.

The following is an example of a `UNION` set operation:

```
SELECT sname
FROM   Student
WHERE  major = 'COSC'
   UNION
SELECT sname
```

```
FROM   Student
WHERE major = 'MATH';
```

The resulting display contains the names of students who are majoring in either computer science (COSC) or math (MATH), as follows:

```
SNAME
--------------------
Alan
Brad
Brenda
Elainie
Hillary
Jake
Jerry
Kelly
Lujack
Mario
Mary
Monica
Reva
Sadie
Stephanie
Zelda

16 rows selected.
```

You will find that the result set is sorted and contains no duplicate values. This is because the UNION operation resolves duplicates and in the process sorts each result set and merges them together.

Note: Oracle includes an additional predicate, UNION ALL, which does not resolve duplicates. If we are willing to accept an unsorted result set that contains duplicates, UNION ALL is more efficient because no sorting is required.

The IN and NOT..IN Predicates

Although Oracle has both MINUS and INTERSECT predicates, many implementations of SQL don't have operators for difference (MINUS) or INTERSECT *per se*. However, most SQL versions will have an IN predicate and a corresponding NOT..IN. We will begin our discussion of the IN and NOT..IN predicates from a set point of view. Through these IN and NOT..IN predicates, we can create differences and intersections. Set difference can be defined as follows: If we find the objects from set A that are not in set B, we have found the difference of set A and set B or (A – B). Set intersection can be defined as follows: If we find the objects from set A that are also in set B, we have found the intersection of set A and set B.

A simple IN predicate with constants in a SELECT statement may look like this:

```
SELECT sname, class
FROM   Student
WHERE  class IN (3,4);
```

In this example, the IN (3, 4) is called a *subquery-set*, where the (3, 4) is the set in which we are testing membership. This query says: "Find all student names from the Student table where class is in the set (3, 4)." This query produces the following output:

```
SNAME                    CLASS
-------------------- ----------
Mary                         4
Kelly                        4
Donald                       4
Chris                        4
Susan                        3
Monica                       3
Phoebe                       3
Holly                        4
```

```
Rachel                          3
Jerry                           4
Cramer                          3
Harrison                        4
Francis                         4
Jake                            4
Losmith                         3
Benny                           4
Gus                             3

17 rows selected.
```

There are usually several ways to get information in SQL. The following query produces the same output as the one above:

```
SELECT sname, class
FROM   Student
WHERE  class = 3 OR class = 4;
```

Using IN

We can expand the IN predicate's subquery-set part to be an actual query. For example, consider the following query:

```
SELECT s.sname, s.stno
FROM   Student s
WHERE  s.stno IN
   (SELECT  g.student_number
    FROM    Grade_report g
    WHERE   g.grade = 'A');
```

Note that:

- WHERE s.stno references the name of the column (attribute) in the Student table
- g.student_number is the column name in the Grade_report table

- `stno` in the Student table and `student_number` in the Grade_report table have the same domain

We must have exact column headings (usually qualified column names) and retrieve the information from the same domains (remember the importance of union compatibility).

The preceding query produces this output:

```
SNAME                      STNO
--------------------  ----------
Lineas                        2
Mary                          3
Brenda                        8
Richard                      10
Lujack                       14
Donald                       20
Lynette                      34
Susan                        49
Holly                       123
Sadie                       125
Jessica                     126
Steve                       127
Cedric                      129
Jerry                       142

14 rows selected.
```

Note that we could view the query as a result derived from the intersection of the sets A and B, where set A is the set of student numbers in the student set (the Student table) and set B is the set of student numbers in the grade set (the Grade_report table) that have A's.

To use the `INTERSECT` operator, we can write the following query:

```
SELECT s.stno FROM Student s
   INTERSECT
SELECT g.student_number FROM Grade_report g WHERE g.grade = 'A';
```

This produces the following output:

```
    STNO
----------
         2
         3
         8
        10
        14
        20
        34
        49
       123
       125
       126
       127
       129
       142

14 rows selected.
```

This output contains basically the same information as the previous IN, but gives student numbers instead of names. There is no "name" in the Grade_report table.

The following command will **not** work:

```
SELECT s.sname, s.stno FROM Student s
  INTERSECT
SELECT g.student_number FROM Grade_report g WHERE g.grade = 'A';
```

This query will not work because the set operation has been modified to intersect a name and a number from the Student table and just a number from the Grade_report table. Because of the requirement of union compatibility, we must have like types in the same order in both result sets to complete a set operation.

Ordinarily, the internal workings of Oracle will cause the IN version of the above to be more efficient than INTERSECT.

Note: In some implementations of SQL, the use of IN is preferred to joins. Any situation that uses an IN can be achieved with a join, but not vice versa. In Oracle, it is usually better to use a join than a subquery from a performance standpoint. INTERSECT and MINUS are rarely used in SQL because they can be performed with IN more efficiently. UNION is sometimes used, but again, unless you cannot find another way to resolve a problem, IN or join is usually preferred.

Using NOT..IN

In this section, we discuss how to use `NOT..IN` to complete the logical negative of `IN`. There may be some apparent inefficiency with large tables with `NOT..IN` because the `NOT..IN` part of the query must test the outer set with all values in the subquery to find what is not in the set. We say "apparent" because what sometimes seems illogical may have an internal programming workaround that makes it efficient. Clearly, for smaller tables, no difference in performance will likely be detected. Instead of using `NOT..IN`, it is often preferable to use `NOT EXISTS` (discussed in Chapter 9) or the outer join techniques we have already demonstrated.

There are times when the `NOT..IN` predicate may seem to more easily describe the desired outcome or may be used for a set difference. For a simple example, consider the following query:

```
SELECT sname, class
FROM   Student
WHERE  class IN (1,3,4)
ORDER BY class, sname;
```

This would produce the following output:

```
SNAME                CLASS
-------------------- ---------
Brad                         1
Elainie                      1
Fraiser                      1
George                       1
Hillary                      1
Lindsay                      1
Lineas                       1
Lujack                       1
Lynette                      1
Richard                      1
Steve                        1
Cramer                       3
Gus                          3
Losmith                      3
Monica                       3
Phoebe                       3
Rachel                       3
Susan                        3
Benny                        4
Chris                        4
Donald                       4
Francis                      4
Harrison                     4
Holly                        4
Jake                         4
Jerry                        4
Kelly                        4
Mary                         4

28 rows selected.
```

Ordering was added to the query and those following to make them easier to compare. Contrast this last query to the following one:

```
SELECT sname, class
FROM   Student
WHERE  class NOT IN (2)
ORDER BY class, sname;
```

This produces the following output:

```
SNAME                     CLASS
--------------------  ----------
Brad                          1
Elainie                       1
Fraiser                       1
George                        1
Hillary                       1
Lindsay                       1
Lineas                        1
Lujack                        1
Lynette                       1
Richard                       1
Steve                         1
Cramer                        3
Gus                           3
Losmith                       3
Monica                        3
Phoebe                        3
Rachel                        3
Susan                         3
Benny                         4
Chris                         4
Donald                        4
Francis                       4
Harrison                      4
Holly                         4
Jake                          4
Jerry                         4
Kelly                         4
Mary                          4

28 rows selected.
```

In this case we get the same output as the previous query because the Student table only has classes 1, 2, 3, and 4. You would expect the same result provided you knew all the classes were in the set (1,2,3,4). If counts did not match, this would indicate that some value of class was not 1, 2, 3, or 4.

As another example, suppose you want the name of students who are not computer science or math majors. We could use the following query:

```
SELECT sname
FROM   Student
WHERE  major NOT IN ('COSC','MATH');
```

This would give:

```
SNAME
--------------------
Lineas
Richard
Harley
Donald
Chris
Lynette
Susan
Bill
Phoebe
Holly
Jessica
Steve
Cedric
Rachel
George
Cramer
Fraiser
Harrison
Francis
Smithly
Sebastian
Losmith
Genevieve
Lindsay
Benny
Gus
```

```
Romona
Ken

28 rows selected.
```

You must be very careful with the `NOT..IN` predicate for two reasons:

- The logic of "NOT *something*" may not be what you think it is. (We'll look at this in more detail in Exercise 6-7 at the end of the chapter.)
- If nulls are present in the data, you get odd answers with `NOT..IN`.

Consider the following Stumajor table:

```
Name        Major
----------  -------------
Mary        Biology
Sam         Chemistry
Alice       Art
Tom
```

Note: The Stumajor table has not been created for you — you will have to create it in order to try out the following queries.

If you perform the following query:

```
SELECT *
FROM  Stumajor
WHERE major IN ('Chemistry','Biology');
```

It produces the following output:

```
NAME                  MAJOR
-------------------   -------------------
Mary                  Biology
Sam                   Chemistry
```

```
2 rows selected.
```

If you execute this query:

```
SELECT *
FROM Stumajor
WHERE major NOT IN ('Chemistry','Biology');
```

It produces the following output:

```
NAME                MAJOR
------------------- -------------------
Alice               Art

1 rows selected.
```

The value of null is not equal to anything. You might expect that NOT..IN would give you <Tom, NULL>, but it does not. Why? Because nulls in the selection field (here, major) are ignored, or do not return a "True" test.

The Difference Operation

To illustrate the difference operation, suppose set A is the set of students in classes 2, 3, or 4 and that set B is a set of students in class = 2. We could use the NOT..IN predicate to remove the students in set B from set A (thereby using a difference operation). For example, suppose we use the following query:

```
SELECT sname
FROM   Student
WHERE  class IN (2,3,4)
   AND NOT class IN (2)
ORDER BY class, sname;
```

The produces the following output:

```
SNAME                     CLASS
-------------------- ----------
Cramer                        3
Gus                           3
Losmith                       3
Monica                        3
Phoebe                        3
Rachel                        3
Susan                         3
Benny                         4
Chris                         4
Donald                        4
Francis                       4
Harrison                      4
Holly                         4
Jake                          4
Jerry                         4
Kelly                         4
Mary                          4

17 rows selected.
```

This output is actually the same as the output we get when we use the following query:

```
SELECT sname, class
FROM   Student
WHERE  class IN (3,4)
ORDER BY class, sname;
```

In Oracle, we can also use the MINUS predicate as follows:

```
SELECT sname, class
FROM   Student
WHERE  class IN (2,3,4)
   MINUS
SELECT sname, class
FROM   Student
WHERE  class IN (2)
```

```
ORDER BY class, sname;
```

Which produces the following output:

```
SNAME                    CLASS
------------------  ---------
Cramer                       3
Gus                          3
Losmith                      3
Monica                       3
Phoebe                       3
Rachel                       3
Susan                        3
Benny                        4
Chris                        4
Donald                       4
Francis                      4
Harrison                     4
Holly                        4
Jake                         4
Jerry                        4
Kelly                        4
Mary                         4

16 rows selected.
```

A more interesting, less obvious example of set difference is a situation in which sets are created on the fly. Suppose you want to find the names of students who are not majoring in COSC or MATH but you want to delete from that set those who have made an A in some course. Finding the names of students who are not COSC or MATH majors is completed as before (again, ordering added for readability):

```
SELECT sname, major
FROM   Student
WHERE  major NOT IN ('COSC','MATH')
ORDER BY major, sname;
```

This produces the following output:

```
SNAME                MAJO
-------------------- ----
Chris                ACCT
Donald               ACCT
Francis              ACCT
Harrison             ACCT
Sebastian            ACCT
Gus                  ART
Benny                CHEM
Losmith              CHEM
Cedric               ENGL
Cramer               ENGL
Lineas               ENGL
Phoebe               ENGL
Rachel               ENGL
Richard              ENGL
Romona               ENGL
Smithly              ENGL
Steve                ENGL
Susan                ENGL
Bill                 POLY
Fraiser              POLY
George               POLY
Harley               POLY
Holly                POLY
Jessica              POLY
Ken                  POLY
Lynette              POLY
Genevieve            UNKN
Lindsay              UNKN

28 rows selected.
```

The set of students who have made A's can be found as follows:

```
SELECT s.sname name, major
FROM   Student s
WHERE  s.stno IN
```

```
   (SELECT  g.student_number
    FROM    Grade_report g
    WHERE   g.grade = 'A')
ORDER BY major, sname;
```

This produces the following output:

```
NAME                 MAJO
-------------------- ----
Donald               ACCT
Brenda               COSC
Jerry                COSC
Lujack               COSC
Mary                 COSC
Cedric               ENGL
Lineas               ENGL
Richard              ENGL
Steve                ENGL
Susan                ENGL
Sadie                MATH
Holly                POLY
Jessica              POLY
Lynette              POLY

14 rows selected.
```

Therefore, the difference operation would be to find the difference of the two sets as follows:

```
SELECT s1.sname name, s1.major
FROM   Student s1
WHERE  s1.major NOT IN ('COSC','MATH')
   MINUS
SELECT s2.sname name, s2.major
FROM   Student s2
WHERE  s2.stno IN
   (SELECT gr.student_number
    FROM   Grade_report gr
    WHERE  gr.grade = 'A')
ORDER BY major, name;
```

Which produces the following output:

```
NAME                 MAJO
-------------------- ----
Chris                ACCT
Francis              ACCT
Harrison             ACCT
Sebastian            ACCT
Gus                  ART
Benny                CHEM
Losmith              CHEM
Cramer               ENGL
Phoebe               ENGL
Rachel               ENGL
Romona               ENGL
Smithly              ENGL
Bill                 POLY
Fraiser              POLY
George               POLY
Harley               POLY
Ken                  POLY
Genevieve            UNKN
Lindsay              UNKN

19 rows selected.
```

Exercises for Chapter 6

As you do the exercises, unless it is stated otherwise, you will be using the tables from our standard Student-Course database. Also, as you do the exercises, it will be a good idea to copy/paste your query as well as your query result into a word processor file.

6-1. In this exercise, you will test the `UNION` operator. Having seen how the `UNION` operator works, demonstrate some permutations to see what will work "legally" and what will not. First, create two tables:

Table1			Table2			
A	**B**		**A**	**B**	**C**	**D**
x1	y1		x2	y2	z2	w2
r1	s1		r2	s2	T2	u2

Let the type of A's and B's be `CHAR(2)`. Let the type of C in Table2 be `VARCHAR2(2)` and D in Table2 be `VARCHAR2(3)`.

Try the following statements and note the results:

```
SELECT * FROM Table1 UNION SELECT * FROM Table2;
SELECT * FROM Table1 UNION SELECT A,B FROM Table2;
SELECT * FROM Table1 UNION SELECT B,A FROM Table1;
SELECT * FROM Table1 UNION SELECT A,C FROM Table2;
SELECT * FROM Table1 UNION SELECT A,D FROM Table2;

CREATE OR REPLACE VIEW viewx AS
SELECT A,B FROM Table2;

SELECT * FROM Table1 UNION SELECT * FROM viewx;
```

Feel free to experiment with any other combinations that seem appropriate or that you wonder about.

6-2. Create and print the result of a query that generates the name, class, and course numbers of students who have B's in computer science courses. Store this query as Q62. (Be sure to store the result too.) Then, revise Q62 to delete from the result set those students who are sophomores (class = 2) using `NOT..IN` to `SELECT` sophomores. Repeat this exercise using `MINUS` instead of `NOT..IN`.

6-3. Find the student names, grades, and course numbers of students who have earned an A in computer science or math courses. Create a join of the Section and Grade_report tables (be careful to not create the Cartesian product), then `UNION` the set of course numbers `COSC____` and `A` with the set of course numbers `MATH____` and `A`.

Hint: Start with the query to get names, grades, and course numbers for `COSC___` and `A`, then turn this into a view. Do the same for `MATH___` and `A`, then execute the `UNION` statement like this (using your view names):

```
SELECT * FROM view1a UNION SELECT * FROM view1b;
```

6-4. Find the names and majors of students who have earned a C in any course. Make the section "who have earned a C in any course" a subquery for which you use `IN`.

6-5. A less obvious example of a difference query would be to find a difference that is not based on simple, easy-to-achieve sets. Suppose that set A is the set of students who have earned an A or B in computer science (COSC) courses. Suppose further that set B is the set of students who have taken math courses (regardless of what grade they earned).

Then, set A minus set B would contain the names of students who have earned an A or B in computer science courses, less those who have taken math courses. Similarly, set B minus set A would be the set of students who took math courses, less those who took COSC courses and earned an A or a B in COSC*xxxx*.

Build these queries into set difference queries as views based on student numbers and execute them.

a. First, run a query that gives the student number, name, course, and grade for each set. Save each query as Q65a and Q65b.

b. After saving each query, reconstruct it into a view of just student numbers, verify that it works, and then use `CREATE VIEW` to create set A and set B. Verify that you have the same number of tuples in set A as you have in Q65a and the same in set B as in Q65b.

c. Then, display the student numbers of students in each set difference — show (set A minus set B) and (set B minus set A). Look at the original queries, Q65a and Q65b, to verify your result.

6-6. Create two tables, R1 and R2, that contain a name and a salary. In the first table, order the attributes as name, salary. In the second table, order the attributes as salary, name. Use the same types for each (`VARCHAR2(20)`, `NUMBER(2)`, for example). Populate the tables with three tuples each. Can you `UNION` these two tables with `SELECT * FROM R1 UNION SELECT * FROM R2`? Why or why not? If not, can you force the `UNION` of the two tables? Illustrate how. Be sure to `DROP` the tables when you are finished.

Optional Exercise

6-7. (De Morgan's Theorem) Find the result set for all sections that are offered in building 13 and call this set A. Find the result set for all sections that are offered in building 36 and call this set B. Construct the SQL query to find the following result sets:

a. The result of set A OR set B (i.e., use `WHERE bldg = 13 OR bldg = 36`).

b. The result of the complement of (a): `NOT(set A OR set B)`.

c. The result of `NOT(A) AND NOT(B)`.

d. The count of all rows in the Section table.

Is the count in d = a + b? Is the result of c the same as the result of b? Explain why or why not in each case.

Chapter 7

Subqueries versus Joins

The purpose of this chapter is to demonstrate how you can use subqueries as alternatives to joins. There are two main issues to consider in choosing between subqueries and joins (and/or other techniques as well):

- You must consider how you get information, which is often subjective. By understanding the limitations of joins and subqueries (and sets and other techniques, for that matter), you will broaden your choices as to how to get information from a database.
- You must consider performance. You usually have choices about how to get information, such as by joins, sets, subqueries, views, and so on. In large databases you need to be flexible and consider other choices if a query is used often but performs poorly.

Note: Although set operations are also viable choices for retrieving data from multiple tables, they are less common and usually less efficient than joins and subqueries.

The IN Subquery

Suppose a query requires that we "List the names of students who have earned an A or B in any course." Where is this data? Student names are in the Student table and grades are in the Grade_report table. This query can be completed as either a subquery or as a join. As a subquery, it would take the following form:

```
SELECT Student.sname
FROM Student
WHERE "link to Grade_report"
  IN ("link to Student" - subquery involving Grade_report)
```

The link between the Student table and the Grade_report table is the student number. In the Student table, the appropriate attribute is stno, and in the Grade_report table the corresponding attribute is student_number. When using a link between tables with the `IN` subquery, only the linking attributes can be mentioned in the `WHERE ..IN` and in the result set of the subquery. Thus, the above request in a subquery will be as follows:

```
SELECT s.sname
FROM   Student s
WHERE  s.stno
   IN (SELECT gr.student_number
       FROM  Grade_report gr
       WHERE gr.grade = 'B' OR gr.grade = 'A');
```

Note: The part of the query before the IN is called the *outer query*. The part after the IN is called the *inner query*.

This produces the following output:

```
SNAME
--------------------
Lineas
Mary
Zelda
Ken
Mario
Brenda
Richard
Kelly
Lujack
Reva
Harley
Donald
Chris
Lynette
Susan
Hillary
Phoebe
Holly
Sadie
Jessica
Steve
Cedric
George
Jerry
Cramer
Fraiser
Francis
Smithly
Sebastian
Lindsay
Stephanie

31 rows selected.
```

The Subquery as a Join

An alternative way to perform the preceding query would be to perform a join and not use a subquery, as follows:

```
SELECT s.sname
FROM   Student s, Grade_report gr
WHERE  s.stno = gr.student_number
   AND (gr.grade = 'B' OR gr.grade = 'A');
```

This will give:

```
SNAME
--------------------
Lineas
Lineas
Lineas
Lineas
Mary
Mary
Mary
Mary
Mary
Mary
Zelda
Ken
Mario
Brenda
Brenda
Brenda
Brenda
Richard
Kelly
Kelly
Lujack
Lujack
Lujack
.
.
.
```

```
Lindsay
Stephanie

67 rows selected.
```

If a join is used, then any Student-Grade_report row that has equal student numbers and a grade of A or B is selected. Thus, there are a lot of duplicate names in the output. To get the desired result without duplicates, we may add the qualifier DISTINCT to the join query as follows:

```
SELECT DISTINCT Student.sname
FROM Student, Grade_report gr
WHERE ...
```

This query will give the same output as we got from the subquery (31 rows). In the subquery version of the query, there is no duplication of names in the output because the subquery may be viewed as a set from which we will choose the names — a given name is either in the subquery set or it is not.

Depending on which version of SQL we are using, the join or the subquery may be more efficient. Database systems such as Oracle parse queries and execute them according to a plan, much like a programming language compiles source code and generates an object module for execution. The program that creates the execution plan in Oracle is called the *optimizer*. Even if we write a query as a subquery, the Oracle optimizer may indeed internally convert our query to a join (or vice versa).

As we have seen earlier, using DISTINCT may not be efficient performancewise for large tables because of the internal sorting that occurs. So, when using a query that uses a join and DISTINCT versus using one that uses a subquery, the Oracle optimizer is confronted with an interesting problem. Internally, when joining with DISTINCT, the Oracle optimizer must choose between joining and then sorting versus creating a result set for the subquery and actually doing the query with the subquery result set. For small tables, no difference is likely to be noted. For large tables in production databases, we would have to test each type of query to see how it performed.

When the Join Cannot Be Turned into a Subquery

If the original query had been one that asked for output from the Grade_report table, such as "List the names and grades of all students who have earned an A or B in any course," the query would be asking for information from both the Student and Grade_report tables. In this case, we must join the two tables to get the information. That is, when columns from both the tables have to be in the result set, a join is necessary.

Now, refer to the first query example presented in this chapter in which we were asked to list the names of students who have earned an A or B in any course. This query asked for information from only the Student table. In this query example, the query used the Grade_report table but nothing from the Grade_report table was in the outer result set, so a subquery was used. But, this query could also have been written as a join.

Now, the answer to the question posed here (a result set that lists the names and grades of all students who have earned an A or B in any course) would be:

```
SELECT DISTINCT Student.sname, gr.grade
FROM Student, Grade_report gr
WHERE Student.stno = gr.student_number    -- join condition
   AND (gr.grade = 'B' OR gr.grade = 'A');
```

This produces the following output:

```
SNAME                G
-------------------- --
Brenda               A
Brenda               B
Cedric               A
Cedric               B
Chris                B
Cramer               B
Donald               A
Fraiser              B
Francis              B
George               B
Harley               B
Hillary              B
Holly                A
Holly                B
Jerry                A
Jessica              A
Jessica              B
Kelly                B
Ken                  B
Lindsay              B
Lineas               A
Lineas               B
Lujack               A
Lujack               B
Lynette              A
Lynette              B
Mario                B
Mary                 A
Mary                 B
Phoebe               B
Reva                 B
Richard              A
Sadie                A
Sadie                B
Sebastian            B
Smithly              B
```

```
Stephanie            B
Steve                A
Steve                B
Susan                A
Zelda                B

41 rows selected.
```

If information from a table is needed in a result set, then that table cannot be buried in a subquery — it must be in the outer query.

More Examples Involving Joins and IN

The purpose of this section is to show several queries that will and will not allow the use of the subquery. As we have discussed, some joins can be expressed as subqueries, while others cannot. In addition, all subqueries with the IN predicate can be reformed as a join. How do we know whether we can use a subquery? It depends on the final, outer result set. Some additional examples will help clarify this point.

Example 1

In this example, we will find the names of all departments that offer a course with "INTRO" in the title.

In order to create an appropriate query, we need the Course table (to find the course information) and the Department_to_major table (to find the names of the departments). It is usually a good idea to first look at the tables with the DESC command to be sure that the information can be found in them. Thus, we begin by showing the Course and Department_to_major tables using DESC as follows:

```
SQL> DESC Course;
```

Which gives:

```
Name                              Null?     Type
------------------------------    --------  --------
COURSE_NAME                                 CHAR(20)
COURSE_NUMBER                     NOT NULL  CHAR(8)
CREDIT_HOURS                                NUMBER(2)
OFFERING_DEPT                               CHAR(4)
```

```
SQL> DESC Department_to_major;
```

Which gives:

```
Name                Type
----------------    --------
DCODE               CHAR(4)
DNAME               CHAR(20)
```

The query we posed (find the names of all departments that offer a course with "INTRO" in the title) only asks for department names, not the names of the INTRO courses. We can find this result using a subquery because all the information in the result set is contained in the outer query, which uses the Department_to_major table as follows:

```
SELECT d2m.dname
FROM   Department_to_major d2m
WHERE  d2m.dcode
IN (SELECT Course.offering_dept
FROM  Course
WHERE Course.course_name LIKE '%INTRO%');
```

This produces the following output:

```
DNAME
--------------------
Chemistry
Computer Science
Political Science
```

This query can also be done as a join:

```
SELECT d2m.dname
FROM   Department_to_major d2m, Course c
WHERE  d2m.dcode = c.offering_dept
AND    c.course_name LIKE '%INTRO%';
```

When done as a join, the query produces the following output:

```
DNAME
--------------------
Chemistry
Computer Science
Computer Science
Political Science
```

Since DISTINCT was not used for the result set with the join, all occurrences of matching rows are reported.

Example 2

In this example, we will list the student name, student major code, and section identifier of students who earned a C in courses taught by Professor Jones (JONES).

The first question we must ask ourselves is: *Which tables are needed for the overall query?* By looking at the information we need to collect, we can see that we will need the following tables: Student (for student name, student major code), Grade_report (for grades), and Section (for the teacher name). As noted above, it is usually a good idea to first look at the descriptions of the tables with the DESC command to verify the names of the columns. Thus, we begin by showing the Student, Grade_report, and Section tables using DESC as follows:

```
SQL> DESC Student;
```

Which gives:

```
Name          Null?               Type
------------  ------------------  -----------
STNO          NOT NULL            NUMBER(3)
SNAME                             VARCHAR2(20)
MAJOR                             CHAR(4)
CLASS                             NUMBER(1)
```

```
SQL> DESC Grade_report;
```

Which gives:

```
Name            Null?              Type
--------------  -----------------  -----------
STUDENT_NUMBER  NOT NULL           NUMBER(3)
SECTION_ID      NOT NULL           NUMBER(6)
GRADE                              CHAR(1)
```

```
SQL> DESC Section;
```

Which gives:

```
Name                Null?          Type
-----------------   -------------- -----------
SECTION_ID          NOT NULL       NUMBER(6)
COURSE_NUM                         CHAR(8)
SEMESTER                           VARCHAR2(6)
YEAR                               CHAR(2)
INSTRUCTOR                         CHAR(10)
BLDG                               NUMBER(3)
ROOM                               NUMBER(3)
```

The next question we must ask ourselves is: *In which tables are the columns that are needed in the result set?* The query asks, "List the student name, student major code, and section identifier of students who earned a C in courses taught by Professor Jones (JONES)." We need the names and major codes from the Student table, and we can get the section identifiers from the Grade_report table. Therefore, the result set part of the query — that is, the outer query — must contain the Student and Grade_report tables. The rest of the query can contain any other tables we need to answer the question. The resulting query may look like this:

```
SELECT s.sname, s.major, g.section_id
FROM   Student s, Grade_report g
WHERE  g.student_number = s.stno
          /* join condx Student-Grade_report */
AND    g.grade = 'C'
AND    g.section_id IN
   (SELECT t.section_id
    FROM Section t
    WHERE t.instructor LIKE '%JONES%');
```

This produces the following output:

```
SNAME                MAJO SECTION_ID
-------------------- ---- ----------
Richard              ENGL        145
```

In this case, the query could also have been done as a three-table join as shown below:

```
SELECT s.sname, s.major, t.section_id
FROM   Student s, Grade_report g, Section t
WHERE  s.stno = g.student_number
AND    g.section_id = t.section_id
AND    g.grade = 'C'
AND    t.instructor LIKE '%JONES%';
```

Example 3

In this example, we will list the student name and student major code of students who earned a C in courses taught by Professor Jones (JONES).

Note: This is very similar to Example 2, but in this case we are not looking for the section identifier.

Again, the first question we must ask ourselves is: *Which tables are needed?* By looking at the information we need to collect, we can see that we will need the Student, Grade_report, and Section tables. (Since we have already used DESC to view these tables in the previous example, we will not do so again here.) Next, we must ask ourselves: *In which tables are the columns that are needed in the result set?* As we can see, they are all in the Student table. Thus, because the only table needed in the outer query is the Student table, the query can be done in a number of ways. The options include:

- Student Join Grade_report Join Section — a three-table join
- Student Sub (Grade_report Join Section) — Student outer, join in subquery
- Student Join Grade_report Sub (Section) — Done like example 2 (above) with section_id removed from the result set
- Student (Sub Grade_report (Sub Section)) — A three-level subquery

Each of these queries will produce the same result with different efficiencies. We will study them in greater detail in the exercises at the end of the chapter.

Subqueries with Operators

In previous chapters we have seen SELECT statements with conditions like the following:

```
SELECT *
FROM Room
WHERE capacity = 25;
```

In this example, 25 is a constant and = is an operator. The constant can be replaced by a subquery, while the operator can be any logical comparison operator (=, <>, <, >, <=, >=). For example, we could devise a query to tell us which classrooms have a below-average capacity as follows:

```
SELECT *
FROM Room
WHERE capacity <
   (SELECT AVG(capacity)
    FROM Room);
```

This produces the following output:

```
      BLDG       ROOM     CAPACITY  O
----------    -------   ----------  -
        36        123           35  N
        79        179           35  Y
        79        174           22  Y
        36        122           25  N
        36        121           25  N
        36        120           25  N

6 rows selected.
```

The only danger in using subqueries in this fashion is that *the subquery must return only one_row*. If an aggregate function is applied to a table in the subquery in this fashion, we will always get only one row; even if there is a WHERE clause that excludes all rows, the subquery returns one row with a null value. For example, if we changed the preceding query to:

```
SELECT *
FROM Room
WHERE capacity <
   (SELECT AVG(capacity)
    FROM Room
    WHERE bldg = 99);
```

This query would run (without producing any errors), but the result would be "no rows selected."

If we changed the query to:

```
SELECT *
FROM Room
WHERE bldg =
   (SELECT bldg
    FROM Room
    WHERE capacity > 10);
```

We would get:

```
ERROR: single-row subquery returns more than one row
```

When using operators, only single values are acceptable from the subquery. Here the subquery may contain several buildings (bldg) and hence the error. Again, to ensure we get only one row in the subquery and hence ensure a workable query, we can use an aggregate with no GROUP BY or HAVING (which we will discuss in Chapter 8).

Note: As with other queries that include derived results, the caveat to audit the result is always applicable.

Exercises for Chapter 7

As you do the exercises, unless it is stated otherwise, you will be using the tables from our standard Student-Course database. Also, as you do the exercises, it will be a good idea to copy/paste your query as well as your query result into a word processor file.

Use the techniques we discussed in this chapter to construct and execute the following queries.

7-1. Find the student numbers of students who have received an A or B in courses taught in the fall semester. Do this in two ways: First using a subquery, and then using a join.

7-2. Find all students who took a course offered by the accounting department. List the student name and student number, the course taken (course name), and the grade the student earned in that course. Hint: Begin with the Department_to_major table and use an appropriate `WHERE`. Note that this cannot be done with a multi-level subquery. Why?

7-3. Find the names of students who are sophomores (class = 2) as well as the name of their department (based on their major).

7-4. Find the names of departments that offer courses at the junior or senior levels (either one) but *not* at the freshman level. (The course level is the first digit after the prefix. Therefore, AAAA3yyy is a junior course.) *Hint:* Begin by creating the outer query — the names of departments that offer courses at the junior or senior levels. Save this query as q74. Then, construct the subquery — a list of departments that offer courses at the freshman level. Save the subquery as a view. Examine both lists of departments. When you have the outer query and the subquery results, recall the original query that you saved (q74) and add the subquery. Check your result with the department lists you just generated. Re-do the last part of the experiment with your view. You should get the same result.

7-5. Find the names of courses that are prerequisites for other courses. List the course number and name, and the number and name of the prerequisite course.

7-6. List the names of instructors who teach courses that have other than three-hour credits. Do this in two ways: Once with `IN`, and once with `NOT..IN`.

7-7. Create a table called Secretary with the attributes dCode `CHAR(4)` (for department code) and name `VARCHAR2(20)` (for the secretary name). Populate the table as follows:

```
dCode        name
-----------  ------
ACCT         Sally
COSC         Chris
ENGL         Maria
```

a. Create a query that lists the names of departments that have secretaries (use `IN` and the Secretary table in a subquery with the Department_to_major table in the outer query). Save this query as q77a.

b. Create a query that lists the names of departments that do not have secretaries (use `NOT..IN`). Save this query as q77b.

c. Add one more row to the Secretary table that contains <NULL,Brenda>. (This could be a situation in which we have hired Brenda but have not yet assigned her to a department.)

d. Recall q77a and re-run it.

e. Recall q77b and re-run it.

The behavior of NOT..IN when nulls exist may surprise you. If nulls may exist in the subquery, then NOT..IN should either:

- Not be used. (We will see how to use another predicate, NOT EXISTS, in Chapter 9, which is a workaround to this problem.)
- Should include AND whatever IS NOT NULL.

If you use NOT..IN in a subquery, you must ensure that nulls will not occur in the subquery or you must use some other predicate (such as NOT EXISTS). Perhaps the best solution is to avoid NOT..IN unless you cannot figure out another way to solve a problem. To see a correct answer:

f. Add the phrase WHERE dCode IS NOT NULL to the subquery in the IN and NOT..IN cases and run them again.

Save the Secretary table because we will revisit this problem in Chapter 9.

7-8. Devise a list of course names that are offered in the fall semester in rooms where the capacity is equal to or above the average room size.

Optional Exercise

7-9. Set the autotrace facility on with this command:

```
SQL> SET AUTOTRACE ON EXPLAIN
```

Note that AUTOTRACE will only work if the user already owns a proper PLAN_TABLE and the user has sufficient privileges to run AUTOTRACE (that, the PLUSTRACE role, or equivalent privileges).

Then, write and run each of the following queries (these are the same queries that were listed in the Example 3 section earlier in the chapter):

a. Student Join Grade_report Join Section — three-table join
b. Student Sub (Grade_report Join Section) — Student outer, join in subquery
c. Student Join Grade_report Sub (Section) — Like example 2, with section_id removed from the result set
d. Student (Sub Grade_report (Sub Section)) — A three-level subquery

You can modify the queries in the exercise to return only a count of what would be the result set (that is, start with `SELECT * FROM...`). Use the cost = result in the execution plan output to rank order the four queries from least to most efficient.

Chapter 8

GROUP BY and HAVING

In this chapter we will discuss how to use aggregation, grouping, and the HAVING clause in a SELECT. By using these added features, we can group data of a particular type, filter the output with HAVING, and do combinations of aggregate calculations (such as sums, averages, and counts). We will also take another look at nulls.

Aggregates/Column Functions

As we discussed in Chapter 4, an aggregate (or group) function is one that extracts information — such as a COUNT of rows in a table. We can also find an average, minimum, or maximum for some column by operating on multiple rows. Some examples are:

```
SELECT COUNT(*)     -- COUNT(*) counts all rows in the Student table
FROM Student;
```

```
SELECT AVG(credit_hours), MAX(credit_hours) -- two aggregates on
                                            -- the same set of data
FROM Course
WHERE course_number LIKE 'COSC____';

SELECT COUNT(stno) "Student Numbers"   -- alias used for count of
                                       -- non-null student numbers
FROM Student;
```

We can now proceed to expand the use of aggregation in queries.

The GROUP BY Clause

GROUP BY is a clause in a SELECT statement that is designed to be used in conjunction with aggregate functions. GROUP BY will return one row for each *value* of the column(s) that is grouped. For example, you can extract COUNTs of class groups from the Student table with a statement like the following:

```
SELECT class, COUNT(*)
FROM Student
GROUP BY class;
```

This will produce the following output:

```
     CLASS   COUNT(*)
----------   --------
         1         11
         2         10
         3          7
         4         10
                   10
```

This type of statement gives us a new way to retrieve and organize aggregate data. To use the statement, you must GROUP BY *at least* what you are aggregating. A statement like the following will cause a syntax error because it implies that we are to COUNT both class and major, but GROUP BY class only:

```
SELECT class, major, COUNT(*)
FROM Student
GROUP BY class;
```

To be syntactically and logically correct, you must have all of the non-aggregate columns in the GROUP BY clause.

The following is the correct query for the COUNT of class and major:

```
SELECT class, major, COUNT(*)
FROM Student
GROUP BY class, major;
```

This produces the following output:

```
    CLASS MAJO COUNT(*)
--------- ---- --------
        1 COSC        4
        1 ENGL        3
        1 POLY        3
        1 UNKN        1
        2 ACCT        1
        2 COSC        2
        2 ENGL        2
        2 MATH        3
        2 POLY        2
        3 ART         1
        3 CHEM        1
        3 ENGL        4
        3 MATH        1
        4 ACCT        4
        4 CHEM        1
        4 COSC        3
        4 MATH        1
        4 POLY        1
          COSC        1
          ENGL        1
```

```
                MATH          2
                POLY          2
                UNKN          1
                              3

24 rows selected.
```

In a similar vein, the following query would be improper because you must GROUP BY ohead (ohead, an attribute in the Room table, is short for rooms with overhead projectors) to SUM capacities for each ohead value:

```
SELECT ohead, SUM(capacity)
FROM Room;
```

If you SELECT attributes *and* use an aggregate function, you must GROUP BY the non-aggregate attributes.

The correct version of the query is:

```
SELECT ohead, SUM(capacity)
FROM Room
GROUP BY ohead;
```

This produces the following output:

```
O     SUM(CAPACITY)
-     -------------
N               110
Y               142
                100
```

This is the sum of room capacities for all rooms that have no overhead projectors (N), all rooms that have overhead projectors (Y), and all rooms in which the overhead projector capacity is unknown (null).

Observe that in the Room table, some rooms have null values for ohead. Those rows are summed and grouped along with the non-null rows (following is the data of the Room table):

```
      BLDG      ROOM   CAPACITY  O
---------- -------  ---------- -
        13     101          85 Y
        36     123          35 N
        58     114          60
        79     179          35 Y
        79     174          22 Y
        58     112          40
        58     110             Y
        36     122          25 N
        36     121          25 N
        36     120          25 N
```

GROUP BY and ORDER BY

To enhance the display of a `GROUP BY` clause, we can combine it with an `ORDER BY` clause.

Consider the following example:

```
SELECT class, major, COUNT(*)
FROM Student
GROUP BY class, major;
```

This produces the following output:

```
    CLASS  MAJO  COUNT(*)
---------  ----  ---------
        1  COSC          4
        1  ENGL          3
        1  POLY          3
        1  UNKN          1
        2  ACCT          1
        2  COSC          2
        2  ENGL          2
        2  MATH          3
        2  POLY          2
        3  ART           1
        3  CHEM          1
        3  ENGL          4
```

```
        3    MATH        1
        4    ACCT        4
        4    CHEM        1
        4    COSC        3
        4    MATH        1
        4    POLY        1
             COSC        1
             ENGL        1
             MATH        2
             POLY        2
             UNKN        1
                         3

24 rows selected.
```

The result set will be ordered by the class and then by major because of the internal sorting required to do the grouping. Ordering of the result set on any other column(s) including the aggregate can also be used. Consider the following example which orders by `COUNT(*)` in descending order (`DESC` here stands for descending order):

```
SELECT class, major, COUNT(*)
FROM Student
GROUP BY class, major
ORDER BY COUNT(*) DESC;
```

This produces the following output:

```
    CLASS    MAJO   COUNT(*)
---------    ----  ---------
        1    COSC          4
        3    ENGL          4
        4    ACCT          4
        1    ENGL          3
        4    COSC          3
        3
        2    MATH          3
        1    POLY          3
        2    COSC          2
```

```
       2     POLY         2
             POLY         2
             MATH         2
       2     ENGL         2
       1     UNKN         1
       3     ART          1
       3     MATH         1
       4     POLY         1
             UNKN         1
             ENGL         1
             COSC         1
       4     MATH         1
       4     CHEM         1
       3     CHEM         1
       2     ACCT         1

24 rows selected.
```

The HAVING Clause

The HAVING clause is used as a final filter on a SELECT. The HAVING clause filters the result set by a condition *after* the grouping functions have been applied. Consider the following query:

```
SELECT class, COUNT(*)
FROM Student
GROUP BY class;
```

This displays the COUNT of students in various classes (classes of students = 1, 2, 3, 4, which stand for freshman, sophomore, junior, and senior). The result set is:

```
     CLASS   COUNT(*)
----------  ---------
         1         11
         2         10
         3          7
```

```
         4            10
                      10
```

If we are only interested in classes that have more than nine students in them, we could use the following statement:

```
SELECT class, COUNT(*)
FROM Student
GROUP BY class
HAVING COUNT(*) > 9;
```

This would produce the following output:

```
    CLASS      COUNT(*)
---------     ---------
        1            11
        2            10
        4            10
                     10
```

The `HAVING` clause operates on the result set rows after all the selecting, grouping, and other clauses have been applied.

HAVING and WHERE

`HAVING` is a final filter rather than a conditional filter in a `SELECT` statement. The conditional filter is contained in the `WHERE` clause, which excludes non-matching rows from a result set. Note that the following two queries would give the same result:

```
SELECT class, COUNT(*)
FROM Student
GROUP BY class
HAVING class = 3;
```

```
SELECT class, COUNT(*)
FROM Student
WHERE class = 3
GROUP BY class;
```

Both queries would produce this output:

```
     CLASS    COUNT(*)
----------  ----------
         3           7
```

The first of these two queries (the one using HAVING) is less efficient because the query engine must complete the query before filtering rows in which class = 3 from the result set. In the second version (the one using WHERE instead of HAVING), the rows WHERE class = 3 are filtered before grouping takes place. WHERE is not always a substitute for HAVING, but when it can be used instead of HAVING, it should be.

Consider the following query, its meaning, and the processing that is required to finalize the result set:

```
SELECT class, major, COUNT(*)
FROM Student
WHERE major = 'COSC'
GROUP BY class, major
HAVING COUNT(*) > 2;
```

This produces the following output:

```
     CLASS  MAJO    COUNT(*)
----------  ----  ----------
         1  COSC           4
         4  COSC           3
```

In this example, all COSC majors (per the WHERE clause) will be grouped and counted and then displayed only if COUNT(*) > 2. The query might erroneously be interpreted as "Group and count all COSC majors by class, but only if there are more than two in a class." This interpretation is wrong because the way SQL works is to apply the WHERE, then the GROUP BY, and finally filter with the HAVING criterion.

GROUP BY and HAVING: Aggregates of Aggregates

A usual GROUP BY has an aggregate and a column that are grouped as shown below:

```
SELECT COUNT(stno), class
FROM Student
GROUP BY class;
```

This produces the following output:

```
COUNT(STNO)      CLASS
-----------     ------
         11          1
         10          2
          7          3
         10          4
         10
```

This produces a result set of counts by class. While you must have class or some other attribute in the GROUP BY, you do not have to have the class in the result set. Consider the following query:

```
SELECT COUNT(stno)
FROM Student
GROUP BY class;
```

This produces the following output:

```
COUNT(STNO)
-----------
         11
```

```
      10
       7
      10
      10
```

This query generates the same count information as the former query, but the class is not reported in the result set. This latter type of query is useful when you want to determine aggregates of aggregates.

Suppose you wanted to find the class with the minimum number of students. You might try the following query:

```
SELECT MIN(COUNT(stno)), class
FROM Student
GROUP BY class;
```

However, this query will not work. The `MIN` function is an aggregate, and aggregates operate on tables that contain rows. In this case, we are asking `MIN` to operate on a table of counted classes that have not yet been calculated. The point is that SQL cannot handle this mismatch of aggregation and grouping. The way to find the class with the minimum number of students would be to first display the counts of classes, grouped by class as follows:

```
SELECT COUNT(stno)
FROM Student
GROUP BY class;
```

We then find the minimum students in a class as follows:

```
SELECT MIN(COUNT(stno))
FROM Student
GROUP BY class;
```

This produces the following output:

```
MIN(COUNT(STNO))
----------------
               7
```

We then use this information in a subquery with a HAVING clause like this:

```
SELECT COUNT(stno), class
FROM Student
GROUP BY class
HAVING COUNT(stno) =
   (SELECT MIN(COUNT(stno))
    FROM Student
GROUP BY class);
```

This produces the following output:

```
COUNT(STNO)      CLASS
-----------     ------
          7          3
```

Auditing IN Subqueries

In this section, we consider a potential problem of using aggregation with subqueries. As with Cartesian products and joins, aggregation hides detail and should always be audited. Consider the following two tables: GG and SS.

Table GG contains section numbers that the students are registered in (num), grades (gd), and student names (sname).

Table GG:

```
NUM    GD    SNAME
----   --    ----------------
100    A     BRENDA
110    B     BRENDA
120    A     BRENDA
200    A     BRENDA
210    A     BRENDA
220    B     BRENDA
100    A     RICHARD
```

```
100     B     DOUG
200     A     RICHARD
110     B     MORRIS
```

Table SS contains a section identifier (sec) and an instructor name (iname).

Table SS:

```
SEC     INAME
----    ------------
100     JONES
110     SMITH
120     JONES
200     ADAMS
210     JONES
```

Suppose we want to find out how many A's each instructor awarded. We might start with a join of table GG and table SS to show all the information ungrouped and unfiltered. A normal equi-join would be as follows:

```
SELECT *
FROM  GG, SS
WHERE GG.num = SS.sec   -- join condition
;
```

This produces the following output:

```
SEC     INAME         NUM     GD     SNAME
----    ----------    ----    --     ------------------
100     JONES         100     A      BRENDA
100     JONES         100     A      RICHARD
100     JONES         100     B      DOUG
110     SMITH         110     B      MORRIS
110     SMITH         110     B      BRENDA
120     JONES         120     A      BRENDA
200     ADAMS         200     A      BRENDA
200     ADAMS         200     A      RICHARD
210     JONES         210     A      BRENDA
```

The following query will tell us that there are six A's in the GG table:

```
SELECT COUNT(*)
FROM GG
WHERE gd = 'A';
```

Now, if we execute the following query looking for A's by instructor:

```
SELECT SS.iname           -- instructor name
FROM SS, GG
WHERE SS.sec = GG.num     -- join condition
   AND GG.gd = 'A';
```

We get this output:

```
INAME
------------
JONES
JONES
ADAMS
JONES
JONES
ADAMS
```

With a COUNT and GROUP BY applied to the join, our query becomes:

```
SELECT SS.iname, COUNT(*)
FROM SS, GG
WHERE SS.sec = GG.num     -- join GG to SS
   AND GG.gd = 'A'
GROUP BY SS.iname;
```

We get the following output:

```
INAME        COUNT(EXPRESSION 1)
-----------  -------------------
ADAMS                          2
JONES                          4
```

So far, so good, and everything appears normal. You may note that the final count/grouping has the same number of A's as the original tables — the sum of the counts equals 6. Now, if we had devised a count query with a sub-SELECT, we could get an answer that looks correct but in fact is not. For example, consider the following subquery version of the preceding join query:

```
SELECT SS.iname, COUNT(*)
FROM SS
WHERE SS.sec IN
   (SELECT GG.num
    FROM GG
    WHERE GG.gd = 'A')
GROUP BY SS.iname;
```

This produces the following output:

```
INAME           COUNT(EXPRESSION 1)
--------------  -------------------
ADAMS                             1
JONES                             3
```

Why did we get this output? The answer is that the second query is counting names of instructors and whether an "A" is present in the set of courses that this instructor teaches; not how many A's are in the set, just whether there are any. The join query gives us all of the A's in the joined table and hence gives the correct answer to the question, "How many A's did each instructor award?" The sub-SELECTed query answers a different question: "In how many sections did the instructor award an A?"

The point of this example is that if you are SELECTing and COUNTing, you should audit your results often. If we want to count the number of A's by instructor, we begin by first counting how many A's there are. Then, we can construct a query to join and count. We should be able to total and reconcile the number of A's to the number of A's by instructor.

Nulls Revisited

Nulls present a complication with regard to aggregate functions and other queries. This is because nulls are never equal, less than, greater than, or not equal to any value. Using aggregates by themselves on columns that contain nulls will ignore the null values. For example, suppose we had the following table called Sal.

Sal:

```
NAME             SALARY
----------     --------
Joe                1000
Sam                2000
Bill               3000
Dave
```

Consider the result of the following query:

```
SELECT COUNT(*), AVG(salary), SUM(salary), MIN(salary), MAX(salary)
FROM Sal;
```

This query would produce this output:

```
COUNT(*)   AVG(SALARY)   SUM(SALARY)   MIN(SALARY)   MAX(SALARY)
--------   -----------   -----------   -----------   ------------
       4          2000          6000          1000           3000
```

`COUNT(*)` counts all rows, but the `AVG`, `SUM`, `MIN`, and `MAX` ignore the nulled salary row in computing the aggregate. Counting columns indicates the presence of nulls. If we count with:

```
SELECT COUNT(name)
FROM Sal;
```

We get a result like this:

```
COUNT(NAME)
-----------
          4
```

Or, with the salary column, we get:

```
COUNT(SALARY)
-------------
            3
```

These results indicate we have a null salary. Clearly we have at least four rows but only three salaries. If we want to include nulls in the aggregate, we can use the `NVL` function, which we have discussed in previous chapters. `NVL` returns a value if the value is null. `NVL` has the form `NVL` (*column_name*, *value_if_null*), which is used in place of the column_name. Some examples follow:

```
SELECT name, NVL(salary,0)
FROM Sal;
```

produces the following output:

```
NAME        NVL(SALARY,0)
----------  -------------
Joe                  1000
Sam                  2000
Bill                 3000
Dave                    0
```

```
SELECT COUNT(NVL(salary,0))
FROM Sal;
```

produces the following output:

```
COUNT(NVL(SALARY,0))
--------------------
                   4
```

```
SELECT AVG(NVL(salary,0))
FROM Sal;
```

produces the following output:

```
AVG(NVL(SALARY,0))
------------------
              1500
```

What seems almost contradictory to these examples is that when grouping is added to the query, nulls in the grouped column are included in the result set. So, if we had another column in our table like this:

```
NAME         SALARY    JOB
---------   -------    ------
Joe            1000    Programmer
Sam            2000
Bill           3000    Plumber
Dave                   Programmer
```

And if we ran a query like this:

```
SELECT SUM(salary),job
FROM Sal
GROUP BY job;
```

We would get the following result:

```
SUM(SALARY)    JOB
-----------    ----------
       3000    Plumber
       1000    Programmer
       2000
```

Thus, the aggregate will ignore values that are null, but grouping will compute a value for the nulled column.

Exercises for Chapter 8

As you do the exercises, unless it is stated otherwise, you will be using the tables from our standard Student-Course database. Also, as you do the exercises, it will be a good idea to copy/paste your query as well as your query result into a word processor file.

8-1. Display a list of courses (course names) that have prerequisites and the number of prerequisites for each course. Order the list by the number of prerequisites.

8-2. How many juniors (`class = 3`) are there in the Student table?

8-3. Group and count all math majors by class and display the count if there are two or more in a class. (Remember that class here refers to freshman, sophomore, junior, and senior, and is recorded as 1, 2, 3, and 4.)

8-4. Print the counts of A's, B's, and so on from the Grade_report table.

8-5. Print the counts of course numbers offered in descending order by count. Use the Section table only.

8-6. Create a table with names and number of children (NOC). Populate the table with five or six rows. Use `COUNT`, `SUM`, `AVG`, `MIN`, and `MAX` on the NOC attribute in one query and check that the numbers you get are what you expect.

8-7. Create a table of names, salaries, and job locations. Populate the table with at least 10 rows and no fewer than three job locations. (There will be several employees at each location.) Find the average salary for each job location with one `SELECT`.

8-8. Print an ordered list of instructors and the number of A's they assigned to students. Order the output by number of A's (lowest to greatest). You can (and probably will) ignore instructors who assign no A's.

8-9. Create a table called Employees with name, salary, and title fields. Include exactly six rows. Make the salary null in one row, the job title null in another, and both the salary and the job title null in another. Use the data shown below.

Employees:

```
Name          Salary      Title
------------  ---------   ---------------
Mary          1000        Programmer
Brenda        3000
Stephanie                 Artist
Alice
Lindsay       2000        Artist
Christina     500         Programmer
```

a. Display the table.
b. Display count, sum, maximum, minimum, and average salary.
c. Display count, sum, maximum, minimum, and average salary, counting salary as 0 if no salary is listed.
d. Display the average salary grouped by job title on the table.
e. Display the average salary grouped by job title when null salary is counted as 0.
f. Display the average salary grouped by job title when salary is counted as 0 if it is null and include a value for "no job title."

8-10. Find the instructor and the course where the maximum number of A's were awarded.

Optional Exercise

8-11. Find the count of the number of students by class who are taking classes offered by the computer science (COSC) department. Turn on autotrace (`SET AUTOTRACE ON EXPLAIN`). Do the query in two ways: First using a condition in the `WHERE` clause, and then by filtering with a `HAVING` clause. Which is more efficient, `WHERE` or `HAVING`? Hint: These queries need a five-table join.

Delete (`DROP`) all of your "scratch" tables (the ones you created just for this exercise, including Employees, NOC, and any others you may have created).

Chapter 9

Correlated Subqueries

A correlated subquery is one in which both of the following are true:

- There is a subquery (and hence a main, outer query).
- The information in the subquery is referenced by the outer, main query such that the inner query may be thought of as being executed repeatedly.

In this chapter, we will take a look at correlated subqueries. We will discuss existence queries and correlation as well as `NOT EXISTS`. We will also take a look at SQL's universal and existential qualifiers. Before discussing correlated subqueries in detail however, let's make sure we understand what a non-correlated subquery is.

Non-Correlated Subqueries

A *non-correlated subquery* is a subquery that is independent of the outer query. The subquery could be executed on its own. The following is an example of a query that is not correlated:

```
SELECT s.sname
FROM   Student s
WHERE  s.stno IN
   (SELECT gr.student_number
    FROM   Grade_report gr
    WHERE  gr.grade = 'A');
```

Note: The part of the query in parentheses is the subquery (also referred to as a *nested query* or *embedded query*). Note that the subquery is an independent entity — it would work by itself if run as a stand-alone query.

We have seen in earlier chapters that Oracle may rearrange queries to gain efficiency. Rearrangement aside, the subquery:

```
(SELECT gr.student_number
FROM   Grade_report gr
WHERE  gr.grade = 'A');
```

can be thought of as being evaluated first, creating the set of student numbers that have A's. The subquery result set is then used to determine which rows in the main query will be SELECTed.

Consider the following:

```
SELECT s.sname                    -- outer
FROM   Student s                  -- outer
WHERE  s.stno IN                  -- outer
   (SELECT  gr.student_number         -- inner
    FROM    Grade_report gr           -- inner
    WHERE   gr.grade = 'A')           -- inner
;
```

This produces the following output:

```
SNAME
--------------------
Lineas
Mary
```

```
Brenda
Richard
Lujack
Donald
Lynette
Susan
Holly
Sadie
Jessica
Steve
Cedric
Jerry

14 rows selected.
```

Correlated Subqueries

At the beginning of this chapter we stated that correlated subqueries are subqueries in which there is a subquery (and hence a main, outer query) and the information in the subquery is referenced by the outer, main query.

Correlated queries present a different execution scenario to the Data Manipulation Language (DML) from ordinary, non-correlated subqueries. The correlated subquery cannot stand alone because it depends on the outer query; therefore, completing the subquery prior to execution of the outer query is not an option. Since the efficiency of the correlated subquery varies, it may be worthwhile to test it against joins or sets.

Note: One situation in which you cannot avoid correlation is the "for all" query, which we will discuss later in this chapter.

The following is an example of a correlated query:

```
SELECT s.sname
FROM   Student s
WHERE  s.stno IN
   (SELECT gr.student_number
    FROM  Grade_report gr
    WHERE gr.student_number = s.stno
       /* s.stno references outer query */
AND   gr.grade = 'B');
```

This produces the following output:

```
SNAME
--------------------
Lineas
Mary
Brenda
Kelly
Lujack
Reva
Harley
Chris
Lynette
Hillary
Phoebe
Holly
Sadie
Jessica
Steve
Cedric
George
Cramer
Fraiser
Francis
Smithly
Sebastian
Lindsay
Stephanie
Zelda
Mario
```

```
Ken

27 rows selected.
```

Here, the inner query references the outer one — observe the use of s.stno in the WHERE clause of the inner query. Rather than thinking of this query as creating a set of student numbers that have B's, each row from the outer query is SELECTed individually and tested against all rows of the inner query one at a time until it is determined whether a given student number is in the inner set and whether that student earned a B.

This situation is like a nested DO loop in a programming language, where the first row from the Student table is SELECTed and tested against rows from the Grade_report table, then the second row from the Student table is SELECTed and tested against rows from the Grade_report table. The following is the DO loop in pseudo-code:

```
LOOP1: For each row in Student s DO
   LOOP2: For each row in Grade_report gr DO
      IF (gr.student_number = s.stno) then
         IF (gr.grade = 'B') THEN TRUE
      END LOOP2;
   if TRUE, then Student row is SELECTed
END LOOP1;
```

This particular query could have been done without correlation in a manner similar to our first example in this chapter; however, it demonstrates the difference in query execution.

You might think that correlated queries are less efficient than simple subqueries because the simple subquery is done once and the correlated subquery is done once for each outer row. However, the internal handling of how the query executes depends on the SQL and the optimizer for that database engine. In Oracle, the database engine is designed so that queries containing correlation are actually quite efficient.

Existence Queries and Correlation

Correlated subqueries are often written so that the question in the inner query is one of existence. For example, assume we want to find the names of students who have taken a computer science (COSC) class and have earned a grade of B in that course. This query can be written in several ways. For example, we can use a non-correlated subquery as follows:

```
SELECT s.sname
FROM   Student s
WHERE  s.stno IN
   (SELECT gr.student_number FROM Grade_report gr, Section
    WHERE Section.section_id = gr.section_id
         /* join condition Grade_report-Section */
    AND Section.course_num LIKE 'COSC____'
    AND gr.grade = 'B');
```

This would produce the following output:

```
SNAME
--------------------
Lineas
Mary
Brenda
Lujack
Reva
Harley
Chris
Lynette
Hillary
Phoebe
Holly
George
```

```
Cramer
Fraiser
Francis
Lindsay
Stephanie

17 rows selected.
```

Since this query is non-correlated, we can think of the query as first forming the set of student numbers of students who have earned B's in COSC courses — the inner query result set. In the inner query, we must have both the Grade_report and the Section tables because the course numbers are in the Section table and the grades are in the Grade_report table. Once we form this set of student numbers (that is, once we complete the inner query), the outer query looks through the Student table and SELECTs only those students who are in the inner query result set.

Note: This query could also be done by creating a double-nested subquery containing two INs, or it could be written using a three-table join.

Had we chosen to write the query with an unnecessary correlation, it might look like this:

```
SELECT s.sname
FROM   Student s
WHERE  s.stno IN
   (SELECT gr.student_number
    FROM  Grade_report gr, Section
    WHERE Section.section_id = gr.section_id
              /* join condition Grade_report-Section */
    AND   Section.course_num LIKE 'COSC____'  /* correlation */
    AND   gr.student_number = s.stno
    AND   gr.grade = 'B');
```

The final result of this query would be the same as the previous one. In this case, using the Student table in the subquery is unnecessary. Although correlation is unnecessary, we have provided this example for several reasons:

- To show when correlation is necessary
- To show how to untangle unnecessarily correlated queries
- To show how you might migrate your thought process toward correlation, should it be necessary

First, let's look at situations in which correlation *is* necessary, and, in particular, introduce a new predicate: EXISTS.

EXISTS

As noted earlier, there will be situations in which the correlation of a subquery *is* necessary. Another way to write the correlated query is with the EXISTS predicate, which looks like this:

```
SELECT s.sname
FROM   Student s
WHERE  EXISTS
   (SELECT 1 FROM Grade_report gr, Section
    WHERE Section.section_id = gr.section_id
          /* join condition Grade_report-Section */
    AND Section.course_num LIKE 'COSC____'
    AND gr.student_number = s.stno          /* correlation  */
    AND gr.grade = 'B');
```

This correlated query produces the same output (17 rows) as both of the previous queries. Let us dissect this version.

The EXISTS predicate says, "Choose the row from the Student table in the outer query if the subquery is true." (That is, if a row in the subquery *exists* that satisfies the condition in the subquery WHERE clause.) Since no actual result set for the inner query is formed, SELECT 1 is used as a "dummy" result set to indicate that the subquery is true (1 is returned) or false (no rows are returned). In the non-correlated case, we tied the student number in the Student table to the inner query by the IN predicate as follows:

```
SELECT s.stno
FROM   Student s
WHERE  s.stno IN
   (SELECT "student number...")
```

When using the EXISTS predicate, we use the Student table in the subquery (i.e., it's correlated) and hence we are seeking only to find whether the subquery WHERE can be satisfied.

What is the SELECT 1 doing in the subquery? Using the EXISTS predicate, the subquery does not form a result set *per se*, but rather returns true or false. SELECT * in the subquery may be used; however, from an "internal" standpoint, SELECT * causes the SQL engine to check the data dictionary unnecessarily. Because the actual result of the inner query is only true or false, it is suggested that SELECT 'X'... (or SELECT 1...) instead of SELECT * be used so that a constant is SELECTed instead of some "sensible" entry. The SELECT 'X'... or (SELECT 1...) is simply more efficient.

In the EXISTS case, we do not specify what attributes need be SELECTed in the inner query's result set; rather, we use SELECT 1 to select something (a 1) if the subquery WHERE is satisfied (that is, true) and to select nothing (no rows would give false) if the condition in the subquery WHERE is not met. The EXISTS predicate forces us to correlate the query. To illustrate that correlation is usually necessary with EXISTS, consider the following query:

```
SELECT s.sname                    /* exists-uncorrelated  */
```

```
FROM   Student s
WHERE  EXISTS
   (SELECT 'X' FROM Grade_report gr, Section t
    WHERE t.section_id = gr.section_id
            /* join condition Grade_report-Section */
    AND   t.course_num LIKE 'COSC____'
    AND   gr.grade = 'B');
```

This produces the following output:

```
SNAME
--------------------
Lineas
Mary
Brenda
Richard
Kelly
.
.
.
Bill
Hillary
Phoebe
Jake

48 rows selected.
```

This query uses `EXISTS`, but has no correlation. This syntax infers that for each student row, we test the joined Grade_report and Section tables to see whether there is a course number like COSC and a grade of B (which, of course, there is). We unnecessarily ask the subquery question over and over again. The result from this latter, uncorrelated `EXISTS` query is the same as:

```
SELECT s.sname
FROM Student s;
```

The point is that the correlation is necessary when we use `EXISTS`.

Consider another example in which a correlation could be used. Suppose we want to find the names of all students who have three or more B's. A first pass at a query might be something like this:

```
SELECT s.sname
FROM   Student s WHERE "something" IN
   (SELECT "something"
    FROM   Grade_report
    WHERE  "count of grade = 'B'" > 2);
```

This query can be done with a HAVING clause as we saw previously, but we want to show how to do this in yet another way. Suppose we arrange the subquery to use the student number from the Student table as a filter and count in the subquery only when a row in the Grade_report table correlates to that student. The query looks like this:

```
SELECT s.sname
FROM   Student s
WHERE  2 < (SELECT COUNT(*)
   FROM   Grade_report gr
   WHERE  gr.student_number = s.stno
   AND    gr.grade = 'B');
```

This results in the following output:

```
SNAME
--------------------
Lineas
Mary
Lujack
Reva
Chris
Hillary
Phoebe
Holly

8 rows selected.
```

Although there is no EXISTS in the query, it is implied. The syntax of the query does not allow an EXISTS, but the sense of the query is "where exists a count of 2 which is less than...." In this correlated query, we must examine the Grade_report table for each member of the Student table to see whether the student has two B's (correlation). We test the entire Grade_report table for each student row in the outer query.

If it were possible, a subquery without the correlation would be more desirable. The overall query might be:

```
SELECT s.sname
FROM   Student s
WHERE  s.stno in ...
```

We might attempt to write the following subquery:

```
SELECT s.sname
FROM   Student s
WHERE  s.stno IN
   (SELECT gr.student_number
    FROM   Grade_report gr
    WHERE  gr.grade = 'B');
```

However, this would give us only students who had made at *least* one B, as seen in the following output:

```
SNAME
--------------------
Lineas
Mary
Brenda
Kelly
Lujack
Reva
Harley
Chris
Lynette
Hillary
Phoebe
```

```
Holly
Sadie
Jessica
Steve
Cedric
George
Cramer
Fraiser
Francis
Smithly
Sebastian
Lindsay
Stephanie
Zelda
Mario
Ken

27 rows selected.
```

To get students who have earned three B's, we could try the following query:

```
SELECT s.sname
FROM   Student s
WHERE  s.stno IN
   (SELECT gr.student_number, COUNT(*)
    FROM   Grade_report gr
    WHERE  gr.grade = 'B'
    GROUP  BY gr.student_number
    HAVING COUNT(*) > 2);
```

However, this will not work because the subquery cannot have two attributes in its result set unless the main query has two attributes in the `WHERE..IN`. Here, the subquery must have only gr.student_number to match s.stno. We might then construct an inline view as with the following query:

```
SELECT s.sname
FROM   Student s
WHERE  s.stno IN
```

```
   (SELECT student_number
   FROM (SELECT student_number, COUNT(*)
      FROM  Grade_report gr
      WHERE gr.grade = 'B'
      GROUP BY student_number having COUNT(*) > 2));
```

This succeeds in Oracle but fails in some other SQLs. The output of this query would be:

```
SNAME
--------------------
Lineas
Mary
Lujack
Reva
Chris
Hillary
Phoebe
Holly

8 rows selected.
```

As you can see, we can query the database using various methods with SQL. In this case, the correlated query may be the easiest to see and perhaps the most efficient.

From IN to EXISTS

A simple example of converting from `IN` to `EXISTS`, or from uncorrelated to correlated queries (or vice versa), would be move the set test in the `WHERE..IN` of the uncorrelated query to the `WHERE` of the `EXISTS` in the correlated query. For example, note the placement of the set test in the following uncorrelated query:

```
SELECT *
FROM Student s
WHERE s.stno IN
   (SELECT g.student_number
```

```
   FROM Grade_report g
   WHERE grade = 'B');
```

Now note the placement of the set test in the following correlated query:

```
SELECT *
FROM  Student s
WHERE EXISTS          -- replace IN with EXISTS
   (SELECT 1          -- g.student_number change the result set to 1
    FROM  Grade_report g
    WHERE grade = 'B'
    AND   s.stno = g.student_number)   -- correlate the subquery
;
```

These two queries produce the following output:

```
   STNO  SNAME                 MAJO  CLASS  BDATE
-------  --------------------  ----  -----  ---------
      2  Lineas                ENGL      1  5-APR-80
      3  Mary                  COSC      4  16-JUL-78
      8  Brenda                COSC      2  13-AUG-77
     13  Kelly                 MATH      4  12-AUG-80
     14  Lujack                COSC      1  12-FEB-77
     15  Reva                  MATH      2  10-JUN-80
     19  Harley                POLY      2  16-APR-81
     24  Chris                 ACCT      4  12-FEB-78
     34  Lynette               POLY      1  16-JUL-81
    121  Hillary               COSC      1  16-JUL-77
    122  Phoebe                ENGL      3  15-APR-80
    123  Holly                 POLY      4  15-JAN-81
    125  Sadie                 MATH      2  12-AUG-80
    126  Jessica               POLY      2  16-JUL-81
    127  Steve                 ENGL      1  11-MAR-80
    129  Cedric                ENGL      2  15-APR-80
    132  George                POLY      1  16-APR-81
    143  Cramer                ENGL      3  15-APR-80
    144  Fraiser               POLY      1  16-JUL-81
    146  Francis               ACCT      4  11-JUN-77
    147  Smithly               ENGL      2  13-MAY-80
    148  Sebastian             ACCT      2  14-OCT-76
```

```
    155  Lindsay            UNKN        1  15-OCT-79
    157  Stephanie          MATH           16-APR-81
      5  Zelda              COSC           12-FEB-78
      7  Mario              MATH           12-AUG-80
      6  Ken                POLY           15-JUL-80

27 rows selected.
```

This example gives us a pattern to move from one kind of query to the other and to test the efficiency of both kinds of queries. Note that in the EXISTS version we changed the result set for the subquery to 1 by commenting out the original result set of g.student_number.

NOT EXISTS

There are some situations in which the EXISTS and NOT EXISTS predicates are necessary. For example, if we ask a "for all" question, it must be answered by "existence" (actually, the lack thereof, or "not existence"). The statement "find *x* for all *y*" is logically equivalent to "do not find *x* where there does not exists a *y*." In SQL, there is no "for all" predicate; instead, the workaround is to use NOT EXISTS. (*A word of caution:* SQL is not simply a logic exercise as we will see.) We will first see how EXISTS and NOT EXISTS work in SQL, and then tackle the "for all" problem. Consider the following query:

```
SELECT s.sname, s.stno, s.major
FROM   Student s
WHERE  EXISTS
   (SELECT  'X'
    FROM  Grade_report gr
    WHERE s.stno = gr.student_number
    AND   gr.grade = 'C')
ORDER BY s.sname;
```

This produces the following output:

```
SNAME                    STNO MAJO
-------------------- --------- ----
Alan                      130 COSC
Benny                     161 CHEM
Bill                       70 POLY
Brenda                      8 COSC
Donald                     20 ACCT
Genevieve                 153 UNKN
Gus                       160 ART
Jake                       31 COSC
Jessica                   126 POLY
Ken                         6 POLY
Lionel                    163
Losmith                   151 CHEM
Mario                       7 MATH
Monica                     62 MATH
Rachel                    131 ENGL
Reva                       15 MATH
Richard                    10 ENGL
Sadie                     125 MATH
Sebastian                 148 ACCT
Smithly                   147 ENGL
Steve                     127 ENGL
Susan                      49 ENGL
Thornton                  158
Zelda                       5 COSC

24 rows selected.
```

The `ORDER BY` was added for comparison purposes. For this correlated query, student names are `SELECT`ed when:

(a) The student is enrolled in a section (`WHERE s.stno = gr.student_number`), and

(b) The same student has a grade of C.

In the `EXISTS` version of this query, both (a) and (b) must be true for the student row to be `SELECT`ed. Recall that we use `SELECT 1` or `SELECT 'X'` in our inner query because we want the subquery to return something if the subquery is true. Therefore, `SELECT..EXISTS` "says" `SELECT..WHERE` true, and the inner query is true if any row is SELECTed in the inner query.

Here is the join version for comparison:

```
SELECT DISTINCT s.sname, s.stno, s.major, g.grade
FROM  student s, grade_report g
WHERE s.stno = g.student_number
   AND g.grade = 'C'
ORDER BY s.sname
```

Which gives:

```
SNAME                      STNO  MAJO  G
--------------------  ----------  ----  -
Alan                        130  COSC  C
Benny                       161  CHEM  C
Bill                         70  POLY  C
Brenda                        8  COSC  C
Donald                       20  ACCT  C
Genevieve                   153  UNKN  C
Gus                         160  ART   C
Jake                         31  COSC  C
Jessica                     126  POLY  C
Ken                           6  POLY  C
Lionel                      163        C
Losmith                     151  CHEM  C
Mario                         7  MATH  C
Monica                       62  MATH  C
Rachel                      131  ENGL  C
Reva                         15  MATH  C
Richard                      10  ENGL  C
Sadie                       125  MATH  C
Sebastian                   148  ACCT  C
Smithly                     147  ENGL  C
Steve                       127  ENGL  C
Susan                        49  ENGL  C
Thornton                    158        C
Zelda                         5  COSC  C

24 rows selected.
```

Now consider the following query, where we change EXISTS to NOT EXISTS:

```
SELECT s.sname
FROM   Student s
WHERE NOT EXISTS
   (SELECT 'X'
    FROM  Grade_report gr
    WHERE s.stno = gr.student_number
    AND   gr.grade = 'C')
ORDER BY s.sname;
```

This produces the following output:

```
SNAME                      STNO  MAJO
-------------------- ---------- ----
Brad                        128  COSC
Cedric                      129  ENGL
Chris                        24  ACCT
Cramer                      143  ENGL
Elainie                      17  COSC
Fraiser                     144  POLY
Francis                     146  ACCT
George                      132  POLY
Harley                       19  POLY
Harrison                    145  ACCT
Hillary                     121  COSC
Holly                       123  POLY
Jake                        191  MATH
Jerry                       142  COSC
Kelly                        13  MATH
Lindsay                     155  UNKN
Lineas                        2  ENGL
Lujack                       14  COSC
Lynette                      34  POLY
Mary                          3  COSC
Phoebe                      122  ENGL
Romona                        9  ENGL
Smith                        88
Stephanie                   157  MATH
```

```
24 rows selected.
```

In this query, we are still SELECTing with the pattern SELECT..WHERE true because all SELECTs with EXISTS work that way. However, the twist is that the subquery must be false to be SELECTed with NOT EXISTS. If the subquery is false, then NOT EXISTS is true and the outer row is SELECTed.

Now, logic implies that if either (a) s.stno <> gr.student_number or (b) gr.grade <> 'C', then the subquery "fails" — that is, it is false for that student row. Because the subquery is false, the NOT EXISTS would return a true for that row. Unfortunately, this logic is not quite what happens. Recall that we characterized the correlated query as follows:

```
LOOP1: For each row in Student s DO
   LOOP2: For each row in Grade_report DO
      IF (gr.student_number = s.stno) THEN
         IF (gr.grade = 'C') THEN TRUE
      END LOOP2;
   if TRUE, then student row is SELECTed
END LOOP1;
```

LOOP2 is completed before the next student is tested. In other words, just because there exists a student number that is not equal, this will not cause the subquery to be false. Rather, the entire subquery table is parsed and the logic is more like this:

For the case EXISTS WHERE s.stno = gr.student_number..., is there a gr.grade = 'C'? If, when the student numbers are equal, no C can be found, then the subquery *fails* — it is false for that outer student row. So with NOT EXISTS we will SELECT students with student numbers equal in the Grade_report and Student tables, but who have no C in the Grade_report table. The point about "no C in the Grade_report table" can only be answered true by looking at all the rows in the inner query.

Consider this join version:

```
SELECT DISTINCT s.sname, g.grade
FROM Student s, Grade_report g
WHERE s.stno = g.student_number
   AND g.grade <> 'C'
```

This gives:

```
SNAME                G
-------------------- -
Brad                 F
Brenda               A
Brenda               B
Cedric               A
Cedric               B
Chris                B
Cramer               B
Donald               A
Fraiser              B
Francis              B
George               B
Harley               B
Harley               D
Harrison             F
Hillary              B
Holly                A
Holly                B
Jerry                A
Jessica              A
Jessica              B
Kelly                B
Ken                  B
Lindsay              B
Lineas               A
Lineas               B
Lineas               D
Lujack               A
Lujack               B
Lynette              A
Lynette              B
Mario                B
Mary                 A
```

```
Mary            B
Phoebe          B
Reva            B
Reva            F
Richard         A
Romona          F
Sadie           A
Sadie           B
Sebastian       B
Smithly         B
Stephanie       B
Steve           A
Steve           B
Susan           A
Zelda           B

47 rows selected.
```

This join returns 47 rows because it is telling us all the Student-Grade_report combinations where there is no C. Remember that a join is a Cartesian product restricted by `s.stno = g.grade_report`. So a student could have a C but also have some other grade, and the query would return that student and his or her non-C grade. The `NOT EXISTS` only returns students who have no C at all.

There is one other point to be made here. The two results from above (`EXISTS` versus `NOT EXISTS`) have the same number of rows, but this is just a coincidence. If the two result sets are examined, you will notice that the people in the two sets are all different. Two people in the second result set show up because they took no courses and hence had no rows in the inner query of the `NOT EXISTS` (<Smith, 88..> and <Jake, 191..>). One has to be careful to account for null situations.

An extra query to check for this situation could be:

```
SELECT s.sname, s.stno, s.major
FROM Student s
WHERE s.stno NOT IN
```

```
(SELECT g.student_number
 FROM Grade_report g);
```

Giving:

```
SNAME                    STNO  MAJO
------------------- ---------- ----
Smith                       88
Jake                       191  MATH
```

SQL Universal and Existential Qualifiers — the "for all" Query

The terms "for all" (or "for each" or "by all") are called *universal qualifiers*, while "there exists" is the *existential qualifier*. SQL has an existential predicate in EXISTS. As we mentioned above, SQL does not have a "for all" predicate; however, the following logical relationship exists:

For all x, WHERE P(x) is true

is logically the same as:

There does not exist an x, WHERE P(x) is not true

A "for all" type SQL query is less straightforward than the other queries we have studied and used. The "for all" SQL query involves a double-nested, correlated query using the NOT EXISTS predicate. Let's look at an example.

Example 1

To show a "for all" type SQL query, we will use tables other than our student records. We have created a table called Cap (for capability). This table has names of students who have multiple foreign language capabilities. We begin by looking at the table with the following query:

```
SELECT *
FROM Cap
ORDER BY name;
```

This produces the following output:

```
NAME                   LANG
--------------------   ---------------
BRENDA                 FRENCH
BRENDA                 CHINESE
BRENDA                 SPANISH
JOE                    CHINESE
KENT                   CHINESE
LUJACK                 FRENCH
LUJACK                 GERMAN
LUJACK                 CHINESE
LUJACK                 SPANISH
MARY JO                GERMAN
MARY JO                CHINESE
MARY JO                FRENCH
MELANIE                FRENCH
MELANIE                CHINESE
RICHARD                GERMAN
RICHARD                SPANISH
RICHARD                CHINESE
RICHARD                FRENCH

18 rows selected.
```

Another view of this table ordered by language is:

```
NAME                   LANG
--------------------   ---------------
BRENDA                 CHINESE
JOE                    CHINESE
KENT                   CHINESE
MARY JO                CHINESE
RICHARD                CHINESE
```

```
MELANIE              CHINESE
LUJACK               CHINESE
BRENDA               FRENCH
RICHARD              FRENCH
MELANIE              FRENCH
MARY JO              FRENCH
LUJACK               FRENCH
LUJACK               GERMAN
RICHARD              GERMAN
MARY JO              GERMAN
BRENDA               SPANISH
RICHARD              SPANISH
LUJACK               SPANISH
```

Suppose we want to find out which languages are spoken by all students. This is a universal qualifier question. For our small practice table, we can answer the question by actually comparing the table sorted two ways as above.

To see how to answer a question of this type for a much larger table where sorting and examining the result would be tedious, we will construct a query. We will show the query and then dissect the result. The query to answer our question "Which language is spoken by all students?" looks like this:

```
SELECT name, lang
FROM   Cap x
WHERE NOT EXISTS
   (SELECT 'X'
    FROM Cap y
    WHERE NOT EXISTS
       (SELECT 'X'
        FROM Cap z
        WHERE x.lang = z.lang
        AND y.name = z.name));
```

As you will see, all of the "for all/for each/by all" questions follow this double-nested, correlated `NOT EXISTS` pattern. It is convenient to use the table aliases (x, y, and z) here for the three instances of Cap.

The result set for this query will be:

```
NAME                 LANG
-------------------- ---------------
BRENDA               CHINESE
RICHARD              CHINESE
LUJACK               CHINESE
MARY JO              CHINESE
MELANIE              CHINESE
JOE                  CHINESE
KENT                 CHINESE

7 rows selected.
```

The Way the Query Works

To SELECT a language spoken by all students, the query proceeds as follows:

a. SELECT a row in Cap (x) (outer query).

b. For that row, begin SELECTing each row again in Cap (y) (middle query).

c. For each of the middle query rows, we want the inner query (Cap (z)) to be true for all cases of the middle query (remember that true is translated to false by the NOT EXISTS). As each inner query is satisfied (it is true), it forces the middle query to continue looking for a match — to look at all cases and eventually conclude false (evaluate to false overall). If the middle query is false, the outer query sees true because of its NOT EXISTS.

To make the middle query (y) find false, all of the inner query (z) occurrences must be true (i.e., the languages from the outer query have to exist with all names from the middle one (y) in the inner one (z)). For an eventual "match," every row in the middle query for an outer query row must be false (i.e., every row in the inner query is true).

These steps are explained in further detail in the next example where we use a smaller table, Cap1, so it will be easier to understand the explanation.

Example 2

Suppose we had this simpler table, Cap1, as shown below:

```
NAME          LANG
-----------   -------
Joe           Spanish
Mary          Spanish
Mary          French
```

Note: Note that this table, Cap1, does not exist. You will have to create it. Keep the attribute names and types similar to the Cap table.

Let's now look at how we can answer the same question "Which language is spoken by all students?" using this smaller table, Cap1. We can see the answer is Spanish.

The query will be similar to the one used in Example 1:

```
SELECT name, lang
FROM   Cap1 x
WHERE  NOT EXISTS
   (SELECT 'X'
    FROM   Cap1 y
    WHERE  NOT EXISTS
      (SELECT 'X'
       FROM  Cap1 z
       WHERE x.lang = z.lang
       AND   y.name = z.name))
ORDER BY lang;
```

The output for this query will be:

```
NAME            LANG
--------------- -------
JOE             SPANISH
MARY            SPANISH
```

How this query works:

1. The row <Joe, Spanish> is SELECTed by the outer query (x).
2. The row <Joe, Spanish> is SELECTed by the middle query (y).
3. The row <Joe, Spanish> is SELECTed by the inner query (z).
4. The inner query is true:

   X.LANG = Spanish
   Z.LANG = Spanish
   Y.NAME = Joe
   Z.NAME = Joe

5. Because the inner query is true, the NOT EXISTS of the middle query translates this to false and continues with the next row in the middle query. The middle query SELECTs <Mary, Spanish> and the inner query begins again with <Joe, Spanish>, seeing:

   X.LANG = Spanish
   Z.LANG = Spanish
   Y.NAME = Mary
   Z.NAME = Joe

   This is false, so the inner query SELECTs a second row, <Mary, Spanish>:

   X.LANG = Spanish
   Z.LANG = Spanish
   Y.NAME = Mary
   Z.NAME = Mary

This is true, so the inner query is true. (Notice that the `X.LANG` has not changed yet, the outer query (x) is still on the first row.)

6. Because the inner query is true, the `NOT EXISTS` of the middle query translates this to false and continues with the next row in the middle query. The middle query now `SELECT`s <Mary, French> and the inner query begins again with <Joe, Spanish>, seeing:

   X.LANG = Spanish
   Z.LANG = Spanish
   Y.NAME = Mary
   Z.NAME = Joe

   This is false, so the inner query `SELECT`s a second row, <Mary, Spanish>:

   X.LANG = Spanish
   Z.LANG = Spanish
   Y.NAME = Mary
   Z.NAME = Mary

   This is true, so the inner query is true.

7. Because the inner query is true, the `NOT EXISTS` of the middle query again converts this true to false and wants to continue, but the middle query is out of rows. This means that the middle query is false.
8. Because the middle query is false, and because we are testing:

```
SELECT DISTINCT name, language
FROM Cap1 x
WHERE NOT EXISTS
   (SELECT 'X' FROM Cap1 y ...
```

   The false from the middle query is translated to true for the outer query and the row <Joe, Spanish> is `SELECT`ed for the result set. Note that Spanish occurs with both Joe and Mary.

9. The second row in the outer query repeats the steps from above for <Mary, Spanish>. The value Spanish will be seen to occur with both Joe and Mary as <Mary, Spanish> is added to the result set.
10. The third row in the outer query begins with <Mary, French>. The middle query SELECTs <Joe, Spanish> and the inner query SELECTs <Joe, Spanish>. The inner query sees:

    X.LANG = French
    Z.LANG = Spanish
    Y.NAME = Joe
    Z.NAME = Mary

    This is false, so the inner query SELECTs a second row, <Mary, Spanish>:

    X.LANG = French
    Z.LANG = Spanish
    Y.NAME = Joe
    Z.NAME = Mary

    This is false, so the inner query SELECTs a third row, <Mary, French>:

    X.LANG = French
    Z.LANG = French
    Y.NAME = Joe
    Z.NAME = Mary

    This is also false. The inner query fails. The inner query evaluates to false, which causes the middle query to see true because of the NOT EXISTS. Because the middle query sees true, it is finished and evaluated to true. Because the middle query evaluates to true, the NOT EXISTS in the outer query changes this to false and X.LANG = French fails. It failed because X.LANG = French did not occur with all values of name.

The "for all" Query as a Relational Division

Consider again the "for all" query we have presented:

```
SELECT name, lang
FROM   Cap1 x
WHERE NOT EXISTS
   (SELECT 'X'
    FROM  Cap1 y
    WHERE NOT EXISTS
      (SELECT 'X'
       FROM  Cap1 z
       WHERE x.lang = z.lang
       AND   y.name = z.name))
ORDER BY lang;
```

The key to determining what a query of this kind means can be found in the innermost query. There you will find a phrase that says, `WHERE x.lang = z. lang....` The x.lang is where the query is testing which *language* occurs *for all* names.

This query is a SQL realization of a relational division exercise. Relational division is a "for all" operation just like those illustrated above. In relational algebra, the query must be set up into a divisor, dividend, and quotient in this pattern:

quotient (B) ← dividend (A, B) divided by divisor (A)

If the question is "What language for *all* names," then the divisor, A, is names, and the quotient, B, is language. It is most prudent to set up SQL like relational algebra with a two-column table (like Cap or Cap1) for the dividend and then treat the divisor and the quotient appropriately. In our query the attribute for language, x.lang, is in the inner query and lang is the quotient. We have also chosen to report the name attribute in the result set.

Example 3

Note that the preceding query is completely different from this one, which asks, "Which students speak all languages?"

```
SELECT DISTINCT name, lang
FROM Cap1 x
WHERE NOT EXISTS
   (SELECT 'X'
    FROM Cap1 y
    WHERE NOT EXISTS
      (SELECT 'X'
       FROM  Cap1 z
       WHERE y.lang = z.lang
       AND   x.name = z.name))
ORDER BY lang;
```

This would produce the following output:

```
NAME          LANG
----------    ----------
MARY          FRENCH
MARY          SPANISH

2 rows selected.
```

Note the phraseology "for all languages," which infers that x.name will occur in the WHERE of the inner query.

Using the table Cap, the following query:

```
SELECT DISTINCT name, lang
FROM Cap x
WHERE NOT EXISTS
   (SELECT 'X'
    FROM Cap y
    WHERE NOT EXISTS
      (SELECT 'X'
       FROM  Cap z
       WHERE y.lang = z.lang
       AND   x.name = z.name))
```

```
ORDER BY lang;
```

Would give:

```
NAME      LANG
--------- -------
LUJACK    CHINESE
RICHARD   CHINESE
LUJACK    FRENCH
RICHARD   FRENCH
LUJACK    GERMAN
RICHARD   GERMAN
LUJACK    SPANISH
RICHARD   SPANISH

8 rows selected.
```

Here note that the inner query contains x.name, which means the question was "Which names occur for *all* languages?" or, put another way, "Which students speak all languages?" The "all" goes with languages for x.name.

Exercises for Chapter 9

As you do the exercises, unless it is stated otherwise, you will be using the tables from our standard Student-Course database. Also, as you do the exercises, it will be a good idea to copy/paste your query as well as your query result into a word processor file.

9-1. List the names of students who have received C's. Do this in three ways:

   a. As a join
   b. As an uncorrelated subquery
   c. As a correlated subquery

   Show each result and account for any differences.

9-2. In the section "Existence Queries and Correlation," we were asked to find the names of students who have taken a computer science class and earned a grade of B. We noted that this could be done in several ways. One query could look like the following:

```
SELECT s.sname
FROM   Student s
WHERE  s.stno IN
   (SELECT gr.student_number
    FROM  Grade_report gr, Section
    WHERE Section.section_id = gr.section_id
           /* join condition Grade_report-Section */
    AND   Section.course_num LIKE 'COSC____'
    AND   gr.grade = 'B');
```

Rewrite this query by putting the finding of the COSC course in a correlated subquery. The query should be: The Student table uncorrelated subquery to the Grade_report table correlated EXISTS to the Section table.

9-3. In the section "SQL Universal and Existential Qualifiers," we illustrated an existence query:

```
SELECT s.sname
FROM   Student s
WHERE EXISTS
   (SELECT 'X'
    FROM  Grade_report gr
    WHERE s.stno = gr.student_number
    AND   gr.grade = 'C');
```

and a NOT EXISTS version:

```
SELECT s.sname
FROM   Student s
WHERE NOT EXISTS
   (SELECT 'X'
    FROM  Grade_report gr
    WHERE s.stno = gr.student_number
    AND   gr.grade = 'C');
```

Show that the EXISTS version is the complement of the NOT EXISTS version by counting the rows in the EXISTS result, the rows in the NOT EXISTS result, and the rows in the Student table. Also, devise a query to test the complement with IN and NOT..IN.

9-4. a. Discover whether all students take courses by counting the students, then count those students whose student numbers are in the Grade_report table and those who are not. Use IN and then NOT..IN and then use EXISTS and NOT EXISTS. How many students take courses and how many students do not?

b. Find out which students have taken courses but have not taken COSC courses. Create a set of student names and courses from the Student, Grade_report, and Section tables (use the prefix COSC to indicate COSC courses). Then use NOT..IN to "subtract" from that set another set of student names where students (who take courses) have taken COSC courses. For this set difference, use NOT..IN.

c. Change NOT..IN to NOT EXISTS (with other appropriate changes) and explain the result. The "other appropriate changes" include adding the correlation and the change of the result attribute in the subquery set.

9-5. There is a table called Plants in our Student-Course database. List the table and then find out what company or companies have plants in all cities. Verify your result manually. *Note:* If you are having trouble finding Plants, think about who owns the table.

9-6. a. Run the following query and print the result:

```
SELECT DISTINCT name, lang
FROM Cap x
WHERE NOT EXISTS
```

```
(SELECT 'X'
 FROM Cap y
 WHERE NOT EXISTS
   (SELECT 'X'
    FROM Cap z
    WHERE X.lang = Z.lang
    AND Y.name = Z.name));
```

Save the query (e.g., `SAVE Forall`) and hand in the result.

b. Recreate the Cap table under your account number (that is, call it some other name such as LANG1). To do this, first create the table and then use the `INSERT` statement with the subselect option (`INSERT INTO LANG1 AS SELECT * FROM Cap;`).

c. Add a new person to your table who speaks only Bengali.

d. Recall your `SELECT` from above (`GET Forall`).

e. Change the table from Cap to LANG1 (for all occurrences use `CHANGE/Cap/LANG1/` repeatedly, assuming that you called your table LANG1).

f. Start the new query (the one you just created with LANG1 in it).

g. How is this result different from the situation when the new person was not in LANG1? Provide an explanation of why the query did what it did.

9-7. The Department_to_major table has a list of four-letter department codes with the department names. In Chapter 7 Exercise 7-7, we created a table called Secretary that should now have data like this:

```
dCode       Name
----------  -----------
ACCT        Sally
COSC        Chris
```

```
ENGL        Maria
null        Brenda
```

In that exercise, we did the following:

a. Create a query that lists the names of departments that have secretaries (use `IN` and the Secretary table in a subquery with the Department_to_major table in the outer query). Save this query as q77a.
b. Create a query that lists the names of departments that do not have secretaries (use `NOT..IN`). Save this query as q77b.
c. Add one more row to the Secretary table that contains <null, 'Brenda'>. (This could be a situation in which we have hired Brenda but have not yet assigned her to a department.)
d. Recall q77a and re-run it.
e. Recall q77b and re-run it.

We remarked in Exercise 7-7 that the `NOT..IN` predicate has problems with nulls. The behavior of `NOT..IN` when nulls exist may surprise you. If nulls may exist in the subquery, then `NOT..IN` should not be used. If you use `NOT..IN` in a subquery, you must ensure that nulls will not occur in the subquery or you must use some other predicate (such as `NOT EXISTS`). Perhaps the best solution is to avoid `NOT..IN`.

Here, we repeat Chapter 7 Exercise 7-7 using `NOT EXISTS`:

a. Re-word query q77a to use `EXISTS`. You will have to correlate the inner and outer queries. Save this query as q99a.
b. Re-word query q77b to use `NOT EXISTS`. You will have to correlate the inner and outer queries. Save this query as q99b. You should *not* have a phrase `IS NOT NULL` in your `NOT EXISTS` query.

c. Re-run q99a with and without <null, Brenda>.

d. Re-run q99b with and without <null, Brenda>.

Note the difference in behavior versus the original question. List the names of those departments that have/do not have secretaries. The point here is to encourage you to use `NOT EXISTS` in a correlated query rather than `NOT..IN`.

References

Earp, R., & Bagui, S. "An In-Depth Look at Oracle's Correlated Subqueries," *Oracle SQL Training and CBO Internals*, edited by Kimberly Floss. Rampant Press, 2004.

Chapter 10

CREATE TABLE and SQLLOADER

In previous chapters we concentrated primarily on retrieving information from an existing database. This chapter revisits the creation and loading of tables and shows some of the constraints that we can place on table definitions. In particular, we will review the "simple" `CREATE TABLE` command and discuss the `NOT NULL` as well as `PRIMARY KEY` constraints. We will also discuss the `UNIQUE` and `CHECK` constraints and referential integrity. Finally, we will examine SQLLOADER and look at a couple of examples of it in use.

The "Simple" CREATE TABLE

You have seen "simple" CREATE TABLE statements in earlier chapters. To refresh your memory, consider the following example:

```
CREATE TABLE Test1
   (name         VARCHAR2(20),
    ssn          CHAR(9),
    dept_number  INTEGER,
    acct_balance NUMBER(9,2));
```

In this example, we create a table called Test1.

- name is a variable character string with a maximum length of 20
- ssn (Social Security number) is a fixed-length string of 9 characters
- dept_number is an integer (which means no decimals are allowed)
- acct_balance is a number column that can have up to nine digits with the last two assumed after the decimal

Some notes:

1. Oracle uses relatively few data types. For numeric values there is NUMBER, INTEGER, SMALLINT, or FLOAT. For numeric values with decimals, you should use NUMBER with values like NUMBER(9,2) or NUMBER(3,1). INTEGER(INT) is the same as NUMBER except that it does not accept decimal digits as an argument. If we define a column to be of type INTEGER and insert a value with decimal parts, the decimal parts will be truncated. SMALLINT or FLOAT can be used like NUMBER; the SMALLINT data type will also truncate decimal places. SMALLINT, INTEGER, and FLOAT data types are ANSI SQL data types. Oracle will automatically convert them to an equivalent NUMBER data type with appropriate scale and

precision. You can also specify DOUBLE PRECISION, REAL, or DECIMAL which are also ANSI standard, and these will convert to NUMBER with appropriate scale and precision.

2. VARCHAR2 is preferred by Oracle and is in line with the correct SQL standard.
3. Beyond choosing types for columns, you may need to make other choices to create an effective database. Some of these "add-ons" are called constraints because they force you to enter good data and hence maintain the integrity of the database. In the following sections, we will explore these constraints, including NOT NULL, PRIMARY KEY, UNIQUE, CHECK, and referential constraints.

When you are finished with the Test1 table, delete (DROP) it with the following statement:

```
SQL> DROP TABLE Test1;
```

Note: We will recreate Test1 and similar tables with other options in the following sections, so if you are doing the exercises as they are presented, delete (DROP) the tables when you are finished with them.

The NOT NULL Constraint

What is a constraint? In database, a *constraint* is a mechanism to insure integrity. So, what is integrity? *Integrity* means that we can believe or trust in the data in the database. Suppose we construct a table that contains customer numbers and names. Further suppose that we want to ensure that all customers have a name associated with that customer number. What we are saying is that no name can be null — every customer number must have a name. Looking at this from another angle, if we give you this database and we say that the name field has a NOT NULL constraint associated with it, then you trust that the database will contain no null values in the name field. Now, if you were to find a null in the name field, then you would say that the database lacked integrity. Therefore, if we enact a NOT NULL constraint, this ensures that we cannot insert nulls in the name column; hence, this is called an "integrity constraint."

Next we illustrate the CREATE TABLE command with a NOT NULL constraint on a field. The NOT NULL constraint will not allow nulls to be inserted in a column. Here the dept_number column has a NOT NULL constraint:

```
CREATE TABLE Test1
   (name         VARCHAR2(20),
    ssn          CHAR(9),
    dept_number  INTEGER NOT NULL,
    acct_balance NUMBER(9,2));
```

This command produces the following output:

```
Table created.
```

We insert some data to show the integrity constraint in action:

```
INSERT INTO Test1 VALUES
   (null,'123456789',101,null);
```

Will give:

```
1 row created.
```

```
INSERT INTO Test1 VALUES
   ('Ricardo','123456789',null,null)
   /
```

Will give:

```
('Ricardo','123456789',null,null)
*
ERROR at line 2:
ORA-01400: cannot insert NULL into ("******"."TEST1"."DEPT_NUMBER")
```

If we type:

```
SQL> SELECT *
FROM Test1;
```

We will see the following:

```
NAME                 SSN       DEPT_NUMBER ACCT_BALANCE
-------------------- --------- ----------- ------------
                     123456789         101
```

The NOT NULL constraint can also be added to a column after the table is created, provided there are no nulls in that column. To add a NOT NULL constraint to an existing table, an ALTER TABLE command is used. For example:

```
ALTER TABLE Test1
MODIFY ssn NOT NULL;
```

This produces the following output:

```
Table altered.
```

This ALTER TABLE command placed the NOT NULL constraint on the column ssn. To view the constraints on Test1, we can DESCribe the table:

```
DESC Test1
```

This would produce:

```
Name                              Null?    Type
--------------------------------- -------- ------------
NAME                              NOT NULL VARCHAR2(20)
SSN                               NOT NULL CHAR(9)
```

```
DEPT_NUMBER                                  NUMBER(38)
ACCT_BALANCE                                 NUMBER(9,2)
```

The ALTER TABLE works as above provided that there are no nulls already present. Had we used the data from above with a null name, this is what we would have gotten:

```
ALTER TABLE Test1
  MODIFY name NOT NULL;
```

Giving:

```
ALTER TABLE Test1
    *
ERROR at line 1:
ORA-02296: cannot enable (******.) - null values found
```

PRIMARY KEY Constraints

When creating a table, a PRIMARY KEY constraint will disallow duplicate values in a column. Internally, the designation of a primary key also creates a primary key index. The designation of a primary key will be necessary for the referential integrity constraints that follow.

A fundamental rule of relational databases is that primary keys cannot be null; the non-null primary key rule is called "the entity integrity constraint." The designation of PRIMARY KEY also automatically puts the NOT NULL constraint in the definition of the column(s).

You may recall that in a previous chapter we said that a relational table is like a mathematical set. The relational table has no order and should have no duplicate rows. The way the "no duplicate rows" integrity constraint is enforced is by using a primary key.

Creating the PRIMARY KEY Constraint

There are several ways to create a primary key: at the column level, the table level, or by using an ALTER TABLE command, as the following examples show.

At the Column Level

The first way to create a primary key is to add CONSTRAINT *key-name* PRIMARY KEY to the column upon creation, like this:

```
CREATE TABLE newStudent
   (ssn  CHAR(9) CONSTRAINT ssn_pk PRIMARY KEY,
    name VARCHAR2(20), etc.)
```

This technique is called adding the constraint at the "column level." ssn_pk is the name of the PRIMARY KEY constraint for ssn. It is conventional to name all constraints (although most people don't bother to name NOT NULL constraints). If we do not give a constraint a name, the system will define one; so, it's much better if we know what the name is (or should be) so that we can manipulate the constraint (using ENABLE, DISABLE, or DROP).

At the Table Level

The second way to create a primary key is at the table level. In this method, the CREATE TABLE looks like this:

```
CREATE TABLE Customer
   (ssn CHAR(9),
    ...
    ...,
    acct_balance NUMBER,
    CONSTRAINT ssn_pk PRIMARY KEY (ssn))
```

Using the ALTER TABLE Command

The third way to create a primary key is at the table level by adding the stipulation of the primary key *post hoc.* This can be done by using the ALTER TABLE command. Here is an example:

```
ALTER TABLE newStudent
ADD CONSTRAINT ssn_pk PRIMARY KEY (SSN);
```

Adding a Concatenated Primary Key

The second and third ways of creating a primary key at the table level are the only ways to designate a concatenated primary key. A statement like this is syntactically incorrect:

```
CREATE TABLE Student_teacher
   (ssn    CHAR(9)      PRIMARY KEY,
    salary NUMBER(9,2) PRIMARY KEY);
```

However, we can add the primary key at the table level in the following way:

```
CREATE TABLE Student_teacher
   (ssn    CHAR(9),
    salary NUMBER(9,2),
    CONSTRAINT ssn_salary_pk PRIMARY KEY (ssn, salary));
```

We can also add our primary key in two separate statements with a CREATE TABLE and then an ALTER TABLE command. First the CREATE TABLE command:

```
CREATE TABLE Student_teacher
   (ssn   CHAR(9),
   salary NUMBER(9,2));
```

Then the ALTER TABLE command can be used to add the PRIMARY KEY constraint:

```
ALTER TABLE Student_teacher
ADD CONSTRAINT ssn_salary_pk PRIMARY KEY (ssn, salary);
```

Note: If the primary key is a single-column primary key, then it can be added at the column level when the table is created. If the primary key is a concatenated key, it must be added at the table level (either at creation or later). If the primary key is added after the table is created, it must be added at the table level, regardless of the number of columns in the key.

Another Example of Adding a Concatenated Primary Key

In our Grade_report table, a grade cannot be determined by either student_number or section_id alone; it requires both columns to uniquely identify a grade. The CREATE TABLE and ALTER TABLE commands for the Grade_report table are shown next. If first we created the Grade_report table like this:

```
CREATE TABLE Grade_report
   (student_number  CHAR(9),
    section_id      CHAR(9),
    grade           CHAR(1));
```

We could then add a PRIMARY KEY constraint using the ALTER TABLE command, as shown below:

```
ALTER TABLE Grade_report ADD CONSTRAINT snum_section_pk
   PRIMARY KEY (student_number, section_id);
```

The UNIQUE Constraint

Like PRIMARY KEY, UNIQUE is another column integrity constraint. UNIQUE will disallow duplicate entries for a column even though the column is not a primary key. The UNIQUE constraint is different from the PRIMARY KEY constraint in three ways:

- Unique keys can exist in addition to (or without) the primary key.
- Unique does *not* necessitate NOT NULL, whereas primary key does.
- There can be more than one unique key, but only one primary key.

As an example of the UNIQUE constraint, suppose that we created a table of names and occupational titles in which everyone was supposed to have a unique title. Suppose further that the table had an employee number as a primary key. The CREATE TABLE might look like this:

```
CREATE TABLE Emp
   (empno  NUMBER(3),
    name   VARCHAR2(20),
    title  VARCHAR2(20)
    CONSTRAINT empno_pk PRIMARY KEY (empno),
    CONSTRAINT title_uk UNIQUE (title));
```

When adding a UNIQUE constraint, an index will be built automatically for those columns included in the unique key.

The CHECK Constraint

In addition to the PRIMARY KEY and the UNIQUE constraints, we can put a CHECK constraint on our column definition in Oracle. A CHECK constraint will disallow a value that is outside the bounds of the CHECK. Consider the following example:

```
CREATE TABLE StudentA
   (ssn   CHAR(9),
    class NUMBER(1)
    CONSTRAINT class_ck CHECK (class BETWEEN 1 AND 4),
    name  VARCHAR(2));
```

Here we could not, for example, successfully execute:

```
INSERT INTO StudentA VALUES ('123456789',5,'Smith');
```

We could, however, enter a null value for class, which technically does not violate the integrity constraint (unless we so specify by making class also NOT NULL).

Note: Technically speaking, NOT NULL is also a form of a CHECK constraint.

Referential Integrity

Relationships in relational databases are logical connections between tables. Relationships are realized via foreign key–primary key constraints. Not only do we make logical connections by defining constraints, but we also enforce referential integrity constraints, or foreign key–primary key constraints. A *referential integrity constraint* is one in which a row in one table cannot exist if a value in that table refers to a value in another table that does not exist. To clarify the idea of referential integrity, suppose we have the following two tables named Department and Employee:

Department

deptno	deptname
1	Accounting
2	Personnel
3	Development

Employee

empno	empname	dept
100	Jones	2
101	Smith	1
102	Adams	1
104	Harris	3

And suppose that deptno is the primary key of the Department table, and dept is the foreign key in the Employee table. If we were trying to perform a join, the deptno field of the Department table would be joined to the dept field of the Employee table. The relationship between the Department and Employee tables is through the primary key of the Department table (deptno), and the foreign key of the Employee table (dept).

To maintain referential integrity, it would be inappropriate to enter a row in the Employee table that did not have a department number defined in the Department table. To try to insert the row:

<105,'Walsh',4>

in the Employee table would be a violation of the integrity of the database because department number 4 does not exist (that is, it has no integrity).

It would likewise be invalid to try to change a value in an existing row (that is, perform an `UPDATE`) to make it equal to a value that did not exist. If, for example, we tried to change

<100,'Jones',2>

to

<100,'Jones',6>

it would be an operation that violated database integrity because there is no department 6.

While deptno in the Department table cannot be null due to the entity integrity constraint (primary keys cannot be null), dept in the Employee table can be null. It is acceptable for dept to be undefined, but it is not acceptable for dept to point to a nonexistent deptno. If the Employee table were created with dept as `NOT NULL`, this is said to constitute a "mandatory relationship." If dept could be null, then the relationship would be an "optional relationship."

Finally, it would be invalid to `DELETE` a row in the Department table that contained a value for department number that was already in the Employee table. For example, if

<2,'Personnel'>

were deleted from the Department table, then the row

<100,'Jones',2>

would then refer to a nonexistent department. It would therefore be a reference or relationship with no integrity.

In each case (`INSERT`, `UPDATE`, and `DELETE`), we say that there needs to be a referential integrity constraint on the dept column in the Employee table referencing deptno in the Department table. When this primary key–foreign key (deptno in the Department table and dept in the Employee table) is defined, we have defined the relationship of the Employee table to the Department table.

In the INSERT and UPDATE cases from earlier, we would expect (correctly) that the usual action of the system would be to deny the action. In the case of the DELETE, there are options we will explore that allow us to either disallow (RESTRICT) the DELETE or CASCADE the delete operation. Some versions of SQL, including later versions of Oracle, also have a DELETE option to set newly unreferenced foreign keys to null.

Note: A foreign key constraint must point to the primary key of another table (or the same table), or it must be null. If a NOT NULL constraint is placed on the foreign key column, it enforces a mandatory relationship between parent and child entities, while allowing null values allows an optional relationship.

Defining the Referential Integrity Constraint

To enable a referential integrity constraint, it is necessary for the column that is being referenced to be first defined as a primary key. In the Employee-Department example above, we have to first create the Department table with a primary key. The creation statement for the Department table (the *referenced* table) could look like this:

```
CREATE TABLE Department
   (deptno   NUMBER(3),
    deptname VARCHAR2(20),
    CONSTRAINT deptno_pk PRIMARY KEY (deptno));
```

The Employee table (the *referencing* table) would then be created using the following statement:

```
CREATE TABLE Employee
   (empno   NUMBER(4) CONSTRAINT empno_pk PRIMARY KEY,
    empname VARCHAR2(20),
```

```
dept    NUMBER(3)
CONSTRAINT dept_fk REFERENCES Department(deptno));
```

The CREATE TABLE Employee... statement defines a column, dept, to be of type NUMBER(3), but the statement goes further in defining dept to be a *foreign* key that references another table, Department. Within the Department table, the referenced column, deptno, must be an already defined primary key.

Also note that the CREATE TABLE Department... statement must be executed and populated first. If we use CREATE TABLE as illustrated for the Employee table before the Department table was created, we would be trying to reference a nonexistent table and we would get an error. Likewise, if department numbers did not exist in the Department table, then data could not be added to the Employee table.

Note: However, if both CREATE TABLE statements were enclosed within a CREATE SCHEMA statement, you can create the Employee table before the Department table.

Adding the Foreign Key after Tables Are Created

As we have seen with other constraints, the foreign key can be added after tables are created. To do so, we must have set up the primary key of the referenced table. The syntax of the ALTER TABLE command would look like this:

```
ALTER TABLE Employee
ADD CONSTRAINT dept_fk
FOREIGN KEY (dept)
REFERENCES Department(deptno);
```

The (optional) name of the constraint is dept_fk. Note that the column names must match exactly, so it would be prudent to do a DESC *tablename* before actually writing the ALTER TABLE command so that you can be sure of the column names.

Using DELETE and the Referential Constraint

There are three possibilities in the DELETE subcategory of foreign key referential constraint enforcement in Oracle: ON DELETE RESTRICT, ON DELETE CASCADE, and ON DELETE SET NULL. ON DELETE RESTRICT will not allow you to delete a referenced key in the referenced table. ON DELETE CASCADE will not only allow the deletion, but it will also delete all dependent references to the table. ON DELETE SET NULL will delete the entry in the primary key table and then set the dependent values to null. Next we explain and illustrate each of these three options in more detail.

ON DELETE RESTRICT

ON DELETE RESTRICT is the default referential integrity delete option and is not explicitly allowed in Oracle. In the previous CREATE TABLE Employee... example, the delete defaults to being a RESTRICT. Because of this constraint, we cannot violate the referential constraint; we will get an error message if we try to do so.

After the two tables are created, it is necessary to populate the Department table first so that when employees are added to the database, valid department numbers can be used. This population ordering can be overcome by using ALTER TABLE..DISABLE and disabling the constraint by name. However, this constraint disabling is not advisable unless a great number of rows must be loaded at once.

ON DELETE CASCADE

The referential integrity delete option of ON DELETE CASCADE is more dangerous than the other options in that it tells the database to delete the rows in the "dependent table" (in this case, the Employee table) that are affected by the deletion of rows in the referenced table (in this case, the Department table). Suppose, for example, we had a deptno = 3 in the Department table. Also suppose we had the Employee table referencing the Department table, and we had employees in department 3. If we deleted department 3 in the Department table, then with ON DELETE CASCADE we would also delete all employees in the Employee table with dept = 3.

When adding the ON DELETE CASCADE option, the option is added after the REFERENCES clause of CREATE TABLE as shown below:

```
CREATE TABLE Employee
   (empno     NUMBER(3) CONSTRAINT empno_pk PRIMARY KEY,
    empname   VARCHAR2(20),
    dept      NUMBER(3)
    REFERENCES department(deptno) ON DELETE CASCADE);
```

Warning: There is no warning in Oracle that you have deleted rows in the dependent table when ON DELETE CASCADE is in effect — the dependent rows just disappear. Thus, you should audit your database before and after issuing a DELETE command that involves referential CASCADEs.

Because DELETE is not an auto-COMMIT statement, you can ROLLBACK from a CASCADEd delete but you must specifically perform the ROLLBACK. If you sign off or do an explicit COMMIT or an implied COMMIT (as with a CREATE TABLE), you will have accepted the CASCADEd delete effect.

ON DELETE SET NULL

In later versions of Oracle, the ON DELETE SET NULL option for referential integrity was added. Remember that a foreign key, if allowed to be null, indicates an optional relationship. If the relationship is mandatory, a foreign key cannot be null. If the relationship is optional, then the ON DELETE SET NULL may be appropriate for the referential constraint. The syntax for the CREATE TABLE is similar to our previous examples except for the REFERENCES clause:

```
CREATE TABLE Employee
  (empno NUMBER(3) CONSTRAINT empno_pk PRIMARY KEY,
   empname VARCHAR2(20),
   dept NUMBER(3) REFERENCES department(deptno) ON DELETE SET NULL);
```

If a department in the Department table is deleted and if there are dependent rows from the Employee table, then the dependent rows will have their values for the dept field set to null.

More on Constraint Names

The table USER_CONSTRAINTS contains the constraint information we have placed on your table(s). The following is the DESC of USER_CONSTRAINTS:

```
Name                     Null?      Type
------------------------ ---------- --------------
OWNER                    NOT NULL   VARCHAR2(30)
CONSTRAINT_NAME          NOT NULL   VARCHAR2(30)
CONSTRAINT_TYPE                     VARCHAR2(1)
TABLE_NAME               NOT NULL   VARCHAR2(30)
SEARCH_CONDITION                    LONG
R_OWNER                             VARCHAR2(30)
R_CONSTRAINT_NAME                   VARCHAR2(30)
DELETE_RULE                         VARCHAR2(9)
STATUS                              VARCHAR2(8)
```

Thus, if we had created a table called Test1 with an unnamed constraint (for example, an unnamed primary key) in it, we could see the constraints with a query like the following:

```
SELECT table_name, constraint_name, constraint_type
FROM USER_CONSTRAINTS;
```

This would produce the following output:

```
TABLE_NAME          CONSTRAINT_NAME         C
----------------    -------------------     -
TEST1               SYS_C001930             P
```

Test1 is the name of the table on which the constraint was created. The SYS_C001930 is a system-allocated constraint name. This is what happens when you do not name the constraint yourself. The P tells us that this is a primary key constraint. The C stands for constraint type. The values for the available constraint types are as follows:

P stands for primary key
U stands for unique key
R stands for foreign key
C stands for a check constraint
V stands for a `WITH CHECK OPTION` for views

In an earlier chapter, we learned how to create a view in Oracle. As we discussed, a view can provide restrictions on what can be viewed (selected). When a view is created, we can specify a `WITH CHECK OPTION`, which would also disallow `INSERT`s or `UPDATE`s to the original table via a view. Here is an example of the `WITH CHECK OPTION` in action:

```
CREATE TABLE Employee (empno number(3), salary number(8,2));
```

Which gives:

```
Table created.
```

```
CREATE VIEW ve AS
SELECT *
FROM employee
WHERE empno = 101 WITH CHECK OPTION;
```

Which gives:

```
View created.
```

Now,

```
SELECT *
FROM ve;
```

Will give:

```
     EMPNO     SALARY
---------- ----------
       101      40000
```

But,

```
INSERT INTO ve VALUES (103,50000);
```

Will give:

```
INSERT INTO ve VALUES (103,50000)
*
ERROR at line 1:
ORA-01402: view WITH CHECK OPTION where-clause violation
```

SQLLOADER

In earlier chapters, we loaded (populated) SQL tables with INSERT INTO...VALUES... or INSERT INTO...SELECT..., but neither of these commands is particularly appropriate for larger tables. For larger tables, Oracle has a utility called SQLLOADER. Oracle uses this utility (also called SQLLDR in some systems) to populate existing tables (in Oracle) from a host file in the host mode (outside of SQLPLUS). There are two important caveats about SQLLOADER:

- The SQL table must be created first within SQLPLUS.
- The SQLLOADER facility is fussy about format and stingy with error elucidation.

Next we will take a look at a couple of examples using the SQLLOADER.

SQLLOADER Example 1

1. The first step would be to create a table in SQL like this:

```
CREATE TABLE Auto
   (vin    NUMBER(3) CONSTRAINT vin_pk PRIMARY KEY,
    make   VARCHAR2(15),
    model  VARCHAR2(15));
```

2. Once the table has been created in SQL, we can then exit to the host system by typing:

```
SQL> HOST
```

3. Then, in the host, we need to use an editor to create a file. So, at the host prompt type (for the vi editor):

```
[bagui@cs-whelk ~]$ vi auto.ctl
```

This will open up the vi editor in your host and you can type the following script:

```
LOAD DATA
INFILE *
   REPLACE
   INTO TABLE Auto
      (vin   POSITION (01:03) INTEGER EXTERNAL,
       make  POSITION (05:11) CHAR(7),
       model POSITION (12:20) CHAR(9))
BEGINDATA
111 Chevy  Lumina
222 Honda  Accord
333 Ford   Mustang
444 Volks  Bug
```

Note: In the host, the file can be named anything you want. We named our file auto.ctl. The file extension convention is .ctl, as in auto.ctl. Other file extensions are allowable, but it is recommended that you keep the default extension.

4. Save your file.
5. Now you are ready to load the data from the host to the SQL files. Suppose your SQL user ID is Studentxx and your password is yyy. You would then execute (from the host) the following command:

   ```
   sqlloader Studentxx/yyy auto.ctl
   ```

   or

   ```
   sqlldr Studentxx/yyy auto.ctl
   ```

   The file auto.ctl contains one SQLLOADER scenario for loading a file. There are other scenarios, but the one we are demonstrating should work well for us. We used a load scenario where data is input from the auto.ctl file, but this could be done with another file instead of the one designated by `INFILE *...BEGINDATA`.

If data were loaded from a file, the first few lines would be:

```
LOAD DATA
INFILE *
REPLACE
INTO TABLE Auto
```

BEGINDATA would not be appropriate (we will look at an example in the following section). The REPLACE option can be used instead of APPEND or INSERT. REPLACE replaces whatever is in the Auto table with the data provided, so be careful if you really mean to "append" rather than "replace." You can also INSERT into an empty table.

The phrase INTO TABLE Auto implies that the Auto table has been defined in SQL. The column names vin, make, and model must exactly match the names used to create the Auto table. The information after POSITION describes the *incoming* data in the *.ctl file. It does not have to match the defined Auto table, but it does have to match the data after BEGINDATA if any data description is entered (or it must match your file if you use the file option — see the following example). The file ends when you run out of data to input.

The SQLLOADER Studentxx/yyy auto.ctl statement can also be done in a variety of ways. Again, the Studentxx is your user ID (the one you currently use to sign onto Oracle). The yyy is your password. So for "rsmith" with a password of "frog," the statement would be sqlloader rsmith/frog auto.ctl.

When you re-enter SQL, and type:

```
SELECT *
FROM Auto;
```

The result will be:

```
       VIN  MAKE           MODEL
----------  -------------  ---------------
       111  Chevy          Lumina
       222  Honda          Accord
       333  Ford           Mustang
       444  Volks          Bug
```

If you get an error, you most likely have done one of the following:

- You named the load file with an extension other than .ctl.
- You did not create the Auto table in SQL first.
- You used a different column name in the .ctl file than in the table you created under SQL.
- You are a column off in describing the data.

If the loader doesn't work, look for a file with a .bad extension in the host operating system to help with error elucidation (in this case, it would be auto.bad).

Another SQLLOADER Example

Often it is easier to load data from a file rather than inline. If loading from a file, the `INFILE *` is replaced with the file name. You may also prefer to delimit the input fields with commas (or another character) and you may want to enclose text in quotes. The following is an alternative example of SQLLOADER:

```
LOAD DATA
INFILE 'site.dat'
REPLACE INTO TABLE site
FIELDS TERMINATED BY ',' OPTIONALLY ENCLOSED BY "'"
(site_id, location)
```

where site.dat looks like this:

```
1, 'PARIS'
2, 'BOSTON'
3, 'LONDON'
4, 'STOCKHOLM'
5, 'OTTAWA'
6, 'WASHINGTON'
7, 'LA'
8, 'TORONTO'
```

Exercises for Chapter 10

As you do the exercises, unless it is stated otherwise, you will be using the tables from our standard Student-Course database. Also, as you do the exercises, it will be a good idea to copy/paste your query as well as your query result into a word processor file.

Note: Unless otherwise directed, name all CONSTRAINTs.

10-1. To test choices of type, create a table with various types like this:

```
CREATE TABLE Test1
   (name         VARCHAR2(20),
    ssn          CHAR(9),
    dept_number  INTEGER,
    acct_balance NUMBER(9,2));
```

Then, INSERT values into the table to see what will and will not be accepted. The following data may or may not be acceptable. You are welcome to try other choices:

```
'xx','yy',2,5
'xx','yyy',2000000000,5
'xx','yyyy',2,1234567.89
```

10-2. To test the errors generated when NOT NULL is used, create a table called Test2 that looks like this:

```
CREATE TABLE Test2
   (a CHAR(2) NOT NULL,
    b CHAR(3));
```

INPUT some data and try to enter a null value for A. Acceptable input data for a null is "null."

10-3. a. Create or recreate if necessary Test1 from Exercise 10-1 that does not specify the primary key. Populate the table with at least one duplicate ssn. Then, try to impose the PRIMARY KEY constraint with an ALTER TABLE command. What happens?

b. Recreate the table Test1 from Exercise 10-1, but this time add a primary key of ssn. If you still have Test1 from Exercise 10-3a, you may be able to delete offending rows and add the PRIMARY KEY constraint. Enter two more rows to your table — one containing a new ssn and one with a duplicate ssn. What happens?

10-4. Create the Department and Employee tables as per the examples in the chapter with all the constraints (primary keys, referential and UNIQUE constraints, and CHECK constraints). You can add the constraints at create time or you can use ALTER TABLE to add the constraints. Populate the Department table first with departments 1, 2, and 3. Then populate the Employee table.

Note: Before doing the next few exercises, it is prudent to create two tables called Deptbak and Empbak, which will contain the data you load. This is because you will be deleting, inserting, dropping, recreating, and so on. You can create the Deptbak and Empbak tables with the data we have been using with a command like this:

```
CREATE TABLE Deptbak
AS SELECT *
FROM Dept;
```

Then, when you have added, deleted, updated, and so on, and you want the original table from the start of this problem, you simply run the commands:

```
DROP TABLE Deptbak;

CREATE TABLE Deptbak
AS SELECT *
FROM Dept;
```

a. Create a violation of insertion integrity by adding an employee to a nonexistent department. What happens?

b. Create an `UPDATE` violation by trying to change:

   (i) An existing employee to a nonexistent department.

   (ii) A referenced department number.

c. Try to `DELETE` a department for which there is an employee. What happens? What happens if you try to `DELETE` a department in which no employee has been assigned?

d. Re-do this entire experiment (starting with Exercise 10-4a), except when you create the Employee table, specify the `DELETE` constraint as `CASCADE`.

10-5. In this chapter we used the phrase `ON DELETE CASCADE` in an example where the Employee table was referenced to (depended on) the Department table.

a. Create the Employee and Department tables as shown in the chapter and use SQLLOADER (or SQLLDR) to populate them with three or four rows each (the Department table first). Show the resulting tables and show the `USER_CONSTRAINTS` table entries.

b. Suppose that there were another table that depended on the Employee table, such as Dependent that contained the columns name and empnum. Create the Dependent table, then add the referential constraint where empnum references the Employee table with `ON DELETE CASCADE` (and note that the Employee table also has an `ON DELETE CASCADE`). You are creating a situation in which the Dependent table references the Employee table, which references the Department table. Will the system let you do this? If so, and if you delete a row from the Department table, will it cascade through the Employee table and on to the Dependent table?

10-6. a. Create a table (your choice) with a primary key, a `UNIQUE` constraint, and a `CHECK` option. `INSERT` data into the table and as you do, enter a *good* row and a *bad* row (the bad row violates a constraint). Demonstrate a violation of each of your constraints, one at a time. Show the successes and the errors as you receive them.

b. Display the dictionary view `USER_CONSTRAINTS` and explain the output.

c. Display the dictionary view `ALL_CONSTRAINTS` and list the constraints that are contained in the Student table that you can see.

d. Display the dictionary view `ALL_CONS_COLUMNS` and list the constraints that are contained in the Student table that you can see.

When you are done with the exercises for this chapter, `DROP` the tables that you created to do these exercises.

Chapter 11

Multiple Commands, START Files, and Reports in SQLPLUS

It is sometimes prudent to create a set of commands that we would like to execute as one. In programming languages, we usually do this by creating a procedure or module. In SQLPLUS, this "command set" can be created in several ways. There are two general paths:

- We can write a script that is run with a START command.
- We can write a procedure or function that is compiled and used appropriately.

In this chapter, we will discuss the first general path — writing a script that is run with a START command. Then we will discuss the DECODE, GREATEST, and LEAST functions, which have many useful purposes with respect to displaying result sets. We will also illustrate the CASE function, which is easier to use than DECODE. In addition, we will look at adding reporting features to a START file (a script), as well as using the ACCEPT and PROMPT commands with these files. We will discuss the second general path, writing a procedure or function, in Chapter 12.

Creating a File (a START Table) and Starting It

We have already seen a simple version of a START file, also called a "script," in Chapter 3. To create and store a script, we begin by defining our editor (here, we use vi):

```
SQL> define_editor=vi
```

We then use the editor to create a file named twocomm as follows:

```
SQL> EDIT twocomm
```

This opens the editor screen and creates a blank text file called twocomm.sql. (The .sql extension is automatically added.) Now suppose we want to display the Student table and then the Prereq table in one script. We type the following in the editor:

```
SELECT * FROM Student
/
SELECT * FROM Prereq
/
```

Note: You can use semicolons or slashes, but in scripts, slashes are more readable.

We then save the file, exit the editor, and return to the SQL prompt. The file is saved as twocomm.sql in the host operating system directory. Now, to START the script, we type:

```
SQL> START twocomm
```

The two commands in the file are then executed one after the other.

An alternative, quicker way to START a script is to use the @ symbol, like this:

```
SQL> @twocomm
```

Note: Although the file name is twocomm.sql, we use START twocomm (without the .sql extension).

A START File (Script) with Editing Features

As a preliminary exercise, suppose we executed a simple SELECT as follows:

```
SELECT stno, sname, class, major
FROM Student;
```

When we do this, we get the default headings and column widths in our output. In this case, we get an output that looks like this:

```
    STNO SNAME                 CLASS MAJO
-------- -------------------- ------ ----
       2 BURNS                     1 ENGL
       3 DAVENPORT                 4 COSC
       8 BROWN                     2 COSC
      10 ADAMS                     1 ENGL
...
```

A first embellishment might be to give the headings meaningful descriptors using column aliases, as follows:

```
SELECT stno "Student #",
sname       "Student Name",
class       "Class",
major       "Major"
FROM Student;
```

This would produce the following output:

```
Student # Student Name          Class  Majo
--------  --------------------  -----  ----
       2  BURNS                     1  ENGL
       3  DAVENPORT                 4  COSC
       8  BROWN                     2  COSC
...
```

This is better, but we still can't see all of the major column's alias, so we would want to format the output a bit more. To better display the major column and its alias, we can execute the following formatting statement to format the data in the column:

```
SQL> COLUMN major FORMAT A5
```

Why A5? The data in the column is four characters long, but the alias, Major, is five characters. We want the format to make the alias display along with data under it, but we don't want it to be too long in case we choose to display other information. When we re-run the SELECT, we get the following output:

```
Student #    Student Name          Class  Major
---------    --------------------  -----  ------
        2    BURNS                     1  ENGL
        3    DAVENPORT                 4  COSC
        8    BROWN                     2  COSC
...
```

A better way to format columns is to use headings. With the alias, we make the column's data fit the alias; however, using a column heading and formatting the data is more flexible and useful. A heading has the syntax:

```
COLUMN column-name HEADING "heading string" FORMAT acceptable-format
```

The *column-name* is the name of the column to be formatted. The *heading string* is whatever one wants the column heading to be. The acceptable format is generally: (a) A*nn*, where A means alphanumeric and *nn* is the length, or (b) a series of 9's for numeric data. Other examples of number formatting will follow.

Having formatted the major column as A5, it will retain this format in the current session until we change it, CLEAR it, or sign off from SQL (terminate the session). The CLEAR command has the syntax:

```
CLEAR column-name
```

Here is an example of using a CLEAR, setting a heading and format, and running a query:

```
SQL> CLEAR columns
```

You will get:

```
columns cleared
```

Now if you type:

```
SQL> COLUMN stno HEADING "Student no." format 999
SQL> SELECT *
FROM Student
WHERE rownum <5;
```

You will get:

```
Student no. SNAME                MAJO CLASS BDATE
---------- -------------------- ---- ----- ---------
         2 Lineas               ENGL     1 15-APR-80
         3 Mary                 COSC     4 16-JUL-78
         8 Brenda               COSC     2 13-AUG-77
        10 Richard              ENGL     1 13-MAY-80
```

First we CLEAR columns of any previous formats. Then notice that we are not giving the column an alias, but rather giving the column a heading and formatting the data in the column. Here, the heading will display as written and the data will appear under it, right justified for numeric data and left justified for alphanumeric data.

For simple reports, you can create formats just as we did above and then run the SELECT, all in one script. The following is an example of a simple report script that formats the columns that will be generated by a SQL SELECT:

```
REM Student Report .. April 17, 2008
REM by A. Mozart
REM
COLUMN stno  HEADING 'Student Number'  FORMAT 999
COLUMN sname HEADING 'Student name'    FORMAT A20
COLUMN class HEADING 'Class code'
COLUMN major HEADING 'Major code'      FORMAT A6
SELECT stno, sname, class, major
FROM  Student
   ORDER BY class
/
CLEAR columns
```

Suppose we call this script first.sql. As before, we run the script with:

```
SQL> @first
```

The `REM` in the script is a non-executable statement. Placing the date and author in a script is just sound programming practice. This script illustrates several headings and both alphanumeric and numeric column formatting. Also, we end the script with a `CLEAR columns` command so that any other command in our session will not be affected by our script. The table below shows some examples of formats and their effects.

Suppose that we had a table like Payroll and a column called amount defined as `NUMBER(6,2)`, and we had the following format and value combinations:

```
SQL> COLUMN amount FORMAT
```

The results are shown in the following table:

Format	Value in Amount	Resulting Output
9999.99	0.00	.00
9999.99	1.00	1.00
9999.99	1000.00	1000.00
9990.00	0.00	0.00
9990.00	1.00	1000.00
9990.00	1000.00	10.00
90.00	5555.55	#######
999,990.00	5555.55	5,555,55
$99,990.00	5555.55	$5,555.55
$99,990.00	7.77	$7.77

The ####### in the output will occur if a value is too large for the format.

Using the DECODE, GREATEST, and LEAST Functions

Let us now turn our attention to three functions: DECODE, GREATEST, and LEAST. These three functions will allow us to enhance our display of results.

DECODE

If we want, we can affect our output by using the DECODE function, which is exclusively an Oracle function. We will illustrate both the DECODE and CASE statements in this section.

Note: Oracle also offers its own version of standard CASE statements.

The very useful DECODE function allows us to insert an if-then-else-if logic into a SELECT command. For example, the following statement fragment:

```
DECODE(class,1,'Freshman',2,'Soph',3,'Junior',4,'Senior','Unknown')
```

means:

if class = 1 then return 'Freshman'
else if class = 2 then return 'Soph'
else if class = 3 then return 'Junior'
else if class = 4 then return 'Senior'
else return 'Unknown'

Thus, if we type:

```
SELECT sname, major,
   DECODE(class,1,'Freshman',2,'Soph',3,'Junior',4,'Senior',
         'Unknown') Class
FROM Student
```

```
WHERE rownum < 5;
```

We get the following output:

```
SNAME                MAJO  CLASS
-------------------- ----  --------
Lineas               ENGL  Freshman
Mary                 COSC  Senior
Brenda               COSC  Soph
Richard              ENGL  Freshman
```

In general, in the `DECODE (a,b,c,d,e,f,...)` function, first a is compared to b and c is returned if true (that is, return c if a = b). Then a is compared to d, and e is returned if true (that is, return e if a = d). Then a is compared to f, and so on.

The comparison of a is to b, d, f and every other second entry in the function. If the number of values in the DECODE is even, the last entry is the "catchall" entry, which is triggered if all other entries compare as not equal. If the number of values in the DECODE is odd, and nothing in the b, d, f, ... stream matches, then a null is returned. Following are some illustrations:

```
DECODE (a,b,c,d,e,f)
```

This means:

If a = b then c
Else if a = d then e
Else f (the "catchall")

```
DECODE (a,b,c,d,e)
```

This means:

If a = b then c
Else if a = d then e
Else null

The problem with the second example (which includes five values, a, b, c, d, e) is that the statement presumes that everyone knows that a null will be returned in such a DECODE *and* that Oracle will continue to have the function work in this way. Both are dangerous programming practices. It would be much better to adopt a convention that one never allows an odd number of arguments in a DECODE, hence always furnishing a "catchall" category. One never knows what data lurks in databases.

While DECODE is common in legacy databases, the CASE statement is probably a clearer and better alternative to DECODE. The equivalent CASE example for the above query would be:

```
SELECT sname, major,
CASE  WHEN class = 1 THEN 'Freshman'
      WHEN class = 2 THEN 'Soph'
      WHEN class = 3 THEN 'Junior'
      WHEN class = 4 THEN 'Senior'
      ELSE 'Undefined'
   END CASE
FROM  Student
WHERE rownum < 5
```

Giving:

```
SNAME                MAJO  CASE
-------------------- ----  ---------
Lineas               ENGL  Freshman
Mary                 COSC  Senior
Brenda               COSC  Soph
Richard              ENGL  Freshman
```

With CASE, each case is clearly defined and the structure ends with an END statement. The spacing within the code is arbitrary, but lining up the cases within the statement is recommended.

GREATEST and LEAST

DECODE only compares for equal, so if we want to "decode" ranges such as:

> if a < 1000 then x
> else if a >= 1000 and a < 2000 then y
> else if a >= 2000 and a < 3000 then z
> else w

we must use the GREATEST or LEAST functions. The LEAST function works like this:

```
LEAST(attribute1, attribute2, attribute3, ...)
```

This returns the LEAST value of all attributes in the list. The previous IF statement coded as a DECODE with LEAST could then be done as follows:

```
DECODE (a, LEAST(a,999), x,
           LEAST(a,1999), y,
           LEAST(a,2999), z, w)
```

In this example, if the value of a were 45, then LEAST(a,999) would return the lower of the two numbers (45), hence returning x from the DECODE function. If the value of a were 1300, then LEAST(a,999) would return 999, which is not equal to a. The DECODE would then look at the value of LEAST (a,1999) and return a as 1300 (the least of 1300 and 1999). It would then compare this 1300 to the first a and find them equal. The overall DECODE would then return y.

Here is the above encoded into SQL:

```
SQL> CREATE TABLE Testrange (num NUMBER(4));
SQL> INSERT INTO Testrange VALUES(123);
SQL> INSERT INTO Testrange VALUES(1234);
SQL> INSERT INTO Testrange VALUES(2500);
SQL> INSERT INTO Testrange VALUES(4444);
```

Now,

```
SQL> SELECT *
FROM Testrange;
```

Would give:

```
       NUM
----------
       123
      1234
      2500
      4444
```

And,

```
SELECT num, DECODE (num, LEAST(num,999), 'x',
   LEAST(num,1999), 'y',
   LEAST(num,2999),'z','w') result
FROM Testrange;
```

Would give:

```
       NUM  R
----------  -
       123  x
      1234  y
      2500  z
      4444  w
```

Note: The logic of DECODE can be inverted to use GREATEST. We will look at this in more detail in the Exercises section at the end of the chapter.

The easiest way to play with the DECODE function is to use the dual table. You can write statements like this:

```
SELECT DECODE (10,11,2,3) FROM dual;
```

This returns a 3 because 10 is not equal to 11.

You can then continue to experiment with statements like:

```
SELECT DECODE (10,10,2,3) FROM dual;
SELECT DECODE (10,11,2,3,10,4) FROM dual;
SELECT DECODE (10,11,2) FROM dual;
SELECT GREATEST (1,3) FROM dual;
```

The above example using the Testrange table encoded as a CASE statement looks like this:

```
SELECT num, case
   WHEN num < 1000 THEN 'x'
   WHEN num < 1999 THEN 'y'
   WHEN num < 2999 THEN 'z'
   ELSE 'w'
   END CASE
   FROM Testrange;
```

Giving:

```
       NUM C
---------- -
       123 x
      1234 y
      2500 z
      4444 w
```

Adding Reporting Features to a START File

We can embellish reports by using the following editing commands in the START file:

- **SET FEEDBACK OFF**: This command prevents messages like "7 rows selected" from appearing.
- **SET ECHO ON**: This command lists each of the commands in a script when the script is run with a START command.

- **SET HEADSEP**: The punctuation that follows the heading separator SET HEADSEP indicates where we want to break a page title or a column heading that runs longer than one line.
- **TTITLE**: This command puts the title at the top of each page. The title should be enclosed in single quotation marks. If a heading separator (as explained above) is used in the TTITLE, it produces a split title (that is, it runs on more than one line).
- **BTITLE**: This command works just like TTITLE except that the title is placed at the bottom of the page.
- **SET LINESIZE**: This command determines the numbers of characters that will appear on a single line.
- **SET PAGESIZE**: This command sets the total number of lines that will be allowed on each page.
- **SET NEWPAGE**: This command prints blank lines before the top line (date, page number) of each page in the report. For example, if we type:

```
SET PAGESIZE 65
SET NEWPAGE 8
```

  This will leave eight blank lines at the top of the page, and each page will have 57 lines. If we increase the size of NEWPAGE, fewer rows of information will be on each page.

- **BREAK ON**: This feature causes the report to be segmented by some attribute and gives a page break when the value of the attribute changes. We must BREAK on the attribute we are ORDERing by or the BREAK makes no sense. We can have only one BREAK in a script. If we use two BREAKs, the second supercedes the first.
- **COMPUTE**: This feature allows us to include SUM, COUNT, AVERAGE, and other attributes with the BREAK. For

example, for a BREAK ON class, we might add a COMPUTE that looks like this:

```
COMPUTE COUNT OF stno ON class;
```

This would cause the COUNT of student numbers to be displayed when a page break occurs on an encounter of "class". Note that we can only use COMPUTE with BREAK.

Some examples if these commands are shown in the next section.

A New and Improved Script

A new and improved script follows. The following report script is in three parts:

- The format part
- The query part
- The reset part

The parts are identified by comments, as shown below:

```
REM ... first SET your parameters

SET FEEDBACK OFF
SET ECHO OFF
SET VERIFY OFF

REM report1.sql - a sample report file        -- format part
REM by R. Earp

SET HEADSEP #
TTITLE 'Student report#List of students'
BTITLE 'From the student file for COP 4710'

COLUMN stno  HEADING 'Student Number'   FORMAT 999
/* 999 is used for numeric formatting */
```

```
COLUMN sname HEADING 'Student Name' FORMAT A20
/* A is used for character formatting */
COLUMN cla HEADING 'Class'      FORMAT A10  /* refs column alias */
COLUMN major HEADING 'Major'    FORMAT A6

BREAK ON cla SKIP 2 -
  ON REPORT                          /* again, refs column alias */

COMPUTE COUNT OF stno ON cla
COMPUTE COUNT OF stno ON report

SET LINESIZE 60
SET PAGESIZE 20
/* intentionally SET small to illustrate what happens */
SET NEWPAGE 0
SPOOL out.x
/* This writes all the output to a file called out.x */

SELECT stno, sname, major            -- query part
DECODE(class,1,'Freshman',2,'Soph',3,'Junior',4,'Senior','Unknown')
/* see below */
  cla,       /* note the column alias, cla, for the DECODE ... */
FROM Student
ORDER BY class
/

REM  query is over .. now reSET all the parameters you SET above
-- reset part

SPOOL OFF
TTITLE OFF
BTITLE OFF

CLEAR COLUMNS
CLEAR BREAKS
CLEAR COMPUTES

SET FEEDBACK ON
SET VERIFY ON
SET ECHO ON
```

At the end of the report file it is a good idea to clean up. Therefore, we use SPOOL OFF, TTITLE OFF, and BTITLE OFF, then we CLEAR the columns, and CLEAR all breaks. It is also a good idea to SET the FEEDBACK, VERIFY, and ECHO back on. These "clean up" commands will reset the system for this session.

The output of the preceding report script will look like this:

```
Fri Nov 21                                        page    1

                      Student report
                     List of students
Student Number  Student Name          Class       Major
--------------  --------------------  ----------  -----
             2  BURNS                 Freshman    ENGL
            10  ADAMS                             ENGL
            17  SMITH                             COSC
            34  FRAZIER                           POLY
           121  HENNESSY                          COSC
           128  ALLENBEE                          COSC
           144  COLBY                             POLY
           132  APPLEGATE                         POLY
           127  ZEBRIN                            ENGL
            70  EARP                              POLY
            14  HARPER                            COSC
--------------  **********
            11  count

From the student file for COP 4710

Fri Nov 21                                        page    2
                      Student report
                     List of students
Student Number  Student Name          Class       Major
--------------  --------------------  --------    -----
             8  BROWN                 Soph        COSC
            19  MCDONALD                          POLY
           147  OSWALD                            ENGL
           130  SMITHSON                          COSC
```

```
          129   WEATHERBY                          ENGL
          126   ZORRO                              POLY
          125   HORNADY                            MATH
           15   WILLIAMSON                         MATH
-------------   **********
            8   count

From the student file for COP 4710

Fri Nov 21                                      page    3
                      Student report
                     List of students
Student Number  Student Name            Class        Major
-------------   ---------------------   ---------    -----
           49   HUGHES                  Junior       ENGL
          122   SIMPSON, B                           ENGL
          131   LOSMITH                              ENGL
          148   MITTERAND                            ACCT
          143   BURNSIDE                             ENGL
           62   HAIRE                                MATH
-------------   **********
            6   count

            3   DAVENPORT               Senior       COSC
           20   JONES                                ACCT

From the student file for COP 4710

Fri Nov 21                                      page    4
                      Student report
                     List of students
Student Number  Student Name            Class        Major
-------------   ---------------------   ---------    -----
          145   SWENSON                 Senior       ACCT
           31   HANEY                                COSC
          146   FRANCIS                              ACCT
          142   MILLER                               COSC
           24   TAYLOR                               ACCT
          123   SMYTHE                               POLY
           13   SIMPSON, A                           MATH
```

```
--------------    **********
             9    count

--------------
            34

From the student file for COP 4710
```

As before, if the script was named report1.sql, it would be invoked like this:

```
SQL> START report1
```

or

```
SQL> @report1
```

Note: We can have only one BREAK in a script, but we can have several ON's. In the following example, the "cla" is a column alias, but it could be a column name. ON REPORT gives us a BREAK on the whole report:

```
BREAK ON cla SKIP 2 -
  ON REPORT    /* again, references column alias */
```

COMPUTEs work in conjunction with BREAKs. We may have a COMPUTE for each ON.. in the break. For example:

```
COMPUTE COUNT OF stno ON cla
COMPUTE COUNT OF stno ON report
```

We used an internal alias for the class column, cla. The following was the result of the COMPUTE COUNT OF stno ON cla:

```
--------------    **********
            11    count
```

We can sum, average, and find the minimum, maximum, standard deviation, and variance if we wish with combinations of computes on breaks.

Note: It is a very good idea to reset all the COLUMNs, BREAKs, SETs, and so on after we finish the report because these values persist until we sign off, unless we reset the parameters.

Using START Files with ACCEPT and PROMPT

We can create a script that contains the commands ACCEPT and PROMPT. In SQLPLUS, ACCEPT is used to accept input from the keyboard, and PROMPT allows us to display a message or prompt on the screen. For example, we may want to create a script that allows the user to SELECT * FROM *whatever*, where *whatever* is any table name that will be typed in by the user. Such a script could look like this (bold added for emphasis):

```
REM     This file uses ACCEPT and PROMPT
SET ECHO OFF
SET VERIFY OFF
ACCEPT tab1 PROMPT ' Enter table name ---> '
SELECT * FROM &tab1;
SET VERIFY ON
SET ECHO ON
```

Once you run this script, the PROMPT command will display the following on the screen (the cursor will be blinking where you are supposed to type in a table name):

```
Enter table name ---> _
```

You can now type any table name. Let's type Student, as shown below:

```
Enter table name ---> Student
```

Student will now be assigned to tab1 (this is done by the use of the ACCEPT command).

So, the next statement in our script,

```
SELECT * FROM &tabl;
```

will now be executed as `SELECT * FROM Student`, displaying the Student table.

If we did not use the `SET ECHO OFF` in our script, then the whole script (in our case the line `SELECT * FROM &tabl;`) will again be displayed on our screen before the execution of the output. To see the full effect of `SET ECHO ON` or `OFF`, try the script again with `SET ECHO ON` at top of the script instead of `SET ECHO OFF` and see what happens.

Using START Files with Positional Input

We can also use positional input with &1, &2, and so on with `START` files. Let's take a look at the data dictionary as an example:

```
SQL> DESC Dict
```

Gives us:

```
Name                              Null?     Type
--------------------------------  --------  --------------------
TABLE_NAME                                  VARCHAR2(30)
COMMENTS                                    VARCHAR2(4000)
```

A useful primitive version of a script for looking up information in the data dictionary would be the following (name the script look.sql):

```
COLUMN tname  FORMAT A20
COLUMN notes  FORMAT A50
SELECT table_name tname, SUBSTR (comments,1,50) notes
FROM Dict
WHERE UPPER (comments) LIKE UPPER ('%&1%')
/
```

Now when you need to look for something in the dictionary, such as all entries having something to do with privileges, we can execute the following command:

```
SQL> @LOOK
```

We will then get the prompt:

```
Enter value for 1:
```

Now to view all comments in the Dict table that have something to do with privileges, type **priv** as shown below:

```
Enter value for 1: priv
```

You will now get:

```
old   3: WHERE UPPER (comments) LIKE UPPER ('%&1%')
new   3: WHERE UPPER (comments) LIKE UPPER ('%priv%')

TNAME                NOTES
------------------   --------------------------------------------------
ALL_POLICIES         All policies for objects if the user has system pr
ALL_REPGROUP_PRIVILE Information about users who are registered for OBJ
GES

DBA_PRIV_AUDIT_OPTS  Describes current system privileges being audited
DBA_REPGROUP_PRIVILE Information about users who are registered for OBJ
GES

DBA_RSRC_CONSUMER_GR Switch privileges for consumer groups
OUP_PRIVS

DBA_RSRC_MANAGER_SYS system privileges for the resource manager
TEM_PRIVS

DBA_SYS_PRIVS        System privileges granted to users and roles
USER_REPGROUP_PRIVIL Information about users who are registered for OBJ
EGES
```

```
USER_RSRC_CONSUMER_G Switch privileges for consumer groups for the user
ROUP_PRIVS
TNAME                NOTES
-------------------- --------------------------------------------------
USER_RSRC_MANAGER_SY System privileges for the resource manager for the
STEM_PRIVS

USER_SYNONYMS        The user's private synonyms
USER_SYS_PRIVS       System privileges granted to current user
ROLE_SYS_PRIVS       System privileges granted to roles
ROLE_TAB_PRIVS       Table privileges granted to roles
SESSION_PRIVS        Privileges which the user currently has set
GV$ENABLEDPRIVS      Synonym for GV_$ENABLEDPRIVS
V$ENABLEDPRIVS       Synonym for V_$ENABLEDPRIVS

17 rows selected.
```

This output gives all tables that have "PRIV" (uppercased) anywhere in the comments column (also uppercased) of the dictionary table (Dict).

Note the first two lines at the beginning of this output:

```
old   3: WHERE UPPER (comments) LIKE UPPER ('%&1%')
new   3: WHERE UPPER (comments) LIKE UPPER ('%priv%')
```

You see these two lines because look.sql did not include a `SET ECHO OFF` command at the beginning of the script.

Exercises for Chapter 11

As you do the exercises, unless it is stated otherwise, you will be using the tables from our standard Student-Course database. Also, as you do the exercises, it will be a good idea to copy/paste your query as well as your query result into a word processor file.

11-1. Create two START files, one called seton and the other called setoff, where setoff contains the SET..OFF commands and seton contains the SET..ON commands.

setoff:

```
SET VERIFY OFF
SET ECHO OFF
```

seton:

```
SET VERIFY OFF
SET ECHO ON
```

Then, create a simple script (called simple.sql) that calls these two scripts:

```
REM Simple script - name is simple.sql
START SEToff
ACCEPT whatever PROMPT 'Enter table name -- '
SELECT * FROM &whatever;
START seton
```

When you get this working, try these variations:

a. What happens if you do not use setoff in the latter script?
b. What happens if you do not use seton?
c. Try other SET commands (set them OFF, then back ON) such as ECHO, VERIFY, and FEEDBACK.

(To see current values of SET parameters, use SHOW, as in SHOW ECHO. To see all SET parameters, you can use SHOW ALL, but you will probably have to spool the output and look at it offline because the listing produced by SHOW ALL is too long for one page.)

11-2. Create a script to display the section number, instructor name, and course title for the Student table. Use variants of the following commands in your script:

The SET commands WRAP, PAGESIZE, LINESIZE, and NEWPAGE. Use TTITLE, BTITLE, column formatting, COMPUTE (used only with BREAK), and number pages with SQL.PNO. Use COL, TAB, LEFT, RIGHT, CENTER, SKIP, SKIP<n>, and FORMAT.

11-3. Write a script that inputs several positional parameters so that you could say something like:

```
START showstudent student 3
```

which would translate into SELECT * FROM Student WHERE class = 3.

11-4. Create a table with the following data in it:

```
Employee        Salary
------------    -------------
Alice           35000
Bob             33000
Sam             55500
Sally           45000
Brenda          88900
```

Then display the table like this:

```
Employee        Salary
------------    --------------
Alice           Low
Bob             Low
Sam             Medium
Sally           Medium
Brenda          High
```

Use the cutoff of 45,000 to differentiate between Low and Medium and 66,000 between Medium and High. Do not use LEAST in the query — use GREATEST.

Chapter 12

Beginning PL/SQL: Anonymous Blocks, Procedures, Functions, and Packages

PL/SQL stands for Procedural Language SQL (also called Programming Language SQL, although the consensus seems to be "Procedural"). PL/SQL is a limited programming language that allows us to go beyond the relational database/SQL bounds by performing procedural (row-level) commands. In this chapter we offer examples of PL/SQL code, which for a programmer is easily extendable. This chapter is not meant to be an exhaustive PL/SQL primer.

SQL is a set-at-a-time operation — you SELECT from a table, CREATE a table, and so on. You can address sets of rows with SQL, but you do not ordinarily address individual rows. With PL/SQL, you can treat a table as a flat file that is accessed one row at a time.

In Chapter 11, "Multiple Commands, START Files, and Reports in SQLPLUS," we introduced scripts, which allow SQLPLUS to execute multiple commands. This chapter presumes that you understand the concept of START files (a.k.a. scripts or blocks).

PL/SQL is used in anonymous blocks, procedures, functions, and packages, all of which are compiled at run time. If the action taken by a procedure or function has to be done repeatedly, the compiled procedure (or function or package) can be distributed to users, providing some security and information hiding.

Note: Triggers also use PL/SQL. We will cover them in the next chapter.

In a nutshell, *procedures* are used for performing a set of SQL commands or operations, *functions* are operations that return a value, and *packages* are umbrellas under which we can group related procedures and functions into one unit. Procedures cannot be used in SQL SELECT statements, whereas functions can be. *An anonymous block* is a set of PL/SQL statements that may be used to perform a series of tasks using the PL/SQL language.

This chapter is not meant to be a complete primer on PL/SQL; rather, it is intended to introduce the concepts and usefulness of PL/SQL and hopefully will provoke further inquiry.

Anonymous Blocks

Anonymous blocks are a good way to begin learning PL/SQL, but they have limited applicability.

PL/SQL blocks are divided into three parts: a declaration section, a program body, and an exceptions section. PL/SQL blocks are often depicted as follows:

```
DECLARE
... declarations
BEGIN
... procedural statements
EXCEPTIONS
... exception commands
END
```

Consider the following example:

```
DECLARE
   amount NUMBER := 0;
BEGIN
   SELECT COUNT(*)
   INTO amount
   FROM Student
   WHERE Student.class = 3;
   DBMS_OUTPUT.PUT_LINE(amount);
END;
```

Only the executable section (the `BEGIN..END`) of the block is required. The `DECLARE` and `EXCEPTIONS` parts are optional; this block has no `EXCEPTIONS` section.

You can create an anonymous block called block1.sql, store it in the host directory, and then execute it from within SQLPLUS with a command such as `@block1`. For example, if the preceding query were saved as "whatever.sql", it would be executed with `@whatever` from the SQL prompt. To see output from a procedure or anonymous block, you can use the dbms_output package, as illustrated in the preceding example. To see the output, you must execute the following command in SQLPLUS before executing the PL/SQL block:

```
SET SERVEROUTPUT ON
```

If you then run @whatever script, you would get the following output:

```
7

PL/SQL procedure successfully completed.
```

Using a block like the one illustrated above is unusual but serves to introduce the look and feel of PL/SQL. The dbms_output package, as used above, is cumbersome and limited in its display. PL/SQL is not usually used to display values as in the preceding example, but rather it is used with procedures and functions to perform tasks.

Elementary Procedures with Sequence Structures

Procedures in SQLPLUS use PL/SQL commands — not SQL commands *per se*. A procedure may also use some Data Manipulation Language (DML) commands (such as `INSERT INTO..VALUES`), but not Data Definition Language (DDL) commands (such as `CREATE TABLE`). In this section we will study some examples of procedures to see how they look and act.

Suppose we wanted to create a procedure to insert values into a table. We could, of course, use a single `INSERT INTO..VALUES` command. We will look at a variant on this theme. A simplified syntax for procedure definition is the following:

```
CREATE OR REPLACE PROCEDURE procedure-name
(parameter list—with types, without lengths)
AS
   Local variable declarations (if any);
         /* if no locals, then no semicolon */
BEGIN
   Statement;
   Statement;
   Statement;
END procedure-name;
```

As with anonymous blocks, there is a `DECLARE` section and a procedure body. (There could be an `EXCEPTIONS` section, but this procedure syntax does not illustrate that feature.) The `CREATE PROCEDURE` includes a procedure name followed by a parameter list (if any), which is where data is passed into the procedure when it is executed. The word `AS` is a necessary syntax marker; however, `IS` can also be used. If there are local variables, they are declared after the `AS` and followed by a semicolon. If there are no local variables, then there is no semicolon. Comments follow the /* ... */ format as in SQL (and C and other languages), and the body of the procedure is surrounded by a `BEGIN..END` pair. `END` can be labeled (and should be). Statements in the body of the procedure involve local variables, `INSERT`, `DELETE`, or `UPDATE` SQL statements, `SELECT` SQL statements with an `INTO` option, or other special-purpose PL/SQL statements (like `EXIT`) as well as assignment and program-control statements.

A Simple Example of a Procedure

Let's look at a step-by-step example of creating a simple PL/SQL procedure. Suppose we have a table named Worker with attributes name, state, salary, and dept and suppose the table contains:

```
NAME                 ST     SALARY      DEPT
-------------------- -- --------- ---------
Sikha                FL      55000         2
Richard              AL      53000         1
George               TX      45000         2
```

The steps to create a simple PL/SQL procedure to insert a value into the Worker table are shown next.

Note: It is a good idea to make a backup of Worker before you begin inserting (or updating or deleting) data in it. You may copy the Worker table to another table, for example Worker1, by typing CREATE TABLE Worker1 AS SELECT * FROM Worker.

---

1. Create a script file called testp1.sql:

```
CREATE OR REPLACE PROCEDURE testp1
AS
BEGIN
   /* Worker(name, state, salary, dept) */
   INSERT INTO Worker VALUES ('Pradeep', 'TX', 25000, 2);
END testp1;
```

2. Save the script file.
3. Compile the procedure by typing:

```
SQL> @testp1
```

You should get:

```
Procedure created.
```

If errors occur, they can be displayed with the following statement:

```
SQL> SHOW ERRORS
```

4. After fixing errors, if there are any, to execute the procedure type:

```
SQL> EXECUTE testp1
```

You will get:

```
PL/SQL procedure successfully completed.
```

Now if you type:

```
SELECT *
FROM Worker;
```

You will get:

```
NAME                 ST    SALARY      DEPT
-------------------- -- --------- ---------
Sikha                FL     55000         2
Richard              AL     53000         1
George               TX     45000         2
Pradeep              TX     25000         2

4 rows selected.
```

Reusing a Procedure

Procedures are stored in compiled form in Oracle. Once the procedure has been compiled (as shown in step 3 of the previous section), the next time you want to use the procedure you do not have to recompile it — you can just re-execute it (as shown in step 4 above).

The example we showed does not use a parameter list or local variables and is, of course, an essentially useless procedure that always inserts the same value into the table. In subsequent sections we will show how to make this procedure much more useful with parameter lists.

Deleting a Procedure

A procedure will be saved unless you specifically delete it.

Note: If you delete the script file called testp1.sql at this point, you will not have deleted the procedure because the procedure is compiled and saved as testp1. The file testp1.sql was just the script file that was used to create and compile the procedure.

To delete the procedure, type:

```
DROP PROCEDURE testp1;
```

You will get:

```
Procedure dropped.
```

Adding a Parameter List to a Procedure

In order to make our testp1 procedure more useful, we need to pass a parameter list to the procedure so that we would be able to insert different values for name, state, salary, and dept into the Worker table. The following is an example of how a parameter list can be passed into a procedure to insert values:

```
CREATE OR REPLACE PROCEDURE testp1
  (namein   VARCHAR2,
   statein  CHAR,
   salaryin NUMBER,
   deptin   NUMBER)
AS
BEGIN
  INSERT INTO Worker VALUES (namein, statein, salaryin, deptin);
END testp1;
```

Save and compile this procedure (as shown in steps 1 through 3 of the previous section). Since this procedure has a parameter list, the procedure will have to be executed differently from the previous example, however. Here you will have to include the parameter list when executing the procedure. To execute this procedure you would type:

```
SQL> EXECUTE testp1 ('Pradeep','AL',18000,3);
```

You could also use an anonymous PL/SQL block to execute testp1, as follows:

```
BEGIN
testp1 ('Pradeep','AL',18000,3);
END;
/
```

Using the EXECUTE command is far more common.

Performing More than One Action in a Procedure

So far, in the above examples, we were only performing one action with the procedure — inserting values into a table called Worker. Procedures can perform more than one action. The following is a procedure that inserts a worker's name, state, and department number but lets the procedure compute the salary to pay the worker. In the procedure, the first three values are passed into the procedure through the parameter list (name, state, and department number). The salary for the new worker will be the average salary of all workers minus 20%. In this procedure we use two local variables for the calculation. Here is the procedure:

```
CREATE OR REPLACE PROCEDURE testp2
  (namein  VARCHAR2,
   statein CHAR,
   deptin  NUMBER)
AS
   avg_salary NUMBER;            /* local variable */
   new_salary NUMBER DEFAULT  0;
```

```
            /* zero is the default salary */
BEGIN
   SELECT AVG(salary) INTO avg_salary FROM Worker;
   new_salary := avg_salary - (avg_salary*0.20);
           /* assignment is by the := operator */
   INSERT INTO Worker VALUES (namein, statein, new_salary, deptin);
END testp2;
```

To execute this procedure, you type:

```
SQL> EXECUTE testp2 ('Pradeep','OH',3);
```

If you then type:

```
SELECT *
FROM Worker;
```

You will get:

```
NAME                 ST     SALARY      DEPT
-------------------- -- --------- ---------
Sikha                FL     55000         2
Richard              AL     53000         1
George               TX     45000         2
Pradeep              OH     40800         3

4 rows selected.
```

This example also illustrates the use of the PL/SQL SELECT..INTO statement. The usual action is to SELECT..INTO a local variable that is then evaluated or used. The control structure of the sequence is the SELECT is executed first, followed by the assignment statement for local variable new_salary, and the INSERT. Because there are no statement sequence altering structures (selection and/or iteration), the statements are executed in a sequential manner from BEGIN to END.

Procedures with Selection and Iteration Control Structures

As with other procedural programming languages, PL/SQL has both selection and iteration in addition to the sequence control structure. Selection is performed by using an IF statement and iteration is performed by a LOOP.

Example of a Procedure with Selection

An example of a selection control structure could be one in which the salary of the worker in the previous example was computed based on the average salary of the department; if the department has no existing workers, then a default salary of $15,000 could be used. This version of the salary procedure would look like this:

```
CREATE OR REPLACE PROCEDURE testp3
  (namein  VARCHAR2,
   statein CHAR,
   deptin  NUMBER)
AS
   avg_salary NUMBER := 0;
               /* default may also be entered this way  */
   new_salary NUMBER;
BEGIN
   SELECT AVG(e.salary) INTO avg_salary
      FROM Worker e WHERE e.dept = deptin;
               /* note the table alias */
   IF avg_salary > 0 THEN
      new_salary := avg_salary - (avg_salary*0.20);
   ELSE
       new_salary := 15000;
   END IF;
INSERT INTO Worker VALUES (namein, statein, new_salary, deptin);
END testp3;
```

The IF..THEN structure always has an END IF. The statement can be written without an ELSE, if necessary. The case structure IF..THEN..ELSE..IF is available, as are nested IF statements.

Example of a Procedure with Iteration

The LOOP control structure in Oracle's PL/SQL is usually used with a *cursor*, which is a local pointer that is declared in a procedure. A cursor allows the programmer to access each row of a table, one row at a time. Suppose in this example we wanted to assign our newest worker a salary that was equal to the average salary of everybody in the company except Tom. We will count the employees (less Tom) and we will sum the salaries (again, less Tom). The procedure could look like this:

```
CREATE OR REPLACE PROCEDURE testp4
  (namein       VARCHAR2,
   statein      CHAR,
   deptin       NUMBER)
AS
   avg_salary  NUMBER := 0;
   sumsal      NUMBER;
   total_emps_less_Tom NUMBER;
   new_salary  NUMBER;
   CURSOR sal_cursor IS
      SELECT salary, name FROM Worker;
BEGIN
   sumsal := 0;
            /* initialize the sum of salaries to zero */
   total_emps_less_Tom := 0;
           /* initialize counter */
   FOR row IN sal_cursor LOOP
      IF row.name 'Tom' THEN
         sumsal := sumsal + row.salary;
         total_emps_less_Tom := total_emps_less_Tom + 1;
      END IF;
           /* an example of IF with no ELSE clause */
```

```
  END LOOP;
  new_salary := sumsal/total_emps_less_Tom;
  INSERT INTO Worker VALUES (namein, statein, new_salary, deptin);
END testp4;
```

Some points about this example:

- The declaration of the CURSOR is done in a similar way to other variables. The syntax assigns a name for the CURSOR (here, it is sal_cursor).
- The LOOP (or iteration) illustrated is a FOR loop, which is common in PL/SQL. There are other loops, but the FOR loop hides some loop complexity and is used in a similar way to the FOR (or DO) in C, C++, and other languages.
- IF requires END IF; LOOP requires END LOOP.
- The variable, row, is not declared! This construction is clearly a language oddity, but that is the way the FOR loop is handled. "row" is the local pointer that points to the CURSOR, which points to values in a cursor table.
- The PL/SQL keyword EXIT can be used in a loop and has the same meaning as in C — that is, it branches to the statement just beyond the loop. EXIT is usually used in an "IF as in IF such-and-such THEN EXIT"; EXIT can also be used in a statement that says, "EXIT WHEN such-and-such," EXITs can only be used inside LOOPs.

In PL/SQL, there are LOOP loops (also called *simple loops*), which almost always use an EXIT command. These are similar to the example in testp4 without the FOR or the cursor. There is also a WHILE LOOP structure.

Functions

A *function* is similar in form to a procedure, but has a different use — it returns a value. This value may be used virtually anywhere, such as in command-line SQL statements, in PL/SQL code, and in procedures and other functions.

The syntax for a function is similar to that of a procedure except that it has a RETURN data type declared and a RETURN statement as follows:

```
CREATE OR REPLACE FUNCTION function-name
(parameter list—with types, without lengths)
RETURN datatype
IS  /* or AS * /  local variable definitions
BEGIN
   Statement;
   Statement;
   Statement;
   Return (local variable);
END function-name;
```

Example of a Function

We can create a function called howmany, which counts the number of rows in the Student table, as follows:

```
CREATE OR REPLACE FUNCTION howmany
RETURN NUMBER
IS num NUMBER;
BEGIN
   SELECT COUNT(*) INTO num FROM Student;
   RETURN (num);
END howmany;
```

As before, we might save this script as howmany.sql. Once we run the script:

```
SQL> @howmany
```

We will get:

```
Function created.
```

Note that a function is different from a procedure in that a function must return a value, whereas procedures cannot return values. You can test the function with the Dual table as shown below:

```
SQL> SELECT howmany FROM Dual;
```

This will give:

```
HOWMANY
---------
48
```

One use of a function is in a PL/SQL procedure or package in which a repetitive operation is performed. As with procedures, functions can have parameter lists.

Deleting a Function

Just like a procedure, the compiled version of the function will be saved unless you delete it. To delete a function, type:

```
DROP FUNCTION function_name;
```

Packages

A *package* is a group of procedures and functions that are combined into one entity. For example, if a programmer wanted to create a personnel package, the package might contain procedures that add workers, delete workers, or update some information for some worker(s). The package might also contain useful functions that would enhance the ability to write procedures. Some information hiding can be accomplished using packages because all of the procedures and functions contained in the package do not have to be visible. Packages are modeled after the Ada language with a specification and body part. The specification has to be created before you can add information to the body.

Creating a Package

Suppose we create part of the aforementioned personnel package. We will create a procedure to add a worker and a function called average_sal that computes the average salary of workers, which will be used in the procedure.

1. The first step would be to create a function as follows:

```
CREATE OR REPLACE FUNCTION average_sal
RETURN  NUMBER
IS num  NUMBER;
     /* IS or AS—either one works */
BEGIN
   SELECT AVG(salary) INTO num FROM Worker;
   RETURN (num);
END average_sal;
```

   Save and compile the function, and make sure that the function works before proceeding.

2. We then incorporate the function into a procedure like testp3 as follows:

```
CREATE OR REPLACE PROCEDURE testp3
  (namein   VARCHAR2,
   statein  CHAR,
   deptin   NUMBER)
AS
BEGIN
```

```
    INSERT INTO Worker VALUES (namein, statein, average_sal,
                               deptin);
END testp3;
```

Note: If you get errors, you may have to use the Worker1 table instead of the Worker table.

Once again, save and compile the procedure (and make sure there are no errors in the procedure) before proceeding.

3. After testing the function and the procedure, both the function, average_sal, and the procedure, testp3, could be put into a package. Suppose we call the package pack1. Packages are created in a two-step process: first the package specification, and then the package body.

   a. A package specification contains the names of the visible procedures to be invoked along with their parameter lists. The specification can be created as follows:

```
CREATE OR REPLACE PACKAGE pack1
AS
   PROCEDURE testp3 (namein VARCHAR2, statein CHAR,
                     deptin NUMBER);
END pack1;
```

   Create this package specification as a script file so that you can save and compile it before proceeding.

   The specification contains the procedure and/or function headings that will be the interfaces for the package. Note that we did not include the function average_sal in the specification. average_sal will be kept inside the package (that is, it will be hidden), used by the procedure in the package (testp3), and unknown and inaccessible outside of the package.

b. Next, the package body has to be created. The format for the package body containing the function average_sal and the procedure testp3 is created as follows:

```
CREATE OR REPLACE PACKAGE BODY pack1
AS
   PROCEDURE testp3 ... details from above
      -- heading must match specification
END pack1;
```

The CREATE OR REPLACE parts of the procedure have been stripped off and the debugged version is put inside the package.

This is shown in the script that you would type, as shown below:

```
CREATE OR REPLACE PACKAGE BODY pack1
AS
PROCEDURE testp3
   (namein VARCHAR2,  statein CHAR,  deptin NUMBER)
AS
BEGIN
   INSERT INTO Worker VALUES (namein, statein, avg_sal,
                              deptin);
END testp3;
END pack1;
```

c. Save this script file as pack_body. Compile the script by typing:

```
@pack_body
```

You will get:

```
Package body created.
```

4. Now that we have created the package, we are ready to use it. Invocation of the procedure is a little different from before because the package name now must be used to qualify the procedure as follows:

```
SQL> EXECUTE pack1.testp3 ('Pradeep','OH',3);
```

Now if you type:

```
SELECT *
FROM Worker;
```

You will get:

```
NAME                 ST    SALARY      DEPT
-------------------- -- --------- ---------
Sikha                FL     55000         2
Richard              AL     53000         1
George               TX     45000         2
Pradeep              OH     51000         3

4 rows selected.
```

Note the newly inserted last line in the above output.

Another Approach to Creating This Package

If we were not concerned about information hiding, we could also create the package specification as:

```
CREATE OR REPLACE PACKAGE pack1
AS
   FUNCTION average_sal RETURN NUMBER;
   PROCEDURE testp3 (namein VARCHAR2, statein CHAR, deptin NUMBER);
END pack1;
```

Note: A RETURN *type* must be included for functions.

In this case, the package body would be compiled as:

```
CREATE OR REPLACE PACKAGE BODY pack1
AS
   FUNCTION average_sal ... details from above
   PROCEDURE testp3 ... details from above
        -- heading must match specification
END pack1;
```

Although this method would work, it would not achieve any information hiding.

Deleting a Package

A package will be saved until it is deleted. To delete a package, use:

```
DROP PACKAGE package_name;
```

Defining a PL/SQL INDEX BY Table

A PL/SQL INDEX BY table is like an array of values, indexed by a number. A useful extension of the previous procedures might be to examine, update, and transfer (INSERT) values in tables, much like we would with a programming language in an array. In the current version of PL/SQL, the array, the PL/SQL table, may contain only one attribute from an existing table. Suppose we have a table named AA, and that table has a column named "x". The following is an example of a simple PL/SQL procedure containing a local table:

```
CREATE OR REPLACE PROCEDURE testtab2 AS
   TYPE inttab IS TABLE OF AA.x%type
                   /* x%type says use whatever AA.x's type is */
      INDEX BY binary_integer;   /* You first define a type */
   itt  inttab;
```

```
               /* Then, you declare a variable of type, inttab */
   n    binary_integer;
BEGIN
   n := 0;
   FOR AArec IN (SELECT * FROM AA) LOOP
      n := n + 1;
      itt(n) := AArec.x;
   END LOOP;
END testtab2;
```

In this example, we have the `CREATE OR REPLACE PROCEDURE` statement as before except that this one does not have parameters. We define a type for our table and then declare a variable of that type as follows:

```
TYPE inttab ...      (defines the type)
int inttab;          (declares a variable of that type)
```

The PL/SQL table will contain values from the AA table's column named "x":

```
type inttab IS TABLE OF AA.x%type
```

The %type means that the internal PL/SQL table will have the same type as whatever the column x type is. The phrase `INDEX BY binary_integer` is required in all `INDEX BY` table definitions. In this procedure, we have also declared a variable called "n", which is of type binary_integer, to be used as an index for our table. After the declare, we have the procedure block (`BEGIN..END`) that defines what the procedure will do. In the example, we select one value into our internal table, itt, from the table AA column x, for every row in AA as follows:

```
BEGIN
   n := 0;
   FOR AArec IN (SELECT * FROM AA) LOOP
      /* note the inline cursor */
      /* AArec assumed as record type of AA
      it is not necessary to declare AArec
```

```
        This is a multi-line comment .... */
        n := n + 1;
        itt(n) := AArec.x;
    END LOOP;
END;
```

As before, the FOR LOOP has the syntax:

```
FOR condition LOOP
...
END LOOP;
```

The *condition* in this case is that there are rows in AA; hence, the way this is written is "while there are rows in AA, do this loop...." Rather than have a BEGIN..END block for the loop or define a cursor, the syntax of PL/SQL may use FOR..LOOP and END LOOP. Within the loop, values from AA column "x" are assigned to itt (our table variable) with this statement:

```
itt(n) := AArec.x
```

If we were to make a mistake in compiling the procedure, the errors can be viewed with SHOW ERRORS. As before, to execute testtab2 we type:

```
SQL> EXECUTE testtab2;
```

Using a PL/SQL Table

Here is a more complex example of a PL/SQL procedure using an INDEX BY table:

```
CREATE OR REPLACE PROCEDURE testtab3 AS
    TYPE inttab IS TABLE OF AA.x%type
        INDEX BY binary_integer;
    itt   inttab;
    n     binary_integer;
    sumx  binary_integer;
    nmax  binary_integer;
```

```
BEGIN
   n := 0; sumx := 0; nmax := 0;
   FOR AArec IN (SELECT * FROM AA) LOOP
           /* AArec assumed as record type of AA */
      n := n + 1;
      itt(n) := AArec.x;
      sumx := sumx + AArec.x;
   IF nmax < itt(n) THEN nmax := itt(n); END IF;
   END LOOP;
   INSERT INTO Result VALUES (n);
   INSERT INTO Result VALUES (nmax);
   INSERT INTO Result VALUES (sumx);
END testtab3;
```

Note: Note that the table called Result has not been created for you. You will have to create it (with one attribute of type NUMBER). You must to do this before you can compile the above script without errors.

This is almost the same example as before, but in this one, we have created two more variables, sumx and nmax. The variable sumx will sum the x values from AA and nmax will tell us what the max value of x was. The `FOR` loop goes through the table creating our PL/SQL table, itt. In addition, the values of AA.x are tested and summed.

Selection is performed in the procedure with the following `IF` statement:

```
IF nmax < itt(n) THEN nmax := itt(n); END IF;
```

This uses the syntax `IF` *`condition`*, *`action`*, `END IF`.

We mentioned before that this process does not have an output procedure such as write, display, or print. To make the procedure do something, we inserted the values for n, nmax, and sumx into a table called Result, which contains only one attribute, a number. We also inserted our results into three rows. We could have used the dbms_output package as we did earlier in the exercise.

Arrays and PL/SQL tables are used for situations in which you must go through the data and collect some information, and then go through the data again for some reason; for example, to determine the median value of a set of values.

Exercises for Chapter 12

For submission purposes, as you do the exercises, it will be a good idea to copy/paste your query (or script) as well as your result into a word processor file.

12-1. Create a test table called Emp2 that is similar to the Worker table in the chapter. (Use `CREATE TABLE Emp2 AS SELECT * FROM WORKER`.) Write a procedure called add_any_emp to insert values into your Emp2 table. If a salary is greater than 20000, then set that salary to 20000. Insert at least three rows into your table with your procedure. In furnishing values for the procedure, include a salary greater than 20000 for one of those rows. Display your populated table.

12-2. Write a procedure called new_emp to access the Emp2 table created in Exercise 12-1. In your procedure, insert a new worker named Madison from WI into the department that has the highest department number. Make the salary equal to the average of all other workers less 15%. Pass the name and state through the parameter list. Save the script you use to create this procedure.

12-3. Write a function called avg_emp that returns the average salary of workers in your Emp2 table. Do not include the lowest salary in the average. Display the average salary using the Dual table.

12-4. Retrieve the script used to create the procedure in Exercise 12-2 and use the function created in Exercise 12-3 in the procedure to add another worker to the table. The parameter list should include name, state, and department number.

12-5. Create a package called Salary that contains both the procedure new_emp and the function avg_emp, but rename the function avg_emp1 for the package. Test new_emp by adding another worker to the Emp2 table and show the table after your addition. Do not put the function in the package specification (you are hiding the function in the package). Try to use avg_emp1 in a `SELECT` (`SELECT Salary.evg_emp1 FROM Dual`). Does it work?

Chapter 13

Introduction to Triggers

This chapter introduces and discusses triggers. We will look at what triggers are, how to create triggers, the difference between row-level and statement-level triggers, enabling and disabling triggers, and deleting triggers. We will also look at triggers in which one table affects another trigger, and we will discuss the issue of mutating tables.

What Is a Trigger?

A *trigger* is a PL/SQL procedure that executes when a table-modifying event (such as an insert, delete, or update) occurs. Triggers may be fired for each *row* affected (`FOR ANY ROW[WHEN] ...`), or may be fired at the *statement* level for an insert, update, or delete operation. Triggers may be fired before or after an event (a triggering action) takes place. There are therefore 12 categories of triggers (`BEFORE` and `AFTER` at row level and statement level for `UPDATE`, `INSERT`, and `DELETE`):

`BEFORE UPDATE` row-level
`BEFORE UPDATE` statement-level
`AFTER UPDATE` row-level
`AFTER UPDATE` statement-level
`BEFORE INSERT` row-level
`BEFORE INSERT` statement-level
`AFTER INSERT` row-level
`AFTER INSERT` statement-level
`BEFORE DELETE` row-level
`BEFORE DELETE` statement-level
`AFTER DELETE` row-level
`AFTER DELETE` statement-level

Note: Oracle also has `INSTEAD OF` triggers. But since this is an introductory chapter on triggers, we will not cover `INSTEAD OF` triggers.

There are four general uses for triggers:

- To enforce complex business rules (rules that are more complex than may be ordinarily available with a SQL constraint or command).
- To compute a value that is based on other values or circumstances.
- To "audit" an insert, delete, or update action. (Oracle provides auditing features, but triggers are a less formal approach to auditing.)
- To implement security measures.

A few well-placed database triggers, written correctly, can reduce application coding and testing times. On the other hand, poorly written database triggers can destroy an application.

A Simple Trigger Example

Triggers are written in special syntax using PL/SQL. Suppose you want to create a trigger such that when you UPDATE the Student table, if there is a change in the major attribute to a Masters in Computer Science (MACS), then you want to set the value of the class attribute to 6. This can be done by creating a BEFORE UPDATE trigger at the row level. We use BEFORE UPDATE because we want to set a value before updating the row. We use the row level because we may want to update more than one row in the table, but we only want to work on one row at a time. We will show a stepwise approach to creating such a trigger and then we will discuss how it works.

Note: Before you begin creating triggers, you need to be aware that there may be privilege problems. You usually cannot set triggers on tables you did not create. There are a couple of ways that you can deal with this problem:

- You may be able to work with the database administrator (DBA), who may be able to grant you permission to set triggers on others' tables. You also need to check that you have the privilege to create a trigger in your account. (To determine whether you have this privilege, check the data dictionary view SESSION_PRIVS.)
- Create a table in your own account identical to the table provided. For example, create a table called Student1 identical to Student by typing: CREATE TABLE Student1 AS SELECT * FROM Student;.

1. First, we will define the editor:

```
SQL> define_editor=vi
```

2. To create the script file that will contain the CREATE OR REPLACE TRIGGER command, type:

```
SQL> EDIT Trigger1
```

3. This will open your editor. Type the following CREATE OR REPLACE TRIGGER script in your editor:

```
CREATE OR REPLACE TRIGGER upd_student_trig
BEFORE UPDATE
OF major
ON Student
FOR EACH ROW
BEGIN
   IF :new.major = 'MACS' THEN :new.class := 6;
   END IF;
END upd_student_trig;
```

4. Save the script file.
5. To compile the trigger, type:

```
SQL> @Trigger1
```

   This will give:

```
Trigger created
```

   You have now created a trigger called upd_student_trig.

   If you get errors upon compiling the CREATE OR REPLACE TRIGGER script, you will need to use the SHOW ERRORS command as shown below:

```
SHOW ERRORS trigger trigger_name;
```

   which in our case would be:

```
SHOW ERRORS trigger upd_student_trig;
```

Note: We did not include any comments in our CREATE OR REPLACE TRIGGER script, but it is generally a good idea to include some comments in your scripts. Comments can include the trigger's function, who you are, and the date you created the trigger.

6. Now suppose we want to issue an UPDATE command on the Student table that will change the major to MACS for student number 2. If we type the following UPDATE command:

```
UPDATE Student
SET major = 'MACS'
WHERE stno = 2;
```

We will get:

```
1 row updated.
```

7. If we now want to see all the students whose major is MACS, we would type:

```
SELECT *
FROM Student
WHERE major = 'MACS';
```

And we would get:

```
     STNO SNAME                MAJO     CLASS BDATE
--------- -------------------- ---- --------- ---------
        2 Lineas               MACS         6 15-APR-80
```

How the Trigger Worked

Our UPDATE command was updating the major to MACS where the student number (stno) was equal to 2. Our trigger, upd_student_trig, was a BEFORE UPDATE trigger, so if the new major was MACS, it changed the class of the student to 6 before the update (as shown in the output above).

This is a BEFORE UPDATE trigger on the Student table for updates involving the major attribute. BEFORE is necessary because you want to compute the value of class before the row is UPDATED. The FOR EACH ROW part of the trigger is necessary when each row in the table might change and should be checked. In this case, although we are updating only one row, the FOR EACH ROW is necessary to use "new" and "old" references (which are not allowed in statement-level triggers). The phrase :new.major refers to the new value for major per the UPDATE command that caused the trigger to fire. If you tried to run this example without FOR EACH ROW, you would get an error message that told you that this could not be a statement-level trigger (and hence you must add FOR EACH ROW).

Row-Level Triggers versus Statement-Level Triggers

Row-level triggers execute once for each row affected by a command. Statement-level triggers execute once for each table-modifying command. For example, if a DELETE command deleted 100 rows from a table, a statement-level trigger would execute only once. Statement-level triggers can be used to enforce undeclared security measures on transactions performed on a table.

Enabling and Disabling Triggers

Triggers are automatically enabled after they are created and compiled (unless they are specifically disabled). Triggers only affect commands of specific types (table-modifying commands), and only while the triggers are enabled. Any transaction created prior to a trigger's creation will not be affected by the trigger; triggers do not retroactively check the database. To enable or disable a trigger after it has been created, the ALTER TRIGGER command is used, as shown below:

```
ALTER TRIGGER trigger_name ENABLE;
```

or

```
ALTER TRIGGER trigger_name DISABLE;
```

Enabling All Triggers for a Table

If a table in Oracle has multiple triggers, the command to enable all triggers for a particular table is:

```
ALTER TABLE table_name ENABLE ALL TRIGGERS;
```

Deleting Triggers

Triggers have to be dropped in order to be deleted. Triggers may be dropped by using the `DROP TRIGGER` command:

```
DROP TRIGGER trigger_name;
```

Values in the Trigger

When referring to values in the table being modified in row-level triggers, the general format is `:new.`*`attribute`* or `:old.`*`attribute`* (with the colons and periods).

In the PL/SQL body, you indicate the attributes in the tables by typing a colon, the word "new" or "old", a period (.), and then the attribute name. For example:

```
:old.stno
```

or

```
:new.class
```

This means the old value of stno or the new value of class, respectively.

Our first trigger example (called upd_student_trig) illustrated a trigger that affected the values being placed into the table. The trigger would be fired with any UPDATE statement involving the major attribute in the Student table, and action would ensue when the new value of the major attribute was set to MACS. Nothing happened if the major was not UPDATEd to MACS. The action in the upd_student_trig example was that you would set the new value of major to MACS, but you would also set the new value of class to 6 (essentially automatically).

Using WHEN

Another way to handle the syntax of the PL/SQL body is to use the WHEN statement. The previous trigger with a WHEN added would look like this:

```
CREATE OR REPLACE TRIGGER upd_student_trig
BEFORE UPDATE
OF major
ON Student
FOR EACH ROW
WHEN (new.major = 'MACS')
BEGIN
   :new.class := 6;
END upd_student_trig;
```

Syntactically, the FOR EACH ROW is necessary if you use the WHEN clause. Also, there is a slight change in the syntax of the "new/old" modifier in the WHEN clause in that it does not use a colon before "new" or "old."

Performance Issues Using WHEN

There are some performance issues regarding triggers in general and the WHEN clause in particular. If triggers are used, there may be multiple triggers on the same table — one for DELETE (BEFORE and/or AFTER), one for UPDATE (with a separate trigger for each different attribute), more BEFORE and AFTER triggers, statement- and row-level triggers, and so on. Generally, the more triggers you put into play, the poorer the performance (but the trade-off may be improved integrity).

The WHEN clause of a trigger is executed first. If the trigger is meant to fire only under a restricted set of circumstances, and particularly if the trigger contains a lot of PL/SQL code, it is prudent to use a WHEN to bypass the PL/SQL if it is not necessary to execute it. In this sense, the WHEN is not strictly an alternative to using IF logic inside of the PL/SQL block — it is generally better to use WHEN.

A Trigger Where One Table Affects Another Trigger

We will now consider several examples of triggers to illustrate their utility. What follows is an example that illustrates a trigger that checks one table and updates another table based on what happens in the first table. Suppose you create a table called Atrig with attributes stno, name, and class, and load data into the Atrig table such that if we type:

```
SQL> SELECT *
FROM Atrig;
```

we get:

```
 STNO  NAME        CLASS
------ ----------- ------
  100  Adam             1
  200  Bob              2
  300  Chuck            3
  400  Dave             1
  500  Ed               2
  600  Frank            4
  700  George           2
  777  Extra            3
```

Also suppose further that you create another "mirror" table called Btrig with attributes st, name, and cl (these are the same attribute types as the Atrig table, but with different attribute names) as follows:

```
SQL> CREATE TABLE Btrig (st, name, cl)
AS SELECT *
FROM Atrig;
```

You will get:

```
8 rows created.
```

Now, if you type:

```
SELECT *
FROM Btrig;
```

You will get:

```
   ST  NAME       CL
------ --------- --
  100  Adam       1
  200  Bob        2
  300  Chuck      3
  400  Dave       1
  500  Ed         2
  600  Frank      4
  700  George     2
  777  Extra      3
```

Now, suppose you want a signal if class is changed to 5. If putting a value of 5 in class is wrong, you would, of course, have created the Atrig table with a CHECK constraint option on class to prevent anyone from changing class to a value of 5. However, let's suppose that changing class to a value of 5 is allowable, but that you want to get an indication if that change were made.

For your signal, you can perform an after-the-fact check on class by using a trigger that fires when the UPDATE to the class attribute makes its value 5. A BEFORE trigger is used to fix a value for a table BEFORE an INSERT or UPDATE takes place. You can also compute a value for INSERTing into (or UPDATing) the table with a BEFORE trigger. An AFTER trigger may be used to "audit" what happened when you INSERTed, UPDATEd, or DELETEd. In this case, the action of notifying you of a change in the value of the class attribute to 5 is more of an auditing action, so we choose to use an AFTER trigger.

To illustrate this trigger, create a script file called Trig1 that contains the CREATE TRIGGER command. This trigger is a row-level, AFTER UPDATE trigger. It looks like this:

```
CREATE OR REPLACE TRIGGER Trig1
AFTER UPDATE
OF class
ON Atrig
FOR EACH ROW
WHEN (new.class=5)
BEGIN
   UPDATE Btrig SET Btrig.name = UPPER (Btrig.name)
   WHERE Btrig.st = :old.stno;
END;
```

When this script is run, it creates a trigger whose name is Trig1. Now, after an UPDATE on table Atrig is performed, the trigger fires if an UPDATE occurs on the class attribute. As the trigger body indicates, the trigger fires after the

UPDATing takes place and each row in the table is checked. If the value of class in the Atrig table is set to 5, the Btrig table gets updated and the name value in Btrig is capitalized for that row. For example, if we type:

```
SQL> UPDATE Atrig
SET class = 5
WHERE stno = 200;
```

You will get:

```
1 row updated.
```

Now if you type:

```
SQL> SELECT *
FROM Btrig;
```

You will get:

```
    ST  NAME            CL
------  ----------   -----
   100  Adam             1
   200  BOB              2
   300  Chuck            3
   400  Dave             1
   500  Ed               2
   600  Frank            4
   700  George           2
   777  Extra            3
```

Here the Btrig table mirrors the Atrig table with the old values for the student number, the old values for the class, and a slightly modified value for name (now shown in capital letters). This is the result of the trigger being fired after the UPDATE was issued.

Mutating Tables

A mutating trigger is a trigger that attempts to modify the same table that initiated the trigger in the first place. You cannot issue an INSERT, DELETE, or UDPATE command from a trigger on the table that is causing the trigger to fire. In the first example (where we created the trigger called upd_student_trig), we simply used "old" and "new" to modify an attribute because the table in question was identified by the trigger. In the second case (where we created the trigger called Trig1), we modified the Btrig table when the problem that caused the trigger was in the Atrig table. When you are modifying the Atrig table, it is said to be "mutating."

In the script below, we create an example of a mutating trigger, Trig. This is an AFTER UPDATE trigger, so after an update has been made to the Atrig table, the trigger (Trig) is supposed to fire by inserting values into the Atrig table. Type the following in a script file called mtrig:

```
CREATE OR REPLACE TRIGGER Trig
AFTER UPDATE
OF class
ON Atrig
FOR EACH ROW
WHEN (new.class=5)
BEGIN
   INSERT INTO Atrig VALUES (555,'XXX',1);
END;
```

Then save mtrig. Now compile the trigger by typing:

```
SQL> @mtrig
```

This will give:

```
Trigger created.
```

The CREATE TRIGGER compiles without errors and everything looks okay. But look at what happens when we execute the following UPDATE command:

```
UPDATE Atrig
SET class = 5
WHERE stno = 700;
```

The command returns this error message:

```
*
ERROR at line 1:
table ATRIG is mutating, trigger/function may not see it
at "TRIG", line 2
error during execution of trigger 'TRIG'
```

This error occurs because you cannot issue an INSERT command on the Atrig table when you have already issued another table-modifying command on the same table. The workaround to this could be to use a temporary table, or to create a view that is identical to the target table, and then update the view.

Exercises for Chapter 13

For these exercises you must create two tables — Atrig and Btrig — in your account. Populate the Atrig table with data as shown in the chapter. Do **not** populate the Btrig table. Then, write the following triggers. Be sure to save the CREATE OR REPLACE trigger code.

13-1. A row-level trigger that fires AFTER a row is DELETEd from the Atrig table — the trigger will INSERT the values that were in Atrig into Btrig. DELETE two rows from the Atrig table. Show the values in the Atrig and Btrig tables. (This is like an automatic backup.)

13-2. A row-level trigger that fires BEFORE UPDATE OR INSERT of a value for class = 6 that puts the old and the new values for the Atrig rows affected into the Btrig table. Show the values in the Atrig and Btrig tables. (This is like an audit table.)

13-3. In this exercise, you will create a statement-level trigger called st_trigger on the Atrig table using the same syntax as shown at the beginning of this chapter. However, you will leave out the line that says FOR EACH ROW and the WHEN.

a. First, create a table called Resultx that has one attribute called out1 of type VARCHAR2(50).

b. Next create your trigger, st_trigger. Have the trigger INSERT a value into the Resultx table whenever an INSERT, DELETE, or UPDATE operation is performed on the Atrig table. Have the value of out1 be a message like "Atrig was modified" concatenated with the system date. (The system date is obtainable with the keyword SYSDATE and concatenation is accomplished with the concatenation operator.) Therefore, the INSERT command might look like this:

```
INSERT INTO Resultx
VALUES ('Atrig was modified'||SYSDATE);
```

c. To trigger more than one action on a table, include the list of actions in the declaration part of the trigger. You would write it like this:

```
CREATE OR REPLACE trigger_name
AFTER UPDATE OR DELETE
ON ...
```

13-4. You can embellish the trigger to perform different operations if you UPDATE, DELETE, and/or INSERT in the same trigger. You can test the action that caused the trigger with an IF statement like this:

```
IF DELETING THEN
operation
END IF;
```

Revise exercise 13-3 to include all three operations (INSERT, DELETE, and UPDATE) in the message sent to the Resultx table so that the Resultx table will say that "Atrig was updated," "Atrig had a delete," or "something was inserted in Atrig," each concatenated with the system date.

13-5. Display a copy of USER_TRIGGERS from the data dictionary.

13-6. Create a partial copy of the Student table in your account like this:

```
CREATE TABLE Student1
AS
SELECT *
FROM Student
WHERE rownum < 5;
```

You can change the attribute names if you wish.

a. Write a BEFORE trigger for your Student1 table that changes the value of the class attribute to 7 if you change the major attribute to MAAC (Masters in Accounting). Do this in two ways: First, using an IF statement, and then using the WHEN.

b. Write an INSERT trigger for the Student1 table such that if you enter any new student, the major is recorded as UNKN (unknown). Test the trigger by using an INSERT like this:

```
INSERT INTO Student1
VALUES ('Juan',777666555,null,null);
```

Also test it using an INSERT like this:

```
INSERT INTO Student1
```

```
VALUES ('Juan',777666555,1,'COSC');
```

Does putting an actual major into the `INSERT` cause the major to be COSC or does the trigger prevail and make the major UNKN?

c. Recreate your trigger (or copy to a new trigger name) and use an `AFTER` trigger. (You only need to do it one way, with the `IF` or with the `WHEN` — it is your choice which you use.) What happens? Try this with a statement-level trigger and note the result. As you will see, it may not work. Why?

References

Earp, R. and Bagui, S. "Oracle's Triggers," *Oracle Internals: Tips, Tricks and Techniques for DBAs*, edited by Donald K. Burleson, Auerbach Publications, Taylor and Francis Group, 2004.

Chapter 14

SQL and XML

EXtensible Markup Language (XML), a meta-markup language developed by the World Wide Web Consortium (W3C) in 1996, is widely used as a standard means of exchanging data over the Internet. XML uses HTML-like tags and attributes to structure data. Tags in XML allow developers to define data items and their relationships. Most relational database products, like Oracle, are now XML enabled. XML-enabled databases provide the capability to transfer data between XML documents and the data structures of a database.

This chapter is intended to be an introductory chapter of examples using SQL and XML. Our goal in this chapter is to introduce XML and illustrate a connection between XML and Oracle databases. The XML extension in Oracle provides SQL operations and functions for processing XML data.

We start the chapter with a brief look at XML. Then we present some SQL/XML functions, show how to create tables using an `XMLType` data type, insert values into those tables, and introduce `XPATH` queries.

Overview of XML

Below is an example of an XML document containing information about employees.

```
<employees>
   <employee>
      <lastname>Smith</lastname>
      <firstname>John</firstname>
      <title>Software Engineer</title>
      <salary>50000</salary>
   </employee>
   <employee>
      <lastname>Saha</lastname>
      <firstname>Piyali</firstname>
      <title>Engineer</title>
      <salary>60000</salary>
   </employee>

   <!-- Additional employees not shown for brevity -- >
   ...
</employees>
```

The first tag is named employees, indicating that information for multiple employees will appear within the opening and closing tags. The angle brackets surround the opening tag name, as in <employees>, and the closing (or ending) tag is created with the inclusion of a forward slash, as in </employees>. In XML, tags are user-defined. The next opening tag is employee. The tags lastname, firstname, title, and salary document the information that is recorded for each employee. Also, the lastname, firstname, title, and salary are enclosed within an outer employee tag "wrapper":

```
<employee> ... </employee>
```

XML requires every opening tag to have a closing tag. Also, tags are case sensitive and may not have whitespace.

In this example, employees is said to be the root element, employee is the child of employees, and lastname, firstname, title, and salary are children of employee. XML has a hierarchical structure, and references to XML documents often use a parent-child terminology. Only two employee instances are shown in this example.

Oracle and XML

A relational model like Oracle is particularly suited for data that is highly structured and well known. XML data, on the other hand, is not very well structured and has more of an evolving and flexible structure.

Oracle provides extensive support for XML data storage and processing; it also has an `XMLType` that is used to store and query XML data. An *XML fragment* is an XML instance that does not have a single top-level (root) element. You can store XML documents and fragments natively as columns of the new `XMLType` data type. You can also create columns, parameters, and variables of the new XML data type and store XML instances in them. The `XMLType` data type can be manipulated using XQuery and XML Data Manipulation Language (DML). `XMLType` also provides member functions to access, extract, and query XML data and XML fragments.

You can create Oracle `SELECT` queries to instruct Oracle to return database values in XML format. In the next few sections we will present some `SELECT` queries using SQL/XML functions like `XMLFOREST`, `XMLELEMENT`, and `XMLATTRIBUTES`.

XMLFOREST

The XMLFOREST function allows you to read values from Oracle tables and present them in XML format. The general format for the XMLFOREST function is:

```
SQL> SELECT XMLFOREST(Table.field_name1, Table.field_name2, ...)
"alias"
FROM TableName;
```

This function converts each of its argument parameters (field names from tables) to XML and returns an XML fragment that is a concatenation of each of the arguments (field names) converted to XML. The "alias" is a required part of the XMLFOREST function.

As an example, in the following query we will read two attributes, stno and sname, from the Student table and present the query in XML format using the XMLFOREST function:

```
SQL> SELECT XMLFOREST(s.stno, s.sname) "Student name and number"
FROM Student s;
```

This will give us:

```
Student name and number
-----------------------------------------------------------------
<STNO>2</STNO>
<SNAME>Lineas</SNAME>

<STNO>3</STNO>
<SNAME>Mary</SNAME>

<STNO>8</STNO>
<SNAME>Brenda</SNAME>

<STNO>10</STNO>
<SNAME>Richard</SNAME>
.
.
```

```
.
<STNO>191</STNO>
<SNAME>Jake</SNAME>

48 rows selected.
```

Here the XML tags default to the field names and the data is placed between the XML tags.

Using XMLELEMENT

The XMLELEMENT function, in addition to allowing you to read values from Oracle tables and present them in XML format, allows you to wrap the values in descriptive XML tags. The general format for XMLELEMENT is:

```
SQL> SELECT XMLELEMENT("tag_name", Table.field_name1),
XMLELEMENT("tag_name", Table.field_name2)
FROM TableName;
```

The XMLELEMENT function creates an XML element in XMLType by taking the *tag_name* and the information from the specified field of a table as arguments. The *tag_name* is used to create an XML tag.

For example, in the following query we will read the same two attributes, stno and sname, from the Student table and present the query in XML format, wrapped in descriptive XML tags:

```
SQL> SELECT XMLELEMENT("Student_Number", stno),
XMLELEMENT("Name", sname)
FROM Student;
```

Will give us:

```
XMLELEMENT("STUDENT_NUMBER",STNO)
-----------------------------------------------------------------
XMLELEMENT("NAME",SNAME)
-----------------------------------------------------------------
```

```
<Student_Number>2</Student_Number>
<Name>Lineas</Name>

<Student_Number>3</Student_Number>
<Name>Mary</Name>

<Student_Number>8</Student_Number>
<Name>Brenda</Name>
.
.
.
<Student_Number>191</Student_Number>
<Name>Jake</Name>

48 rows selected.
```

Here, note the tag names in XML — Student_Number and Name. Also notice that the data is between the XML tags.

XMLELEMENT can also be used to list field names within a single XML tag as follows:

```
SQL> SELECT XMLELEMENT("tag_name", Table.field_name1,
Table.field_name2, ...)
FROM TableName;
```

So, if we type:

```
SQL> SELECT XMLELEMENT("Student", sname, bdate)
FROM Student;
```

We will get:

```
XMLELEMENT("STUDENT",SNAME,BDATE)
--------------------------------------------------------------------
<Student>Lineas15-APR-80</Student>
<Student>Mary16-JUL-78</Student>
<Student>Brenda13-AUG-77</Student>
<Student>Richard13-MAY-80</Student>
.
.
```

```
.
<Student>Jake10-JUN-80</Student>

48 rows selected.
```

In this output the data is all strung together, so we will have to concatenate spaces to the above query as follows:

```
SQL> SELECT XMLELEMENT("Student", sname|| ' ' ||  bdate)
FROM Student;
```

This will give:

```
XMLELEMENT("STUDENT",SNAME||''||BDATE)
--------------------------------------------------------------
<Student>Lineas 15-APR-80</Student>
<Student>Mary 16-JUL-78</Student>
<Student>Brenda 13-AUG-77</Student>
.
.
.

<Student>Smith 15-OCT-79</Student>
<Student>Jake 10-JUN-80</Student>

48 rows selected.
```

In the following example we are concatenating the field names with some additional text:

```
SQL> SELECT XMLELEMENT("Student", s.sname || ' was born on ' ||
s.bdate) AS "STUDENT's BIRTHDATE"
FROM Student s;
```

This gives:

```
STUDENT's BIRTHDATE
--------------------------------------------------------------
<Student>Lineas was born on 15-APR-80</Student>
<Student>Mary was born on 16-JUL-78</Student>
<Student>Brenda was born on 13-AUG-77</Student>
<Student>Richard was born on 13-MAY-80</Student>
```

```
.
.
.
<Student>Jake was born on 10-JUN-80</Student>

48 rows selected.
```

Using XMLELEMENT and XMLFOREST together we can also display XML output in the format of elements and tagged attributes within elements, as shown below:

```
SQL>SELECT XMLELEMENT("STUDENT",
XMLFOREST(s.stno, s.sname, s.class)) "Student Element"
FROM Student s;
```

This gives us:

```
Student Element
-----------------------------------------------------------------
<STUDENT><STNO>2</STNO><SNAME>Lineas</SNAME><CLASS>6</CLASS></STUDENT>
<STUDENT><STNO>3</STNO><SNAME>Mary</SNAME><CLASS>4</CLASS></STUDENT>
<STUDENT><STNO>8</STNO><SNAME>Brenda</SNAME><CLASS>2</CLASS></STUDENT>
<STUDENT><STNO>10</STNO><SNAME>Richard</SNAME><CLASS>1</CLASS></STUDENT>
.
.
.
<STUDENT><STNO>88</STNO><SNAME>Smith</SNAME></STUDENT>
<STUDENT><STNO>191</STNO><SNAME>Jake</SNAME><CLASS>2</CLASS></STUDENT>

48 rows selected.
```

In this XML output, we have a student element, with attributes stno and sname.

Using XMLATTRIBUTES

Another way of displaying attributes is by using XMLATTRIBUTES. XMLATTRIBUTES, when used within XMLELEMENT, is employed to specify attributes of that element. The following query displays the student number (stno), student name (sname), and birthdate (bdate), as attributes of the element Student.

```
SQL>SELECT XMLELEMENT("STUDENT", XMLATTRIBUTES(s.stno AS
"STUDENT_NO", s.sname AS "STUDENT_NAME", s.bdate))
FROM Student s;
```

This gives us:

```
XMLELEMENT("STUDENT",XMLATTRIBUTES(S.STNOAS"STUDENT_NO",
S.SNAMEAS"STUDENT_NAME",
--------------------------------------------------------------------
<STUDENT STUDENT_NO="2" STUDENT_NAME="Lineas"BDATE="15-APR-80">
</STUDENT>
<STUDENT STUDENT_NO="3" STUDENT_NAME="Mary" BDATE="16-JUL-78">
</STUDENT>
<STUDENT STUDENT_NO="8" STUDENT_NAME="Brenda" BDATE="13-AUG-77">
</STUDENT>
<STUDENT STUDENT_NO="10" STUDENT_NAME="Richard" BDATE="13-MAY-80">
</STUDENT>
.
.
.
<STUDENT STUDENT_NO="88" STUDENT_NAME="Smith" BDATE="15-OCT-79">
</STUDENT>
<STUDENT STUDENT_NO="191" STUDENT_NAME="Jake" BDATE="10-JUN-80">
</STUDENT>

48 rows selected.
```

In order to include a more descriptive heading we should include an alias, as shown below:

```
SQL> SELECT XMLELEMENT("STUDENT", XMLATTRIBUTES(s.stno AS
"STUDENT_NO", s.sname AS "STUDENT_NAME", s.bdate)) AS "STUDENT_INFO"
FROM Student s;
```

And this gives us:

```
STUDENT_INFO
--------------------------------------------------------------------
<STUDENT STUDENT_NO="2" STUDENT_NAME="Lineas" BDATE="15-APR-80">
</STUDENT>
<STUDENT STUDENT_NO="3" STUDENT_NAME="Mary" BDATE="16-JUL-78">
</STUDENT>
<STUDENT STUDENT_NO="8" STUDENT_NAME="Brenda" BDATE="13-AUG-77">
</STUDENT>
<STUDENT STUDENT_NO="10" STUDENT_NAME="Richard" BDATE="13-MAY-80">
</STUDENT>
.
.
.

<STUDENT STUDENT_NO="88" STUDENT_NAME="Smith" BDATE="15-OCT-79">
</STUDENT>
<STUDENT STUDENT_NO="191" STUDENT_NAME="Jake" BDATE="10-JUN-80">
</STUDENT>

48 rows selected.
```

Creating a Table Using the XMLType Data Type

To create a table using the XMLType, we use the regular CREATE TABLE command as follows:

```
SQL> CREATE TABLE Studentxml(stu NUMBER(3), info sys.xmltype);
```

You will get:

```
Table created.
```

And, to see the description of the Studentxml table, type:

```
SQL> DESC Studentxml;
```

You will get:

```
Name                            Null?    Type
------------------------------- -------- ----------------------
STU                                      NUMBER(3)
INFO                                     SYS.XMLTYPE
```

Inserting Values into Tables with an XMLType Data Type

In this section we demonstrate how to insert values into tables with an XMLType data type using INSERT INTO..VALUES.

If you type:

```
INSERT INTO Studentxml VALUES (101,
XMLTYPE('<STU_INFO>
<sname>Pramit</sname>
<major>Statistics</major>
</STU_INFO>'));
```

You will get:

```
1 row created.
```

To display what you inserted, type:

```
SQL> SELECT *
FROM Studentxml;
```

This will give:

```
       STU
----------
INFO
----------------------------------------------------------------------
       101
 <STU_INFO>
  <sname>Pramit</sname>
  <major>Statistics</major>
</STU_INFO>
```

Another insert statement:

```
INSERT INTO Studentxml VALUES(102,
XMLTYPE('<STU_INFO>
<sname>Amit</sname>
<major>Math</major>
</STU_INFO>'));
```

And you will get:

```
1 row created.
```

Again, to display all the data in Studentxml, type:

```
SQL> SELECT *
FROM Studentxml;
```

You will get:

```
       STU
----------
INFO
--------------------------------------------------------------------
       101
 <STU_INFO>
  <sname>Pramit</sname>
  <major>Statistics</major>
</STU_INFO>

       102
<STU_INFO>
  <sname>Amit</sname>

       STU
----------
INFO
--------------------------------------------------------------------
  <major>Math</major>
</STU_INFO>
```

Extracting Information Using XPATH

In this section we demonstrate how to extract information from a table with an XMLType data type using an XPATH expression. XPATH is used to query data from tables with XMLTypes, where the data is in XML format. We will illustrate XPATH through the use of the EXTRACTVALUE and EXISTSNODE functions.

Using EXTRACTVALUE

EXTRACTVALUE returns values based on an XPATH expression.

The general format for the EXTRACTVALUE function is:

```
SQL> SELECT EXTRACTVALUE(Table.field_name, 'XPATH_expression')
FROM TableName;
```

For example, to display the student names (sname) of all students from the Studentxml table, we would type:

```
SQL> SELECT EXTRACTVALUE(info, '/STU_INFO/sname') AS "Student Names"
FROM studentxml;
```

This would give us:

```
Student Names
--------------------------------------------------------------------
Pramit
Amit
```

Using EXISTSNODE

EXISTSNODE reads in an XPATH expression and returns true (or 1) if the XML document contains the node specified in the XPATH.

The general format for the EXISTSNODE function is:

```
EXISTSNODE(Table.field_name, 'XPATH = [Table.field_name =
"Some_data_value"]')=1
```

To display the names of all the students who major in Statistics, we would type:

```
SELECT EXTRACTVALUE(info, 'STU_INFO/sname') AS "Statistics Majors"
FROM Studentxml
WHERE EXISTSNODE(info, '/STU_INFO[major = "Statistics"]')=1;
```

And this would give us:

```
Statistics Majors
--------------------------------------------------------------------
Pramit
```

Exercises for Chapter 14

As you do the exercises, it is a good idea to copy/paste your query as well as your query result into a word processor file.

14-1. List the student names and majors of all the seniors in XML format. First present the information using the XMLFOREST function, and then using the XMLELEMENT function.

14-2. Display the majors of all the seniors in the following format:

```
<Student_name is a XXXX major>
```

For example,

```
<Mary is a COSC major>
```

14-3. Display as attributes the course names, course numbers, and credit hours of all courses that are more than three credit hours. First display this using the XMLATTRIBUTES function, and then using the XMLELEMENT/XMLFOREST combination.

14-4. At the beginning of this chapter we presented a sample XML document. Create a table called Employee with an `XMLType` data type and insert those two employees (and the rest of the information) into the Employee table. Add two more employees: One as a statistician with a salary of $85,000, and another as a painter with a salary of $40,000.

a. Display the name of the painter.

b. Display the names and the titles of all the people with salaries greater than $49,000.

Include descriptive headings in your output.

Appendix A

Some UNIX Commands

In this appendix we list some commonly used UNIX commands and UNIX editor commands.

Commonly Used UNIX Commands

The following commands are entered from a UNIX prompt, such as goblin%.

To display your user ID:

```
goblin% whoami
```

To list the files in your directory:

```
goblin% ls
```

To list the files in your directory with size and date:

```
goblin% ls -l
```

To list the files in your directory with size and date that start with the letter "m":

```
goblin% ls -l m*
```

To list the files in your directory that start with the letters "ma" (no size or date):

```
goblin% ls ma*
```

To see how to use the `ls` command, invoke the UNIX built-in manual for `ls`:

```
goblin% man ls
```

To see what directory you are in:

```
goblin% pwd
```

To display the contents of a file use `cat` *`filename`*. For example:

```
goblin% cat showc.sql
```

For longer file listings you can pause at the end of each page (and press the Spacebar to continue) by using the pipe operator and pipe the "cat" result to "more."

```
cat filename | more
```

or

```
goblin% cat showc.sql | more
```

or

```
goblin% more showc.sql
```

Note: You may find it easier to view a file from an editor like vi or joe than to list it with cat. Sometimes cat listings go by too quickly.

To copy three files, ex11, ex12, and ex13, into one file, ex1all:

```
goblin% cat ex11 ex12 ex13 > ex1all
```

To copy a file use `cp` *`fromfile tofile`*. For example, at a UNIX prompt type:

```
goblin% cp ex1.lst ex1.bak
```

To rename a file use `mv` *`oldname newname`*. For example:

```
golbin% mv ex1.lst newex1.lst
```

To move up one directory (change directory):

```
goblin% cd ..
```

To create a subdirectory, mysub, in your directory:

```
goblin% mkdir mysub
```

To move to your newly created subdirectory:

```
goblin% cd mysub
```

To get back to your home directory:

```
goblin% cd
```

To see who else is signed on to this machine:

```
goblin% who
```

or, even better:

```
goblin% finger
```

To delete (remove) the file named frog:

```
goblin% rm frog
```

To print the file named ex1all:

```
goblin% lp ex1all
```

Summary Table

Several of the commands used in UNIX can be abbreviated. Below is a list of some important commands and their abbreviations, for example, the abbreviation for the "change directory" command is "cd."

Change directory:	`cd`
Copy:	`cp`
Delete:	`rm`
Display:	`cat` or `more`
Help manual:	`man`
List:	`ls`
Move:	`mv`
Show directory:	`pwd`

Other Miscellaneous Commands

Following are some additional UNIX commands.

To display a 2012 calendar, you can type:

```
cal 2012
```

To show the first 10 lines of a file, you can type:

`head` *`filename`*

To show the last 20 lines of a file, type:

`tail -20` *`filename`*

To show the time and date, type:

```
date
```

To see what processes you are running, type:

```
ps
```

To kill a process by number, type:

```
kill
```

Note: The commands ps and kill are useful if you lock up and have to sign back on to kill a previous session.

Editors

There are several editors you can use for editing text files in UNIX. Most UNIX gurus use the vi editor; however, many people find vi cumbersome and prefer one of the "easier" editors, such as joe or pico. Some notes on each of these follow.

Using vi as Your Editor

To use the vi editor from a UNIX machine with a prompt like triton%, type:

```
triton% vi filename
```

This command initiates the file and gives it a name.

To switch to the Insert mode in vi, press <Esc> and then type **i** to insert. You can then start typing your script.

Note: In the vi editor, you need to get into the habit of pressing <Esc> a lot. <Esc> is used to change from one mode to another in the vi editor.

From within vi:

Press <Esc> and type **x** to delete a character.

Press <Esc> and type **:wq** to write and quit.

Press <Esc> and type **:q!** to quit *without* saving (generally to start over).

Other vi Commands

Below are some additional vi commands. Remember that you will need to press the <Esc> key before you can use any of the following commands. Remember that <Esc> is used to switch from any mode to any other mode in vi.

a:	Appends to the end of a line if you are at the end of a line (<Esc> to quit)
<Shift>a:	Moves to the end of a line and then appends (and <Esc> to quit).
o (lowercase):	Opens a new line below the present line.
O (uppercase):	Opens the line above.
dd:	Deletes a line.
5dd:	Deletes five lines.

To move a line, **dd** it, then place the cursor on the line *before* the point where you want the deleted line to be placed and type **p**.

Using joe as Your Editor

If you use joe as your editor, invoke it as follows:

```
joe filename
```

To use joe after you start it, press <Ctrl+KH> (hold down the Control key and type KH). This gives you HELP text that stays at the top of the screen and guides you when editing.

Appendix B

The Data Dictionary

The data dictionary contains the metadata (the data about data) for an Oracle database. The contents of the data dictionary are available through a series of built-in dictionary views. Many of the views are restricted to the database administrator (DBA), but there are other views that are an excellent source of information for the user. What views are there in the dictionary that are available from your account? The table that shows all the dictionary views you can access is called "Dictionary." The public synonym for Dictionary is "Dict."

Before doing a `SELECT * FROM Dict`, be aware that this simple query will give too much information at one time. As we suggested earlier, it is best to approach large tables cautiously. In all queries where the number of rows of output is unknown, you may want to get a count of how many rows are available, so our first query is:

```
SELECT COUNT(*)
FROM Dict;
```

Although the actual number of rows will vary depending on the privileges you have, this query will give you a large number like:

```
COUNT(*)
---------
      817
```

The second task is to DESCribe the dictionary itself:

```
SQL> DESC Dict
```

will give:

```
Name                              Null?    Type
--------------------------------- -------- ----------------------
TABLE_NAME                                 VARCHAR2(30)
COMMENTS                                   VARCHAR2(4000)
```

So, this large dictionary table has lots of rows, but only two columns; however, the second column, Comments, is very wide.

Beginning to Explore the Data Dictionary

To begin exploring the data dictionary, we can begin by entering the following command:

```
SELECT *
FROM Dict
WHERE rownum < 5;
```

`WHERE rownum < 5` will prevent excessive output when a particular command might otherwise give too many rows to handle effectively. The command, as it stands, ends after four rows. You can, of course, use larger `rownum` values or delete the `WHERE` clause and see the whole table, but when exploring we suggest you keep the view short using `rownum < n` and use pause (`SET PAUSE ON`).

If you execute this first command, you will see the very wide Comments column. To more effectively begin looking at the dictionary, you might amend the above query to this:

```
SELECT table_name, SUBSTR(comments,1,30)
FROM Dict
WHERE rownum < 5;
```

Should a table and its comments look interesting, we can always expand the result set and/or rows retrieved.

As you peruse the dictionary table with the above query or variants thereof, you will note that several types of views can be ascertained by the prefix of the view:

Prefix	**Example**
ALL_	ALL_CATALOG
DBA_	DBA_CONSTRAINTS
USER_	USER_TABLES
Other views	V$VERSION or ROLE_ROLE_PRIVS

These views represent information about tables, constraints, database links, and other objects (like triggers, procedures, synonyms, and so on) that are accessible at the level of the USER, ALL users, and DBA:

USER_ These are objects owned by (created by) the account doing the query.

ALL_ This command will display all of the USER_ information plus information on other objects to which access privileges have been given to the user or to "Public."

DBA_ These are DBA database objects (some of which you may not have access to).

You can create other views that don't neatly fall into a USER, ALL, or DBA category. To sample specific portions of the dictionary, we can use a command like this:

```
SELECT table_name, SUBSTR(comments,1,30)
FROM Dict
WHERE table_name LIKE 'ALL%'
/* ALL is case sensitive because it is stored that way in the
dictionary */
AND rownum < 10
```

This will give:

```
TABLE_NAME                     SUBSTR(COMMENTS,1,30)
------------------------------ ------------------------------
ALL_REGISTRY_BANNERS
ALL_XML_SCHEMAS                Description of all XML Schemas
ALL_XML_SCHEMAS2               Dummy version of ALL_XML_SCHEM
ALL_CATALOG                    All tables, views, synonyms, s
ALL_CLUSTERS                   Description of clusters access
ALL_COL_COMMENTS               Comments on columns of accessi
ALL_COL_PRIVS                  Grants on columns for which th
ALL_COL_PRIVS_MADE             Grants on columns for which th
ALL_COL_PRIVS_RECD             Grants on columns for which th
```

As another alternative to exploring the dictionary, we might type:

```
SELECT *
FROM Dict
WHERE table_name LIKE 'USER%'
/* USER is case sensitive because it is stored that way in the
dictionary */
;
```

This query will display only the table names in Dict that begin with USER, as shown below:

```
TABLE_NAME
------------------------------
COMMENTS
```

```
--------------------------------------------------------------------
USER_ALL_TABLES
Description of all object and relational tables owned by the user's

USER_ARGUMENTS
Arguments in object accessible to the user

USER_AUDIT_OBJECT
Audit trail records for statements concerning objects, specifically:
table, cluster, view, index, sequence,[public] database link,
[public] synonym, procedure, trigger, rollback segment, tablespace,
role, user

USER_AUDIT_SESSION
All audit trail records concerning CONNECT and DISCONNECT

USER_AUDIT_STATEMENT
Audit trail records concerning grant, revoke, audit, noaudit and
alter system

USER_AUDIT_TRAIL
Audit trail entries relevant to the user
.
.
.
USER_VARRAYS
Description of varrays contained in the user's own tables

USER_VIEWS
Description of the user's own views

USER_HISTOGRAMS
Synonym for USER_TAB_HISTOGRAMS

143 rows selected.
```

As we illustrated above, it may be good with this second query to first count the number of rows, limit the size of the Comments column, or use `PAUSE` to view the output.

Choosing a View from the Dictionary

Having begun to explore the dictionary, we will choose a view and browse deeper. We will illustrate two choices of objects: CATALOG and TABLES.

Choosing the View You Want to See

We can browse the dictionary by comments or table names. Let's look for dictionary tables that contain the word "catalog" in the comments. The appropriate query would be:

```
SQL> SELECT *
FROM Dict
WHERE UPPER(comments) LIKE '%CATAL%';
```

We uppercase the comments column contents and then compare the word we want to find. This produces the following output:

```
TABLE_NAME
------------------------------
COMMENTS
--------------------------------------------------------------------------------
CAT
Synonym for USER_CATALOG
```

This output tells us we have a table called USER_CATALOG and that there is a synonym for that table, CAT.

We can also browse the dictionary by table name:

```
SQL> SELECT *
FROM Dict
WHERE upper(table_name) LIKE '%CATAL%'
/* Now querying table_name instead of comments */
;
```

The result:

```
TABLE_NAME
------------------------------
COMMENTS
--------------------------------------------------------------------
USER_CATALOG
Tables, Views, Synonyms and Sequences owned by the user
ALL_CATALOG
All tables, views, synonyms, sequences accessible to the user
```

It is usually a good idea to look at both comments and table names when looking for objects in the dictionary.

Describing the View You Want to See

Let's suppose you have chosen an object for further study, ALL_CATALOG. If you type:

```
SQL> DESC ALL_CATALOG;
```

It shows that you have three columns:

```
Name                                       Null?    Type
------------------------------------------ -------- ----------
OWNER                                      NOT NULL VARCHAR2(30)
TABLE_NAME                                 NOT NULL VARCHAR2(30)
TABLE_TYPE                                          VARCHAR2(11)
```

The reason that you want to describe the view is that some dictionary tables are very wide — perhaps 25 or so columns. If you do not restrict what you want to look at, you will get long, hard-to-read listings.

Finding the "Right" Columns

Because ALL_CATALOG is narrow (only three columns), you will likely want to use a command like this:

```
SELECT * ...
```

If there were a lot of columns, you might want to use less than the full complement, like:

```
SELECT table_type, table_name ...
```

Finding out How Many Rows Are in the View

You should always check to see how many rows you would get before you actually try to display all of them. For example, to see how many rows are in ALL_CATALOG, type:

```
SELECT COUNT (*)
FROM ALL_CATALOG;
```

This may give a large number (depending on privileges) such as shown below:

```
 COUNT(*)
---------
     6681
```

As this number is very large (giving you a very long, perhaps useless, display), you can sample the table with a rownum as follows:

```
SELECT *
FROM ALL_CATALOG
WHERE rownum < 5;
```

Which gives:

```
OWNER                     TABLE_NAME                TABLE_TYPE
------------------------- ------------------------- -----------
SYS                       DUAL                      TABLE
PUBLIC                    DUAL                      SYNONYM
SYS                       SYSTEM_PRIVILEGE_MAP      TABLE
PUBLIC                    SYSTEM_PRIVILEGE_MAP      SYNONYM
```

Since there are so many rows, we can look at who owns what with a query like this:

```
SELECT COUNT(*), owner
FROM ALL_CATALOG
GROUP BY owner;
```

Which will give:

```
  COUNT(*) OWNER
---------- ------------------------------
        48 CTXSYS
        67 DMSYS
        21 EXFSYS
        57 MDSYS
       187 OLAPSYS
         5 ORDSYS
     18938 PUBLIC
        20 REARP
      1045 SYS
         9 SYSTEM
        82 WKSYS
         6 WK_TEST
        89 WMSYS
        19 XDB

14 rows selected.
```

There are lots of tables owned by PUBLIC and SYS as well as other tables owned by subsystem components. The following queries display the catalog entries owned by REARP:

```
SELECT owner, table_name, table_type
FROM ALL_CATALOG
WHERE owner = 'REARP';

SELECT *
FROM ALL_CATALOG
WHERE owner = 'REARP';
```

Both the above queries would give:

```
OWNER                    TABLE_NAME                     TABLE_TYPE
------------------------ ------------------------------ -----------
REARP                    BIN$DJdR+bwMBfzgRAgAIMRj0Q==$0 TABLE
REARP                    BIN$DJdR+bwRBfzgRAgAIMRj0Q==$0 TABLE
REARP                    BIN$DJdR+bwVBfzgRAgAIMRj0Q==$0 TABLE
REARP                    BIN$DJdR+bwZBfzgRAgAIMRj0Q==$0 TABLE
REARP                    BIN$DJdR+bwaBfzgRAgAIMRj0Q==$0 TABLE
REARP                    BIN$DJdR+bwfBfzgRAgAIMRj0Q==$0 TABLE
REARP                    BIN$DJdR+bwjBfzgRAgAIMRj0Q==$0 TABLE
REARP                    BIN$DJdR+bwmBfzgRAgAIMRj0Q==$0 TABLE
REARP                    BIN$DJdR+bwpBfzgRAgAIMRj0Q==$0 TABLE
REARP                    BIN$DJdR+bwsBfzgRAgAIMRj0Q==$0 TABLE
REARP                    STUDENT                        TABLE
REARP                    COURSE                         TABLE
REARP                    GRADE_REPORT                   TABLE
REARP                    SECTION                        TABLE
REARP                    DEPARTMENT_TO_MAJOR            TABLE
REARP                    PLANTS                         TABLE
REARP                    PREREQ                         TABLE
REARP                    CAP                            TABLE
REARP                    ROOM                           TABLE
REARP                    TESTSTU                        TABLE
```

This query can then be further filtered by removing more system tables:

```
SELECT *
FROM ALL_CATALOG
WHERE owner = 'REARP
AND table_name NOT LIKE 'BIN%'
```

Giving:

```
OWNER                        TABLE_NAME                     TABLE_TYPE
---------------------------- ------------------------------ -----------
REARP                        STUDENT                        TABLE
REARP                        COURSE                         TABLE
REARP                        GRADE_REPORT                   TABLE
REARP                        SECTION                        TABLE
REARP                        DEPARTMENT_TO_MAJOR            TABLE
REARP                        PLANTS                         TABLE
REARP                        PREREQ                         TABLE
REARP                        CAP                            TABLE
REARP                        ROOM                           TABLE
REARP                        TESTSTU                        TABLE
```

Views of TABLES

The information in ..TABLES (e.g., USER_TABLES, ALL_TABLES, DBA_TABLES) shows the storage characteristics of the physical tables. Much of the information in the tables themselves is specified when tables are created and much of it can be changed with ALTER TABLE for owned tables.

TABS is a synonym for USER_TABLES. Also, there is a useful "old-fashioned" synonym that has been carried forward in later versions of Oracle called TAB. Although TAB is more limited than TABS, many people prefer it because it gives an abbreviated list of tables, views, clusters, and so on, that are owned.

Other Objects — Tablespaces and Constraints

Both ..CATALOG and ..TABLE views tell you about tables and tablespaces. If you have created or use other objects (such as synonyms), you can access a view called USER_OBJECTS, which will tell you what "other" objects you may have. Other objects include clusters, functions, procedures, packages, sequences, synonyms, tables, triggers, and views.

Note: What you can see in the dictionary depends on permissions and privileges that may have to be arranged with the DBA before trying these commands.

Here is an example of some information contained in USER_OBJECTS:

```
SELECT COUNT(*), object_type
FROM USER_OBJECTS
GROUP BY object_type;
```

Giving:

```
 COUNT(*)  OBJECT_TYPE
---------  -------------------
       18  INDEX
        1  LOB
        1  SYNONYM
       40  TABLE
        1  TRIGGER
        1  VIEW
```

Views of Tablespaces

Every table belongs to a tablespace, which is a division of a database. Some authors make the analogy that a database is like a city, the tablespace is like a block in the city, and a table is like a house on a block.

Usually, you use the default database as set up by the database administrator (DBA). Also, you usually don't need to know the database name unless you're doing teleprocessing. In addition to the database, your account is set up to default to some tablespace. Tablespaces were also set by the DBA prior to your account being created. Every tablespace has some size to it defined when the tablespace was created.

A `CREATE TABLESPACE` command might look like this:

```
CREATE TABLESPACE TEMP
DATAFILE 'dog1.dbf' SIZE 100K
```

Such a `CREATE TABLESPACE` command would reserve 100K of disk space under the filename dog1.dbf for your tablespace in your default database. In this command, there are options for `MAXSIZE`, which sets the maximum size of the tablespace, as well as `AUTOEXTEND` options, which allows your tablespace to automatically expand if necessary.

Note: The MAXSIZE is set at the individual data file level and not at the tablespace level. MAXSIZE is used only in conjunction with AUTOEXTEND ON.

As far as you and the dictionary are concerned, you may first want to know which tablespaces you have available. This is done by looking at the `USER_TABLESPACES` view as follows:

```
SELECT *
FROM USER_TABLESPACES;
```

This command will give you a display that looks like this (these will appear on one line in eight columns but are separated here):

```
TABLESPACE_NAME  INITIAL_EXTENT  NEXT_EXTENT  MIN_EXTENTS
---------------  --------------  -----------  -----------
MYSPACE          10240           10240        1
```

```
MAX_EXTENTS  PCT_INCREASE  STATUS    CONTENTS
-----------  ------------  --------  ---------
121          50            ONLINE    PERMANENT
```

This output shows that the tablespace named MYSPACE is available to you and that when you create tables, your initial extent for a table will be 10,240 bytes. If you put a lot of data in your table, the tablespace will allow you another 10,240 bytes (NEXT_EXTENT), up to 121 times (MAX_EXTENTS). The PCT_INCREASE means that when the next extent is allocated, it will increase by 50% each time. ONLINE (STATUS) means that your tablespace is available. The tablespace owner might make it OFFLINE for maintenance purposes.

Note: Tablespaces are not owned by users. All tablespaces reside at the database level and can be taken offline by any user who has the appropriate privileges to do so.

Suppose you want to look at the space available in your tablespace. How do you do this? There are two views of interest: USER_FREE_SPACE and USER_TS_QUOTAS.

If you type:

```
SELECT *
FROM USER_FREE_SPACE;
```

You will get output that looks like this:

```
TABLESPACE_NAME  FILE_ID  BLOCK_ID  BYTES    BLOCKS
---------------  -------  --------  -------  ----------
MYSPACE          12       4         45056    22
OTHERSPACE       11       2         305152   149
```

Here, the tablespaces listed are those that you have access to as a user. Suppose that MYSPACE is the tablespace of interest. If you type:

```
SELECT *
FROM USER_TS_QUOTAS;
```

You will get the following output (and perhaps some other tablespaces):

```
TABLESPACE_NAME  BYTES       MAX_BYTES   BLOCKS      MAX_BLOCKS
---------------  ----------  ----------  ----------  ----------
MYSPACE          104448      -1          51          -1
```

USER_FREE_SPACE shows that you have 45,056 bytes available and USER_TS_QUOTAS shows that you have used 104,448 bytes. The original allocation of space to this tablespace was 150,000 bytes. The "-1" means "unlimited."

Views of Constraints

When you have created tables in a tablespace in a database, you usually have constraints that are placed on values in columns. These constraints include:

- Primary keys (P)
- Unique constraints (U)
- Foreign keys (R)
- Checks (C)
- A special option you can put on views called WITH CHECK OPTION (V)

The letters in the parentheses indicate how the various options are referred to in the USER_CONSTRAINTS table. The columns of USER_CONSTRAINTS can be viewed by typing:

```
SQL> DESCRIBE USER_CONSTRAINTS;
```

This gives us the columns available in USER_CONSTRAINTS, as shown below:

```
Name                     Null?    Type
------------------------ -------- -------------
OWNER                    NOT NULL VARCHAR2(30)
CONSTRAINT_NAME          NOT NULL VARCHAR2(30)
CONSTRAINT_TYPE                   VARCHAR2(1)
TABLE_NAME               NOT NULL VARCHAR2(30)
SEARCH_CONDITION                  LONG
R_OWNER                           VARCHAR2(30)
R_CONSTRAINT_NAME                 VARCHAR2(30)
DELETE_RULE                       VARCHAR2(9)
STATUS                            VARCHAR2(8)
```

Note: Additional columns are not shown for brevity's sake.

Exercises for Appendix B

B-1. How many objects are there in Dict?

B-2. How many objects start with USER? With ALL? With DBA? With something other than USER, ALL, or DBA?

B-3. Which tables in the catalog pertain to synonyms? To tables? To views?

B-4. How many rows are there in ALL_CATALOG?

B-5. Display the USER_CATALOG. Contrast the contents of USER_CATALOG with ALL_CATALOG. How many rows are there in USER_CATALOG? A synonym for USER_CATALOG is CAT. Try the command SELECT * FROM CAT and verify that it is the same as SELECT * FROM USER_CATALOG. How do the rows in USER_CATALOG differ from ALL_CATALOG?

B-6. Investigate and report on the following *x*_TABLES, where x = USER, ALL, and DBA.

How many columns are there in USER_TABLES? In ALL_TABLES? In DBA_TABLES? How many rows are there in USER_TABLES? In ALL_TABLES?

B-7. Display a list of the tables you have created. Show the owner, table_name, and tablespace_name. Use USER_TABLES, TAB, COLS, and TABS.

B-8. Carefully look at ALL_OBJECTS (use rownum, COUNTs, and DESC to explore first). If more information is sought on these other objects, there are tables at various levels (USER, ALL, DBA) for VIEWS, CLUSTERS, SYNONYMS, and SEQUENCES. USER_SYNONYMS and USER_VIEWS are particularly useful.

B-9. Investigate and report on the constraints associated with the Student table.

Appendix C

The Student Database and Other Tables Used in This Book

The Student-Course Database

Student

stno	NOT NULL	NUMBER(3)
	PRIMARY KEY NOT NULL	
sname		VARCHAR2(20)
major		CHAR(4)
class		NUMBER(1)
bdate		DATE

Grade_report

student_number	NOT NULL	NUMBER(3)
section_id	NOT NULL	NUMBER(6)
grade		CHAR(1)
	PRIMARY KEY(student_number, section_id)	

Section

section_id	NOT NULL	NUMBER(6)
	PRIMARY KEY NOT NULL	
course_num		CHAR(8)
semester		VARCHAR2(6)
year		CHAR(2)
instructor		CHAR(10)
bldg		NUMBER(3)
room		NUMBER(3)

Department_to_major

dcode	NOT NULL	CHAR(4)
	PRIMARY KEY NOT NULL	
dname		CHAR(20)

Course

course_name		CHAR(20)
course_number	NOT NULL	CHAR(8)
	PRIMARY KEY NOT NULL	
credit_hours		NUMBER(2)
offering_dept		CHAR(4)

Room

bldg	NOT NULL	NUMBER(3)
room	NOT NULL	NUMBER(3)
capacity		NUMBER(4)
ohead		CHAR(1)
	PRIMARY KEY(bldg, room)	

Prereq

course_number		CHAR(8)
prereq		CHAR(8)
	PRIMARY KEY(course_number, prereq)	

Entity Relationship Diagram of the Student-Course Database

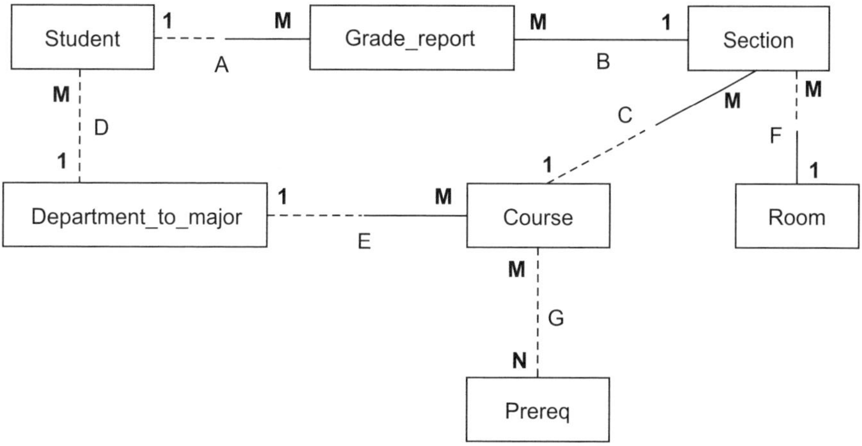

A A Student MAY be registered in one or more (M) Grade_reports. (Grade_report is for a specific Course.)

A Grade_report MUST relate to one and only one (1) Student.

(Students may be in the database and not registered for any Courses, but if a Course is recorded in the Grade_report table, it must be related to one and only one Student.)

B A Section MUST have one or more (M) Grade_Reports. (Sections only exist if they have Students in them.)

A Grade_report MUST relate to one and only one (1) Section.

C A Section MUST relate to one and only one (1) Course.

A Course MAY be offered as one or more (M) Sections.

(Courses may exist where they are not offered in a Section, but a Section, if offered, must relate to one and only one Course.)

D A Student MAY be related to one and only one (1) Department_to_major. (A Student may or may not have declared a major.)

A Department_to_major may have one or more (M) Students. (A department may or may not have Students who major in that department.)

E A Course MUST be related to one and only one (1) Department_to_major.

A Department_to_major MAY offer one or more (M) Courses.

F A Section MUST be offered in one and only one (1) Room.

A Room MAY host one or more (M) Sections.

G A Course MAY have one or more (M) Prereq. (A Course may have one or more prerequisites.)

A Prereq MAY be a prerequisite for one or more (M) Courses.

Other Tables Used in This Book

Plants

company	VARCHAR2(20)
plantlo	VARCHAR2(15)
	PRIMARY KEY(company, plantlo)

Cap

name	VARCHAR2(9)
lang	VARCHAR2(7)
	PRIMARY KEY(name, lang)

AA

X	NUMBER(2)

Worker

name	VARCHAR2(20)
state	CHAR(2)
salary	NUMBER(6)
dept	NUMBER(3)

Appendix D

Glossary of Terms

abstract data type A user-defined data type that allows you to define operations explicitly (in methods).

administrator In this book, the administrator refers to the database administrator (DBA) who has the DBA role. *See* DBA.

aggregate functions A function that returns a result based on multiple rows.

alias A temporary substitute for a name in a query. There can be table aliases and column aliases.

alphanumeric A data type that will accept a combination of characters as well as numbers.

anomaly An undesirable consequence of a data modification.

anonymous block A set of PL/SQL statements that may be used to perform a series of tasks using the PL/SQL language.

attribute Columns in a table or relation are called attributes.

binary intersection A set operation on two sets that generates unique values in common between two sets.

Binary Large Objects (BLOB) A data type used for binary large objects.

binary set difference A set operation on two sets that gives us values in one set less those contained in the other.

binary union A set operation on two sets where the result contains all unique elements of both sets.

Boolean Data type that can only store True or False values (PL/SQL only). The Boolean data type can also be null.

buffer In general terms, this is an area in the computer's memory where data is stored temporarily. The buffer in Oracle's context is the SQL*Plus buffer, which is actually a file called afiedt.buf, stored at the operating system level.

candidate key A column (or group of columns) that identifies a unique row in a table. One of the candidate keys is chosen to be the primary key.

cardinality In a binary relationship, this specifies the minimum and maximum number of relationship instances that an entity can participate in.

Cartesian product A relational operation on two tables, R and S, producing a third table T, with T containing the combination of every row in R with every row in S.

CHAR(*size*) Data type that gives fixed-length character data, *size* characters long.

Character Large Object (CLOB) A data type that declares variables that hold a LOB locator pointing to a large block of single-byte, fixed-width character data.

column Attributes of a table. Columns hold the same kind of values.

column alias A temporary column name.

comment Syntax provided for inserting explanatory statements within a query or program. Comments enhance the readability of a program. They are not read, compiled, or executed by a compiler.

conceptual schema In Oracle, a schema is the collection of objects owned by a single user. Each user has his or her own schema.

copy Command to copy a file in Windows.

correlated subquery A subquery in which the information in the subquery is referenced by the outer, main query. A correlated subquery cannot stand alone; it depends on the outer query.

cp Command to copy a file in UNIX.

cursor The simple definition of cursor is a marker such as a blinking square or line that marks your current position on the screen. In Oracle, "cursor" is used as a synonym for the context area. (The context area is the work area in memory where Oracle stores the current SQL statement.) A cursor is a pointer to a row in a PL/SQL program.

data Facts concerning entities such as people, objects, or events.

data dictionary Catalog information about schemas and constraints, design decisions, usage standards, application program descriptions, and user information. This information can be directly accessed by users or the DBA when needed.

database A shared collection of logically associated or related data.

database administrator (DBA) *See* DBA.

DATE Data type that is used for date and time data.

DBA (database administrator) The DBA has all system privileges and the ability to grant all privileges to other users. The DBA creates and drops users and space.

derived structure A view, snapshot, or temporary table derived from an existing table.

DDL (Data Definition Language) Used by the DBA and database designers to define the internal schema and conceptual schema.

DML (Data Manipulation Language) Users have the ability to manipulate (`INSERT`, `UPDATE`, and `DELETE`) data with the DML.

domain The set of all possible values that an attribute can have.

driving table The table that is accessed first in a join.

entity "Something" in the real world that is of importance to a user and that needs to be represented in a database. An entity may have physical existence (such as a student or building) or it may have conceptual existence (such as a course).

entity integrity constraint A constraint that states that no key value can be null.

entity set The collection of all entities of a particular entity type in a database.

entity type A collection of entities that have the same attributes.

equi-join A join condition with equality comparisons only.

file A collection of logically related records.

first normal form (1NF) State in which the domain of an attribute (column) must include only atomic (simple, indivisible) values and the value of any attribute in a tuple (or row) must be a single value from the domain of that attribute.

foreign account Account that you do not own.

foreign key An attribute that is a primary key of another table. A foreign key allows relationships to be implemented in relational databases.

FLOAT A data type that accepts numbers with decimals (this data type is rarely used).

function Named PL/SQL block that returns a value and can be called with arguments.

functionally dependent A relationship between two attributes (columns) in a table. Attribute Y is functionally dependent on attribute X if attribute X identifies attribute Y.

group function A function that returns a result based on multiple rows is a group function. Also known as an aggregate function.

hierarchical database A data model that represents all relationships using hierarchical trees, where a record represents a node of a tree and all relationships in the tree are represented by a parent-child relationship type. Each record in a hierarchical model may have several offspring but only one parent record.

hierarchical model In a hierarchical model all the data is logically arranged in a hierarchical fashion (also known as a parent-child relationship).

inline view A view that exists only during the execution of a query.

integer A data type that accepts only whole numbers and no decimals.

internal schema Describes the physical storage structure of the database.

join The join operation is used to combine related rows from two tables into single rows based on a logical comparison of column values.

key An attribute or data item that uniquely identifies a record instance or row in a table.

logical model Conceptualizing how data will be organized. It can be considered as the mapping of the conceptual model into a processible data model.

login The process of signing onto a system. Logging in usually requires you to provide your user ID and your password.

Large Object Data Type (LOB) A data type that can store large amounts (up to four gigabytes) of raw data, binary data (such as images), or character text data.

lp UNIX command to send your file to a line printer.

many-to-many (M:N) relationship Relationship in which many rows of one table can be related to many rows in another table.

metadata Data concerning the structure of data in a database that is stored in the data dictionary. Metadata is used to describe tables, columns, constraints, indexes, and so on.

National Character Large Object (NCLOB) A new data type that declares variables that hold a LOB locator pointing to a large block of single-byte, fixed-width character data.

nested table Available in PL/SQL, a nested table is a table structure with a single dimensioned, unbounded collection of homogeneous elements.

network database Represents data as record types, where each record type may have relationships of any cardinality with any other record type in that network.

network model A data model where you are not restricted to having one parent per child. Many-to-one (M:1) and many-to-many (M:N) relationships are acceptable.

noncorrelated subquery A subquery that is independent of the outer query.

normal form The process of decomposing complex data structures into simple tables according to a set of dependency rules.

object Any named element in a Oracle database such as a table, index, synonym, procedure, or trigger.

object privilege Specifies how another user can manipulate the object to which a privilege has been granted (usually by the database administrator).

one-to-one (1:1) relationship Relationship in which one row of one table can be related to only one row in another table.

one-to-many (1:M) relationship Relationship in which one row of one table can be related to more than one row in another table.

optionality A constraint that specifies whether the existence of an entity depends on its being related to another entity via a relationship type (also known as participation).

optimizer Part of an Oracle kernel that determines the best way to use the tables and indexes to complete the request made by a SQL statement.

outer join A join condition where all the rows from one table (for example, the first table) are kept in the result set although those rows did not have matching rows in the other table (the second table).

package Groups of procedures, functions, variables, and SQL statements grouped together into a single unit.

parse Parsing is the mapping of a SQL statement to a cursor. At parse time, several validation checks are made, such as determining whether grants are proper, whether the syntax of the statement is correct, and so on. Decisions regarding execution and optimization are also made during parse time.

physical model A representation of the form and details of how data is stored in the computer.

PL/SQL A programming language that provides procedural extensions to SQL.

primary key A candidate key selected to be the key of a table. The primary key will uniquely identify a row in a table.

privilege Privileges specify what the user can do when he or she is logged on.

procedure A PL/SQL block that can be used to perform a set of SQL commands and operations.

qualifier A prefix used to identify the owner of a table or a particular column of a table. For example, in rearp.Student, rearp is the qualifier for the table Student.

query A SQL instruction to retrieve data from one or more tables or views. Queries begin with the SQL keyword SELECT.

record A named collection of data items. In a relational model, a record is a physical realization of a row.

recursive relationship Relationships among entities in the same class.

redundancy Storing the same data multiple times.

referential integrity The property that guarantees that values from one column that depend on values from another column are present in the "other column."

relation A two-dimensional array containing single-value entries and no duplicate rows. The meaning of the columns is the same in every row, and the order of the rows and columns is immaterial. Often a relation is defined as a populated table. *See also* table.

relational algebra A data manipulation language that provides a set of operators for manipulating relations.

relational database A database consisting of relations (tables). A relational database is structured according to the principles of normalization.

relational model A logical data model in which all data are represented as a collection of normalized tables.

relational select A conditional relational algebra operation performed on a table, R, producing a table, S, with S containing only the rows in R that meet the restrictions specified in the condition.

relationship An association between two entities.

result set Output of a SQL statement.

rows A group of columns in a table. All the columns in a row pertain to the same entity. A row is the same as a tuple.

row filter A command that is used to select rows based on certain criteria.

row function A function that is performed on every single row of a table.

script A set of PL/SQL statements which may be used to perform a series of tasks.

second normal form (2NF) A table that is in first normal form and in which each nonkey attribute (column) is fully functionally dependent on the primary key.

session When you log on to your account, you begin a session.

set A data structure that represents a collection of values with no order and no duplicate values.

set compatibility For two sets (or tables) to be set compatible, both sets must match in number of items and must have compatible data types. Set compatibility is also referred to as union compatibility.

snapshot A means of creating a local copy of remote data.

software engineering A discipline that aims at production of fault-free software that satisfies the user's needs.

spool Copying information from one place to another.

spurious tuples Rows generated as a result of a join of tables that were decomposed incorrectly.

SQL (Structured Query Language) A language for defining the structure and processing of a relational database.

SQL statement SQL statements are used to issue commands to a database.

SQLLOADER Utility for loading data from external files into Oracle.

SQLPLUS (SQL*PLUS) Oracle product that takes your instructions for Oracle, checks them for correctness, submits them to Oracle, and then modifies and reformats the response Oracle gives.

start file File or script that contains SQLPLUS commands.

statement There are two kinds of statements: procedural and SQL. Examples of procedural statements are assignments, procedure calls, and loops. Examples of SQL statements can be divided into DML, DDL, transaction control, or session control.

statement buffer A file called afiedt.buf that contains the last executed SQL command.

string A mixture of letters, numbers, spaces, and other symbols.

string function Function used to manipulate string data.

structural constraint Structural constraints indicate how many of one type of a record is related to another and whether the record must have such a relationship. The cardinality ratio and participation constraints taken together form the structural constraints.

subquery The inner query within the outer (main) query; usually one `SELECT` query within another `SELECT` query.

subset Some group of objects taken from a set.

synonym A name assigned to a table or view that may thereafter be used to refer to the table or view.

system privilege Privilege that allows the user to execute specific sets of commands.

table A table is made of one or more rows of information, each of which contains the same kind of values (columns). It is also referred to as a relation in the relational model.

table alias A temporary name given to a table.

temporary table A derived structure or table where the result of a SELECT can be saved and then used in another SELECT.

theta join A join with one of the following comparison operators: <, <=, >, >=, or not =.

third normal form (3NF) A table that is in second normal form and in which no nonkey attribute (column) is functionally dependent on another nonkey attribute (that is, there are no transitive dependencies in the table).

transaction A series of operations between COMMITs.

trigger A PL/SQL block that gets fired when a table-modifying event occurs.

tuple A row in a table or relation.

union compatibility When working with sets (tables), for two sets to have union compatibility, both sets must match in number of items and must have compatible data types.

user An Oracle user who has a name (user ID) and password and has privileges to use tables, views, and other resources.

VARCHAR An older version of VARCHAR2.

VARCHAR2 A data type that allows you to define an Oracle variable-length string.

view A view is a query that is stored in the data dictionary and is resolved when accessed by a user or some other process.

waterfall model A series of steps that software undergoes, ranging from concept exploration to final retirement.

XML An acronym for EXtensible Markup Language, which is a meta language developed by the World Wide Web Consortium, widely used to exchange data over the Internet.

XPATH Used to query data from tables with XMLTypes.

Appendix E

Important Commands and Functions

ACCEPT SQLPLUS command that takes input from a keyboard and puts it in a named variable. It is used within a script.

ALTER TABLE SQL command that allows a user to add columns to, or modify columns in a table.

ALTER TRIGGER SQL command that allows a user to modify a trigger.

APPEND SQLPLUS command that allows a user to add text to the end of the current line without using an editor. This is a command line function.

AVG SQL function that averages a grouping of data.

BEGIN PL/SQL statement used as an opening statement of a PL/SQL block's executable section.

BREAK SQLPLUS command that performs the action that is specified in the BREAK command. This command is used within a script.

BTITILE SQLPLUS command that puts text (a title) at the bottom of each page; it is used in a script.

CASCADE SQL command that is used in conjunction with DELETE. CASCADE drops (deletes) all referential integrity constraints referring to keys in a dropped table.

CHANGE SQLPLUS line editor command that changes *old text* to *new text*.

CHECK With a CHECK constraint on a column the user can specify a range of values or a set of conditions that a column must have prior to insertion into the database. This is an enforcement of integrity, hence is an integrity constraint.

CLEAR COLUMNS SQLPLUS command that clears options set by the COLUMN command. This is a script command.

COMMIT SQL command that, when issued, makes changes un-ROLLBACKable. Therefore, when issued, changes to a table, INSERTs, UPDATEs, and DELETEs will become permanent.

COMPUTE SQLPLUS script command that performs computations on columns or expressions selected from a table.

CONSTRAINTS Restrictions that can be placed when creating database objects such as tables and views.

COUNT(*) SQL function that counts the total number of rows in a table.

COUNT(*attribute*) SQL group function that counts the number of rows where attribute is not null.

CREATE FUNCTION SQL command that creates a user-defined function.

CREATE PACKAGE SQL command that sets up the specification for a PL/SQL package.

CREATE PACKAGE BODY SQL command that builds the body of a previously specified package.

CREATE OR REPLACE PROCEDURE SQL command that creates the specification and body of a procedure.

CREATE OR REPLACE TRIGGER SQL command that creates and automatically enables a database trigger.

CREATE OR REPLACE VIEW SQL command that creates a view. A view is called a "derived structure."

CREATE SCHEMA SQL command that creates a collection of tables, views, and privilege grants as a single transaction.

CREATE SNAPSHOT SQL command that creates a snapshot (a table that holds the results of a query).

CREATE SYNONYM SQL command that creates a synonym for a table or view.

CREATE TABLE SQL command that creates a table.

CREATE TABLESPACE SQL command used to reserve disk space under a filename for your tables and other objects in your database. This command is usually performed by the DBA.

CREATE TYPE SQL command used to create abstract data types in Oracle.

CURSOR SQL command used as a pointer to a context area. Used in PL/SQL packages; it is declared in the package body.

DECODE SQL command that allows if-then-else logic.

DEL SQLPLUS command-line command that deletes the current line in the buffer.

DELETE SQL command that deletes all rows in a table that satisfy a particular condition specified in a WHERE clause.

DESCRIBE (DESC) SQL command that displays a table's definition (its columns and data types).

DIFFERENCE A set SQL function involving two queries; it returns only those rows from the result of the first query that are not in the result of the second query.

DISABLE SQL command that disables an integrity constraint or trigger.

DISTINCT SQL function that shows unique values that are selected in the result set of a SELECT command. It is formulated as SELECT DISTINCT(*attribute_name*). DISTINCT may also be used with group functions.

DROP FUNCTION SQL command that deletes a specified user-defined function.

DROP PACKAGE SQL command that delete a specified package.

DROP PROCEDURE SQL command that deletes a specified procedure.

DROP SYNONYM SQL command that deletes a synonym.

DROP TABLE SQL command that deletes a table.

DROP TRIGGER SQL command that deletes a trigger.

EDIT SQLPLUS command that calls an external text editor, e.g., vi. The editor allows a user to edit whatever is in the statement buffer.

ENABLE SQL command clause in an ALTER command that enables an integrity constraint or trigger.

EXECUTE SQL command that executes a procedure, package, or function.

EXISTS SQL operator that returns true in a WHERE clause of a SELECT if a subquery following it returns at least one row.

EXISTSNODE SQL/XML function that reads an XPATH expression and returns true (or 1) if the XML document contains the node specified in the XPATH.

EXIT PL/SQL function that takes control out of a currently executing loop.

EXTRACTVALUE SQL/XML function that returns values based on an XPATH expression.

FORCE Option that allows the SQL user to create a view if the underlying tables do not exist or if the user does not have privileges on the underlying table.

FOR EACH ROW SQL command that processes a row at a time in a trigger.

FOR..LOOP SQL command that performs a series of statements a certain number of times in PL/SQL.

GET SQLPLUS command that loads a file from the host system into the statement buffer.

GRANT SQL command that allows someone to pass a privilege to another user.

GREATEST SQL function that returns the highest of a list of values.

GROUP BY SQL clause that produces one summary row for all selected rows that have identical values for the attributes specified in the GROUP BY.

HAVING SQL clause used to determine which groups the GROUP BY will include in the result set.

HELP SQLPLUS command that provides help on various topics.

HOST SQLPLUS command that temporarily takes the user back to the operating system on which Oracle is running.

INDEX BY SQL feature that creates an index on a table. The index will be created by the attribute specified in the INDEX BY.

IF..THEN..ELSE A PL/SQL command. The IF statement will execute one or more statements when a condition evaluates to TRUE. If the condition evaluates to FALSE, the statements in the ELSE section are executed.

IN A logical operator for a WHERE clause, which tests for inclusion in a set.

INPUT SQLPLUS line editor command that allows for the addition a new line of text after the current line in the buffer.

INTERSECT SQL command that combines two queries and returns only those rows from the result of the first query that are identical to the result set in the second query.

INSTR SQL function that returns the location of a pattern in a given string.

INSERT SQL command that allows for the addition of new rows to a table or view.

LEAST SQL function that returns the lowest value from a list of values.

LENGTH SQL function that returns the length of an expression, string, number, or date.

LIKE SQL command that matches a particular pattern. LIKE is used in a SELECT..WHERE clause.

LIST SQLPLUS line editor command that displays lines in the current buffer.

LOOP PL/SQL statement that performs the statements after the LOOP until a constraint has been met.

LOWER SQL function that converts every letter in a string to lowercase.

LPAD SQL string function that stands for "left pad." LPAD inserts characters to the left end of a string.

LTRIM SQL string function that stands for "left trim." LTRIM trims (removes) a set of characters from the left side of a string.

MAX SQL aggregate function that returns the highest of all values from a column in a set of rows.

MIN SQL aggregate function that returns the lowest of all values from a column in a set of rows.

MINUS SQL function which returns only those rows from the result set of the first query that are not in the result set of the second query.

NOT SQL operator that comes before and reverses the logical effect of any logical operator like IN, LIKE, and EXISTS.

NOT EXISTS SQL operator that returns false in a WHERE clause if the subquery following it returns at least one row.

NOT NULL SQL operator-value in a SELECT..WHERE that is true if an attribute has a non-null value.

NULL SQL operator-value that represents an unknown or missing value.

NVL SQL function that allows something to be substituted in place of a NULL value.

OR Logical SQL binary operator that returns a true value in a SELECT..WHERE clause if either one of the expressions are true.

ORDER BY SQL clause that sorts the results of a query before they are displayed.

PRIMARY KEY SQL command; a constraint used to create a primary key in a table.

PRIVILEGE A user permission. There are SYSTEM PRIVILEGEs and OBJECT PRIVILEGEs.

PROMPT SQLPLUS command that displays text to a user's screen from within a script.

REFERENCE A constraint that defines the table name and key used to reference another table.

REM (short for REMARK) Placed at the beginning of a line, REM creates a comment line in a script. It is not read, compiled, or executed by a compiler. It is used for documentation purposes.

RETURN SQL command used in functions. This command causes control to pass from the function or procedure back to the calling environment.

RESTRICT Inter-table constraint that prevents deleting an attribute or value referenced by another table.

REVOKE SQL command that takes specific privileges away from another user.

ROLLBACK SQL command that reverses changes made to uncommitted tables in a database.

ROWNUM A pseudo-column created by Oracle in a result set. Rownum returns the sequence number in which a row was returned when first selected from a table. The first row has a rownum of 1, the second has a rownum of 2, and so on.

RPAD SQL string function that stands for "right pad." RPAD adds characters to the right of a string.

RTRIM SQL string function that stands for "right trim." RTRIM trims (removes) characters from the right side of a string.

SAVE SQLPLUS command that saves the contents of the statement buffer into a file on the host.

SAVEPOINT SQL command that allows the creation of milestones in a transaction.

SELECT SQL command that retrieves rows from tables (or derived structures) in a database.

SET SQLPLUS command that gives a value to a SQLPLUS feature, e.g., `SET PAGESIZE 100`.

SET ECHO ON/OFF SQLPLUS command that allows control of the listing of a command after it is executed.

SET FEEDBACK ON/OFF/*n* SQLPLUS command that controls feedback. For example, `SET FEEDBACK OFF` will prevent the row count from being displayed after the execution of a `SELECT` statement.

SET HEADSEP SQLPLUS command used in a script that identifies the character that tells SQLPLUS to split a title.

SET LINESIZE SQLPLUS command that allows specification of the maximum number of characters that can appear on each line.

SET NEWPAGE SQLPLUS command that allows you to specify how many lines there will be before the top line on each page is displayed.

SET PAGESIZE SQLPLUS command that allows you to set the total number of lines SQLPLUS will place on each page.

SET PAUSE ON/OFF/*character expression* SQLPLUS command that causes output to be displayed a page at a time.

SET SQLPROMPT SQLPLUS command that allows you to change the default prompt.

SET TIMING ON/OFF SQLPLUS command that allows you to show (or not show) timing statistics after a query is run.

SHOW ALL SQLPLUS command that gives a list of all system parameters.

SHOW ERRORS SQLPLUS command that will display line and column numbers for each error in a PL/SQL process if any errors exist.

SPOOL SQLPLUS command that shows the name of the current (or most recent) spool file.

SPOOL *filename* SQLPLUS command that writes the output of a query to the file specified in the SPOOL command.

SPOOL ON SQLPLUS command that, once it is turned on, saves everything that is displayed from that point into host system file until you SPOOL OFF or SPOOL OUT.

SPOOL OFF SQLPLUS command that stops spooling.

SPOOL OUT SQLPLUS command that stops spooling and sends the spooled file to the printer.

START *filename* SQLPLUS command that tells SQLPLUS to execute the instructions contained in a script.

SUBSTR SQL string function that allows SQL to retrieve only a portion of a whole string. The starting position is specified; the ending position may be specified.

SUM SQL aggregate function that adds up all the values for an attribute in a set of rows.

TAB This is a public synonym for a view of the dictionary that gives you the tables and synonyms you have created.

TABS This is basically the same as TAB, but contains a lot more information.

TO_CHAR SQL function that reformats a number or date into a specified character format.

TO_DATE SQL function that converts a string into a given date format.

TTITLE SQLPLUS script command that places a title at the top of each page.

%TYPE A %TYPE attribute can be applied to a variable or table column in PL/SQL. It returns the type of the object.

UNION SQL function that combines the result sets of two queries such that it returns all distinct rows for the result of both queries.

UNION ALL SQL function that combines the result sets of two queries and returns all rows from both the SELECT statements (queries). A UNION ALL also includes duplicate rows.

UNIQUE An column integrity constraint. UNIQUE disallows duplicate entries for a column even though the column is not a primary key. UNIQUE does not necessitate NOT NULL like the primary key does.

UPDATE SQL command that changes values in specified columns in specified tables.

UPPER SQL string function that converts every letter in a string into uppercase.

WHERE SQL clause that allows you to specify qualifiers on columns for rows that are being processed from a table. It is a row filter.

XMLATTRIBUTES SQL/XML function that, used within XMLELEMENT, will specify attributes of that element.

XMLELEMENT SQL/XML function that allows you to read values from Oracle tables and present them in XML format, wrapped in descriptive XML tags.

XMLFOREST SQL/XML function that allows you to read values from Oracle tables and present them in XML format.

Index

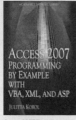

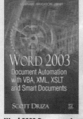

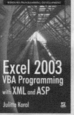

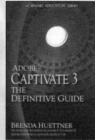

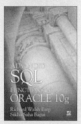

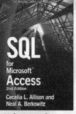

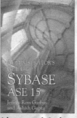

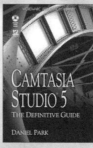

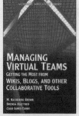

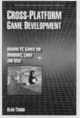

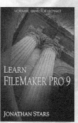

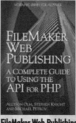

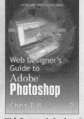

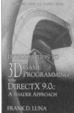

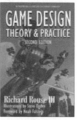

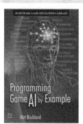

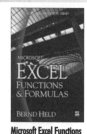